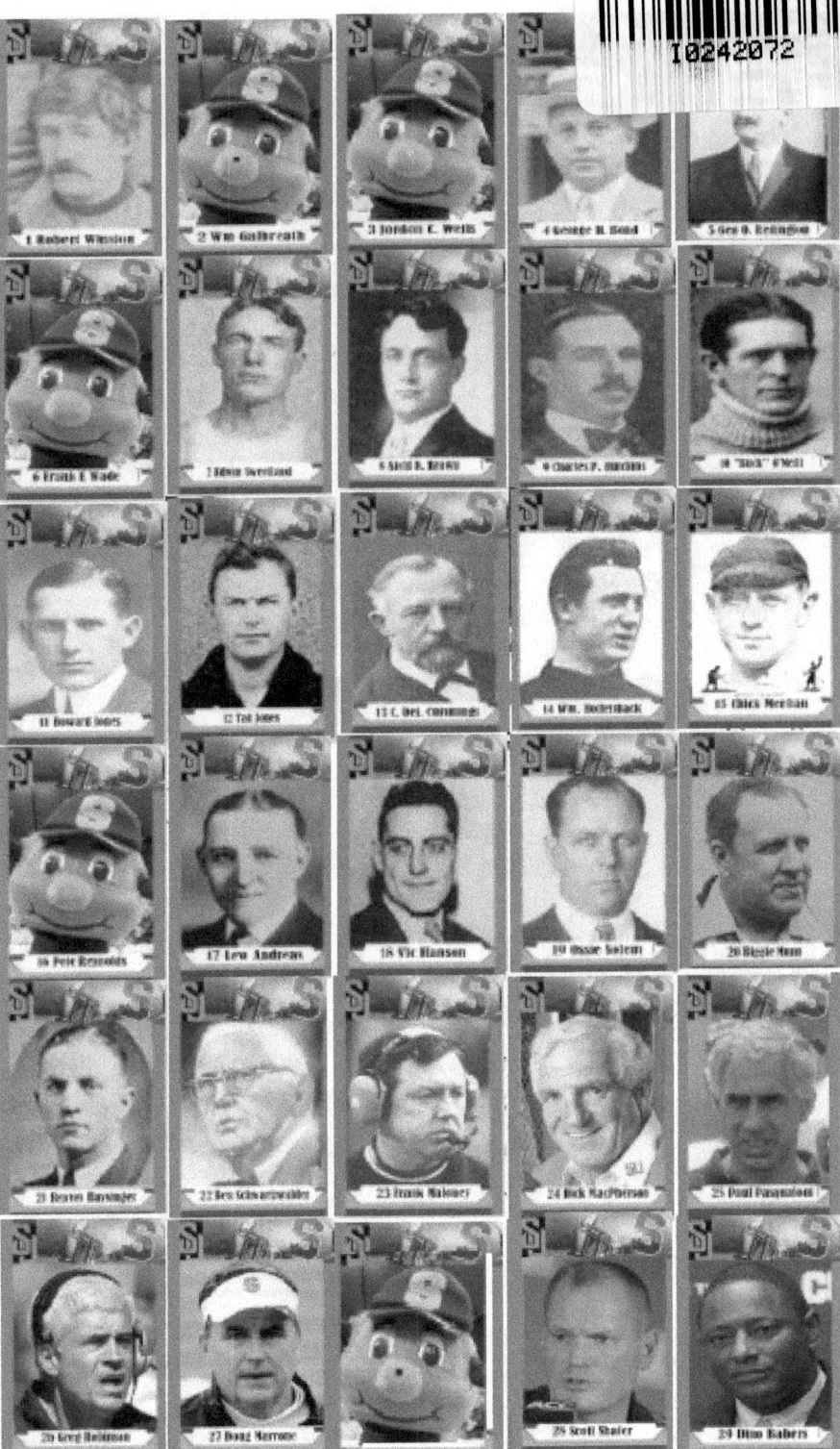

Great Coaches
in
Syracuse Football

From 1st Coach Robert Winston to the Dino Babers era.

This book is written for those of us who love Syracuse University and especially love the Syracuse Orange Football Team. You'll like all the stories from the beginning of the football program, through the great coaches to Syracuse as an annual National Champion contender and as a National Champion. This is a must-have book for Syracuse fans by providing a leg up on the facts missing from the bookshelves of those who do not have this book.

You will learn that the Syracuse Orange, once known as the Orangemen, are fierce and passionate competitors. From the stadium to the classroom to the research lab, the Syracuse Orange always play to win.

The great immortal Syracuse coaches are highlighted—such as —Frank Buck ONeill, Chick Meehan, Ben Schwartzwalder, Dick MacPherson, and Paul Pasqualoni, all the way to the current season with Coach Dino Babers.

This book captures the great moments in Syracuse Football. It takes the reader through stories about the Orange's 29 coaches to great stories about 129 seasons worth of great games (1306 games) with 720 great wins. While examing the era of particular coaches, the book often stops in time and talks about a great player from that era such as Jim Brown, Ernie Davis, Larry Csonka, Floyd Little, Donovan McNabb, Marvin Harrison, Art Monk, John Mackey, Don MacPherson, or Dwight Feeney to add to your reading enjoyment.

This book is your finest source for a great read on your favorite college football team. It is the closest thing to an all-encompassing, full-blown encyclopedia of Syracuse Football coaches. We capture all the seasons with the great Sysracuse coaches helping the players excel in Orange football. This book is for your reading pleasure but also is a great reference for when you want to see how a particular Syracuse game in any year happened to turn out.

You cannot ever get enough of Syracuse greatness, but we do give it a try in this can't miss book. You will not be able to put this book down.

Brian Kelly

Great Coaches in Syracuse Football

Author: Brian W. Kelly
Copyright © 2018 Brian W. Kelly
Publisher/ Editor, Brian P. Kelly

All rights reserved: No part of this book may be reproduced or transmitted in any form, or by any means, electronic or mechanical, including photocopying, recording, scanning, faxing, or by any information storage and retrieval system, without permission from the publisher, LETS GO PUBLISH, in writing.

Disclaimer: Though judicious care was taken throughout the writing and the publication of this work that the information contained herein is accurate, there is no expressed or implied warranty that all information in this book is 100% correct. Therefore, neither LETS GO PUBLISH, nor the author accepts liability for any use of this work.

Trademarks: A number of products and names referenced in this book are trade names and trademarks of their respective companies.

Referenced Material: *The information in this book has been obtained through personal and third-party observations, interviews, and copious research. Where unique information has been provided or extracted from other sources, those sources are acknowledged within the text of the book itself or at the end of the chapter in the Sources Section. Thus, there are no formal footnotes nor is there a bibliography section. Any picture that does not have a source was taken from various sites on the Internet with no credit attached. If resource owners would like credit in the next printing, please email publisher.*

Published by: LETS GO PUBLISH!
Publisher & Editor: Brian P. Kelly
Mail Location: P.O. Box 621, Wilkes-Barre, PA
Email: info@letsgopublish.com
Web site www.letsgopublish.com

Library of Congress Copyright Information Pending
Book Cover Design by Michele Thomas, Editing by Brian P. Kelly

ISBN Information: The International Standard Book Number (ISBN) is a unique machine-readable identification number, which marks any book unmistakably. The ISBN is the clear standard in the book industry. 159 countries and territories are officially ISBN members. The Official ISBN For this book is on the outside cover:

978-1-947402-45-4

The price for this work is : $11.95 USD

10   9   8   7   6   5   4   3   2   1

Release Date: July 2018

LETS GO PUBLISH!

Syracuse Coaching Records from 1889 through 2017

Year	Coach	W	L	T	Year	Coach	W	L	T
1889	No Head Coach	0	1	0	1954	Ben Schwartzwalder	4	4	0
1890	Robert Winston	7	4	0	1955	Ben Schwartzwalder	5	3	0
1891	William Galbreath	4	7	0	1956	Ben Schwartzwalder	7	2	0
1892	Jordon C. Wells	0	8	1	1957	Ben Schwartzwalder	5	3	1
1893	George H. Bond	4	9	1	1958	Ben Schwartzwalder	8	2	0
1894	George H. Bond	6	5	0	1959	Ben Schwartzwalder	11	0	0
1895	George O. Redington	6	2	2	1960	Ben Schwartzwalder	7	2	0
1896	George O. Redington	5	3	0	1961	Ben Schwartzwalder	8	3	0
1897	Frank E Wade	5	3	1	1962	Ben Schwartzwalder	5	5	0
1898	Frank E. Wade	8	2	1	1963	Ben Schwartzwalder	8	2	0
1899	Frank E Wade	4	4	0	1964	Ben Schwartzwalder	7	4	0
1900	Edwin Sweetland	7	2	1	1965	Ben Schwartzwalder	7	3	0
1901	Edwin Sweetland	7	1	0	1966	Ben Schwartzwalder	8	3	0
1902	Edwin Sweetland	6	2	1	1967	Ben Schwartzwalder	8	2	0
1903	Ancil D. Brown	5	4	0	1968	Ben Schwartzwalder	6	4	0
1904	Charles P. Hutchins	6	3	0	1969	Ben Schwartzwalder	5	5	0
1905	Charles P. Hutchins	8	3	0	1970	Ben Schwartzwalder	6	4	0
1906	Frank "Buck" O'Neill	6	3	0	1971	Ben Schwartzwalder	5	5	1
1907	Frank "Buck" O'Neill	5	3	1	1972	Ben Schwartzwalder	5	6	0
1908	Howard Jones	6	3	1	1973	Ben Schwartzwalder	2	9	0
1909	Tad Jones	4	5	1	1974	Frank Maloney	2	9	0
1910	Tad Jones	5	4	1	1975	Frank Maloney	6	5	0
1911	C. Def. Cummings	5	3	2	1976	Frank Maloney	3	8	0
1912	C. Def. Cummings	4	5	0	1977	Frank Maloney	6	5	0
1913	Frank "Buck" O'Neill	6	4	0	1978	Frank Maloney	3	8	0
1914	Frank "Buck" O'Neill	5	3	2	1979	Frank Maloney	7	5	0
1915	Frank "Buck" O'Neill	9	1	2	1980	Frank Maloney	5	6	0
1916	William Hollenback	5	4	0	1981	Dick MacPherson	4	6	1
1917	Frank "Buck" O'Neill	8	1	1	1982	Dick MacPherson	2	9	0
1918	Frank "Buck" O'Neill	5	1	0	1983	Dick MacPherson	6	5	0
1919	Frank "Buck" O'Neill	8	3	0	1984	Dick MacPherson	6	5	0
1920	Chick Meehan	6	2	1	1985	Dick MacPherson	7	5	0
1921	Chick Meehan	7	2	0	1986	Dick MacPherson	5	6	0
1922	Chick Meehan	6	1	2	1987	Dick MacPherson	11	0	1
1923	Chick Meehan	8	1	0	1988	Dick MacPherson	10	2	0
1924	Chick Meehan	8	2	1	1989	Dick MacPherson	8	4	0
1925	Pete Reynolds	8	1	1	1990	Dick MacPherson	7	4	2
1926	Pete Reynolds	7	2	0	1991	Paul Pasqualoni	10	2	0
1927	Lew Andreas	5	3	2	1992	Paul Pasqualoni	10	2	0
1928	Lew Andreas	4	4	1	1993	Paul Pasqualoni	6	4	1
1929	Lew Andreas	6	3	0	1994	Paul Pasqualoni	7	4	0
1930	Vic Hanson	5	2	2	1995	Paul Pasqualoni	9	3	0
1931	Vic Hanson	7	1	1	1996	Paul Pasqualoni	9	3	0
1932	Vic Hanson	4	4	1	1997	Paul Pasqualoni	9	4	0
1933	Vic Hanson	4	4	0	1998	Paul Pasqualoni	8	4	0
1934	Vic Hanson	6	2	0	1999	Paul Pasqualoni	7	5	0
1935	Vic Hanson	6	1	1	2000	Paul Pasqualoni	6	5	0
1936	Vic Hanson	1	7	0	2001	Paul Pasqualoni	10	3	0
1937	Ossie Solem	5	2	1	2002	Paul Pasqualoni	4	8	0
1938	Ossie Solem	5	3	0	2003	Paul Pasqualoni	6	6	0
1939	Ossie Solem	3	3	2	2004	Paul Pasqualoni	6	6	0
1940	Ossie Solem	3	4	0	2005	Greg Robinson	1	#	0
1941	Ossie Solem	5	2	1	2006	Greg Robinson	4	8	0
1942	Ossie Solem	6	3	0	2007	Greg Robinson	2	#	0

Year	Coach	W	L	T	Year	Coach	W	L	T
1944	Ossie Solem	2	4	1	2008	Greg Robinson	3	9	0
1945	Ossie Solem	1	6	0	2009	Doug Marrone	4	8	0
1946	Clarence Biggie Munn	4	5	0	2010	Doug Marrone	8	5	0
1947	Reaves Baysinger	3	6	0	2011	Doug Marrone	5	7	0
1948	Reaves Baysinger	1	8	0	2012	Doug Marrone	8	5	0
1949	Ben Schwartzwalder	4	5	0	2013	Scott Shafer	7	6	0
1950	Ben Schwartzwalder	5	5	0	2014	Scott Shafer	3	9	0
1951	Ben Schwartzwalder	5	4	0	2015	Scott Shafer	4	8	0
1952	Ben Schwartzwalder	7	3	0	2016	Dino Babers	4	8	0
1953	Ben Schwartzwalder	5	3	1	2017	Dino Babers	4	8	0

Total Games   1306
Total Wins   720
Total Losses   537
Total Ties   49   * Prior to Overtime Rules
Stats from   1889   * Through Nov 2017

Dedication

I dedicate this book

To my wonderful brothers and sisters:

Angel Edward J. Kelly, Jr.

Carol & Amelia Kelly

Nancy "Ann" Flannery & Angel Jim Flannery

Mary A. Daniels & Bill Daniels

Joseph A. Kelly & Diane Kelly

I surely am a lucky person to have

Such a great family

Edward J Kelly and Irene McKeown Kelly

.

Acknowledgments:

I appreciate all the help that I have received in putting this book together as well as all of the other 151 books from the past.

My acknowledgments were so large at one time that readers complained that they had to go through too many pages to get to page one.

And, so I put my acknowledgment list online, and it continues to grow. Believe it or not, it would cost about a dollar more to print my books with full acknowledgments.

Thank you and God bless you all for your help. Please check out www.letsgopublish.com to read the latest version of my heartfelt acknowledgments updated for this book.

In this book, I received some extra special help from many fine American patriots including Dennis Grimes, Gerry Rodski, Wily Ky Eyely, Angel Irene McKeown Kelly, Angel Edward Joseph Kelly Sr., Angel Edward Joseph Kelly Jr., Ann Flannery, Angel James Flannery Sr., Mary Daniels, Bill Daniels, Angel Robert Gary Daniels, Angel Sarah Janice Daniels, Angel Punkie Daniels, Joe Kelly, Diane Kelly, Brian P. Kelly, Mike P. Kelly, Katie P. Kelly, Angel Ben Kelly, and Budmund (Buddy) Arthur Kelly.

Thank you all!

Table of Contents

Dedication ix

Table of Contents xiii

Chapter 1 Introduction Syracuse Football 23

Chapter 2 Syracuse Launches its First Football Team 43

Chapter 3 Seven SU Coaches 1889 to 1902 47

Chapter 4 Six SU Coaches 1903 to 1915 69

Chapter 5 Five SU Coaches 1916 to 1929 89

Chapter 6 Vic Hanson 1930 to 1936 109

Chapter 7 Ossie Solem 1937 to 1948 117

Chapter 8 Ben Schwartzwalder 1949 to 1973 135

Chapter 9 Frank Maloney 1974 to 1980 177

Chapter 10 Dick Macpherson 1981 to 1990 185

Chapter 11 Paul Pasqualoni 1991 to 2004 207

Chapter 12 Greg Robinson 2005 to 2008 235

Chapter 13 Doug Marrone 2009 to 2012 243

Chapter 14 Scott Shafer 2013 to 2015 257

Chapter 15 Dino Babers 2016 to ???? 265

Other books by Brian Kelly: (amazon.com, & Kindle) 278

References

I learned how to write creatively in Grade School at St. Boniface. I even enjoyed reading some of my own stuff.

At Meyers High School (HS Diploma) and King's College (BS Data Processing), and Wilkes-University, (MBA Accounting & Finance) learned how to research, write bibliographies and footnote every non-original thought included in my writings. I learned to hate ibid, and op. cit., and I hated assuring that I had all citations were written down in the proper sequence. Having to pay attention to details took my desire to write creatively and diminished it with busy work.

I know it is necessary for the world to stop plagiarism, so authors and publishers can get paid properly, but for an honest writer, it sure is annoying. I wrote many proposals while with IBM and whenever I needed to cite something, I cited it in place, because my readers, IT Managers, and company management, could care less about tracing the vagaries of citations. I always hated to use stilted footnotes, or produce a lengthy, perfectly formatted bibliography. I bet most bibliographies are flawed because even the experts on such drivel do not like the tedium.

I wrote 161 books before this book and several hundred articles published by many magazines and newspapers and I only cite when an idea is not mine or when I am quoting, and again, I choose to cite in place, and the reader does not have to trace strange numbers through strange footnotes and back to bibliography elements that may not be readily accessible or available.

Yet, I would be kidding you, if in a book about the great coaches in Syracuse Football, I tried to bluff my way, so you would think that I knew everything before I began to research and write anything in this book. I spent as much time researching as writing. I might even call myself an expert of sorts now for all the facts that I have uncovered.

Without any pain on your part, you can read this book from cover to cover to enjoy the stories about the many great coaches in Syracuse Football.

This book is not intended for historians per se, but it does teach a lot of history. It is for regular people of all levels of intelligence. It is for people that want to have a fun read, who like smiling when Syracuse

Football is the topic. It is fun reading about each of SU's 720 wins. This book is for people who love Syracuse and perhaps it is also for some Syracuse detractors who want to have command of the facts.

There are lots and lots of facts in this book. This book is not for sticklers about the mundane aspects of writing that often cause creative writers to lay bricks or paint houses instead of writing. It is for everyday people, like you and I, who enjoy Syracuse because it is Syracuse and who enjoy football because it is football. It is that simple.

When Syracuse plays a team and wins or loses, that is a historical fact, but to discover such facts, it does not require fundamental or basic research. The University itself copyrights its material but only so it can say "no" if somebody else's creativity affects the University negatively. Even Syracuse does not own well-known facts that are readily available about legacies such as Dick MacPherson, Ben Schwartzwalder, and championship seasons.

The championships and the coaches and the great players are well known and well defined, though some may think Jim Brown is an Actor and not the greatest Syracuse and Cleveland Browns football player of all time. So, what? As the author of this book, I care but it is a sports book. I use a judicious approach to assure that I am not throwing the bull when I am presenting the facts.

Nonetheless, this is not a book about heavy math algorithms, or potential advances to the internal combustion engine, or space travel, or the eight elements necessary to find a cure for cancer. So, I refuse to treat this book 100% seriously. If you find a fault, I will fix it. This is a book about sports and sports legends and stories about sporting events that have been recorded seven million times already someplace else. Though I tried for sure to get it all right and I used the work of others to assure so, I bet I made a mistake or two.

What is my remedy for the *harmed* if I have made a mistake? I did not write this book to harm anybody. If I did not write this book, would the *harmed individuals* from the book be unharmed. So, at the very least, I can *unpublish* those parts of the book. If any reader is harmed, let me know, and I will do whatever must be done for all to be OK.

Preface:

"It was not a competitive program when we came here, and now everything about it is competitive. We can stay at this level, because Syracuse is that kind of team. But it's not enough. This program and this area deserves a legitimate top 32 team, when you're going to a bowl every year." Quote by Dick Macpherson, a great SU coach

The late Dick Macpherson is one of the more quoted of Syracuse's past coaching masters. It is no wonder why. In his ten great years at Syracuse, Big Mac called it as he saw it.

Everything that is—can be made better. When Clemson came to town in 2017, having had a *much-too-easy* victory against the Orange in 2016, they were planning to leave Syracuse with another big win. But, because everything came together from the pregame to the game, it did not happen.

With Dino Babers as coach, even as it is rebuilding, Syracuse is again a team with a heart. It is a team that cannot be messed with. To get the fans stirring for the Clemson Friday game last fall, the fans planned a big splash. The Orange were back in the Carrier Dome on this Friday for one of the most highly-anticipated games of the season versus the reigning national champion Clemson Tigers. Kickoff between the Orange and the Tigers was at 7:02 p.m. for a game viewable across the world on ESPN.

Syracuse has had many other games like this but none with such meaning and hype as undefeated Clemson was the one and only reigning national championship team in the fall 2017. The Clemson encounter was the 1,300th in the illustrious 128-year history of the Syracuse football program. Lots was happening all day from individually planned trips to the great bookstore and a number of pep filled events leading up to the game including pregame festivities on the Quad that started at 4 p.m. A Quad pep rally featuring the "Pride of the Orange" marching band began at 5:30 p.m. The band performed on the steps of Hendricks Chapel. It was a grand scene.

The band's pregame performance inside the Dome began at 6:48 p.m. and Coach Dino Babers led the Orange team onto the field at 6:57 p.m. It was like clockwork and full precision. This particular week in the ACC was Fall Sportsmanship Week. To showcase their continued dedication to sportsmanship and fair play, the Orange and Tigers met at midfield to shake hands just prior to kickoff.

The last few years, and now with an exciting coach like Dino Babers, Syracuse is looking for the same magic formula for all games including pep rallies and for tailgating festivities. The objective is team spirit and the notion is to bring out the fans in major numbers to help rev the team up for a great game. The Clemson formula worked against Clemson in 2017. Would that not be nice to see a lot more pep and spirit in 2018 and beyond. Look at the results from 2017:

Dungey has 3 TD passes, Syracuse stuns No. 2 Clemson 27-24

"Eric Dungey threw for 278 yards and three touchdowns, Cole Murphy kicked a tiebreaking field goal in the fourth quarter, and Syracuse stunned #2 Clemson 27-24 on Friday night to put a damper on the Tigers' chances to repeat as national champions." Syracuse was at its best. Thank you, Coach Dino Babers, and a spirited group of Orange.

The Syracuse University Bookstore is outstanding for on campus shopping and it is also as good as it gets online at http://shop.und.com/. You can acquire a host of relics and memorabilia and some nice SU wear from the bookstore, plus you can buy books that are all about Syracuse University. I bet the store will also be pleased to sell you some great textbooks about your favorite subjects.

The bookstore is located in the Schine Student Center, 303 University Place, Syracuse, NY 13210: https://bookweb.syr.edu -- 315-443-9900. Give them a call to order this new book for your many Syracuse friends. Of course, you can reach them online at https://bookweb.syr.edu/

This new book by Brian Kelly, which highlights the Great Coaches in Syracuse Football is one of the items that is expected to be available all 52 weeks and in fact all 365 days each year except in LEAP YEAR where the University adds an extra day for your shopping pleasure. The Bookstore is there to add to your Syracuse Orange football experience. Once you get this book, it is yours forever unless, of course you give it away to one of the many SU fans, who will be in awe of your new possession.

Whether you get to the pep rallies and home games on campus or not, this book and its nearly 500 pages brings the glory of Syracuse football right to your bookshelf, your pocket, or right to your hands. Reading this book is like reliving the last game, the last football season, and / or all the seasons before last season without ever having to get on or off a plane. Seeing a game in the Dome, however, is an exhilarating experience, I've done it many times. This book will help you relive that experience over and over. Besides the great read, with this book in your hand at your private venue, there is no limit on the hours for book-tailgating. Moreover, there is no charge, as long as you have stocked up before the read.

The book examines more than just great coaches. There are some coaches that were not so great in every team's football seasons and Syracuse offers no excuses for those times. Your author shows the bad with the good to get the proper perspective for those great moments.

Not all Syracuse coaches, for example, are named Schwartzwalder or MacPherson or Pasqualoni, so not all games are in the W column. However, all teams, no matter who the coach is, were Syracuse tough, nonetheless. That means they all fought hard for wins as the Syracuse Orangemen. I hope you enjoy the contrast.

Opening with a description of Syracuse and moving quickly to the Orange's first football game, this book goes all the way to Coach Dino Babers' last game in 2017. Then, it presents the 2018 season schedule and the outlook for 2018 and the future of the program.

It is written for those of us who love Syracuse Football as played in either Archbold Stadium or the Carrier Dome. You'll enjoy the stories of the seasons as this book moves onward to the great immortal Syracuse Coaches of historical fame—O'Neill, Meehan, Schwartzwalder, MacPherson, and Pasqualoni. What a book!

Predicting that another future immortal great may be in our midst, the book then takes us up to the current season with Coach Dino Babers.

This book is all about the great coaches in Syracuse Football. It touches every aspect of the historical and mythical Syracuse Football Teams. It tells exhilarating stories about SU's 29 coaches and its 129 seasons worth of great games. The book stops every now and then, and it takes the reader on a side excursion in time to learn about a particular event or a great player. The player list always begins with the living immortal, Jim Brown, then moves to the heavenly immortal, Ernie Davis, and on to Floyd Little, Qadry Ismail, Eric Dungey, and a slew of SU All-Americans who have made Syracuse Football a bright light experience for the program's many years and many fans.

In my role as Editor in Chief of Lets Go Publish! and Syracuse fan, as I have been at many games with my dad, your author, I predict that you will not be able to put this book down

You are going to love this book because it is the perfect read for anybody who loves Syracuse University and Syracuse Football and who wants to know more about one of the most revered athletic programs in the Northeast.

Few sports books are a must-read but Brian Kelly's Great Coaches in Syracuse Football will quickly appear at the top of Americas most enjoyable must-read books about sports. Enjoy!

Who is Brian Kelly?

Brian Kelly aka Brian W. Kelly, his pen name for non-sports books, is one of the leading authors in America with this, his 162nd published book. Brian continues as an outspoken and eloquent expert on a variety of topics. Moreover, Kelly also has written several hundred articles on other topics of interest to Americans.

Most of his early works involved high technology. Later, Brian wrote a number of patriotic books and most recently he has been writing human interest books such as The Wine Diet and Thank you, IBM. His books are always well received. If I could get the pen out of Dad's hand for just awhile, I might be able to write a few books of my own, but my editing chores at Lets Go Publish always come first.

Brian Kelly's books are highlighted at www.letsgopublish.com. They are for sale at Amazon, Kindle, and Amazon.com/author/brianwkelly, as well as Barnes & Noble and other fine booksellers.

The best!

Sincerely,

Brian P. Kelly, Editor in Chief
I am Brian Kelly's eldest son

About the Author

Brian Kelly retired as an Assistant Professor in the Business Information Technology (BIT) Program at Marywood University, where he also served as the IBM i and Midrange Systems Technical Advisor to the IT Faculty. Kelly designed, developed, and taught many college and professional courses. He continues as a contributing technical editor to a number of technical industry magazines, including "The Four Hundred" and "Four Hundred Guru," published by IT Jungle.

Kelly is a former IBM Senior Systems Engineer. His specialty was problem solving for customers as well as implementing advanced operating systems and software on his client's machines. Brian is the author of 151 books, including 23 Sports Books, and hundreds of magazine articles. He has been a frequent speaker at technical conferences throughout the United States.

Brian was a candidate for the US Congress from Pennsylvania in 2010 and he ran for Mayor in his home town in 2015. Kelly loves Syracuse and he became a big fan in the 1980's when he was with IBM and he ran many bus trips from Scranton to Syracuse to watch Pennsylvania Teams such as Penn State and Pittsburgh, play the Orangemen.

When PSU stopped playing the Orange, the annual PSU game, which once alternated between PSU and Pitt continued to be billed for Scranton IBMers as the Annual Penn State Game. However, the game itself would feature Army or another appropriate team against the Orangemen of Syracuse. Sometimes our bus parked right alongside the Army busses and our kids loved watching the cadets. This is Brian's seventh "Great Coaches" book about major College Football Teams and writing about Syracuse has been a special treat.

Chapter 1 Introduction Syracuse Football

Syracuse celebrates its 129th year of football

Dino Babers, Syracuse Football Coach Leading the Orange

In 2019, Syracuse will celebrate its 130th year of collegiate football. This book celebrates Syracuse Football; its coaches; its struggles; its greatness; and its long-lasting impact on American life. People like me, who love Syracuse from way back when they were the Orangemen, will love this book. Those not so much incline to love SU football will want their own copy of this book just for additional ammo. Yet, it won't help them! Hah!

In defining the format of the book, we chose to use a timetable that is based on a historical chronology. Within this framework, we discuss the great coaches in Syracuse Football History, and there are many great coaches. No book can claim to be able to capture them all, as it would be a never-ending story, but we sure try. The coaches highlighted in this book helped mold some terrific players.

Jim Brown, Ernie Davis (RIP), Floyd Little, and other Syracuse greats have great reverence for the University for which they played the game of football. Nearly a half century after he left Syracuse to embark on his NFL career, Floyd Little returned to his alma mater in 2011 on a Thursday, quoting lines from a Robert Frost poem to describe why he decided to give up a cushy retirement to be back at school.

"I have promises to keep and miles to go before I sleep," said the Hall of Fame running back, who was introduced as Syracuse's special assistant to the athletic director. The most famous of them all is Jim Brown, who literally is the greatest.

Ernie Davis is one of God's angel's today and surely, he shines on Syracuse University a light that will never be extinguished. Like Brown and Little, Ernie Davis was a Syracuse phenomenon who got sick before the good things happened and he died but his memory lives on.

Every NFL team wanted Ernie Davis to play for them. It was the most lucrative contract for an NFL rookie up to that time. He chose the Cleveland Browns where he would have been teamed with the great Jim Brown. The Browns' dream of pairing Davis with Jim Brown took a tragic turn when Davis was diagnosed with leukemia.

Following his death, the Browns retired his number 45 jersey. Davis was a great man in his short life and we know he is still showering blessings on Syracuse. If asked, by the Browns, I would bet that he would have said that Syracuse jerseys should not be retired because with all of the history of these great teams, there would be no numbers left.

I use my feelings about Ernie Davis as a great human being as an idea to help promulgate the notion that nobody can write a book about Syracuse Football History that is all inclusive, because even if it can be written, it would be too big to ever be read. I hoped this book would come in at a little over 100 pages, but if it had, you would not have liked it. Read what you can when you can. It will be a fun experience.

I capture all the great Syracuse coaches in this book. OK, I get them all but they all don't get the same exact treatment because some, such as Ben Schwartzwalder had more impact on SU than most of them! If I missed any and you tell me, then we'll do another edition. The great coaches naturally include a lot of great people, including players and the 27 great coaches that over time would make or break Syracuse University's football program.

If Syracuse were ever to break because of a coach, as some believe it has at times, simply because it is Syracuse, the University not only would continue, it will always continue.

Syracuse has been able to survive a number of coaches who could not survive themselves, while the university and the football program have both grown in acceptance and popularity.

We all as individuals and as honest institutions, such as Syracuse do our best in life and sometimes it is just enough. Sometimes it is just not enough. Even if we survive and become more than OK, detractors may suggest our success is not enough. I disagree. Let the naysayers say "nay," and go away!

Let me please assure you that I have done my best to portray an accurate depiction of Syracuse Football History, highlighting its great coaching staffs, displayed in a properly summarized format so that none of us are reading this book forever. There are a ton of great stories for sure.

More importantly, none of us should need to search further than this book for the truth about many of the depictions in this book. Let's talk about some Syracuse football moments and some great athletes and coaches now, before we close out the first chapter of this book highlighting the Great Coaches in Syracuse Football.

Brief Overview

Ya just gotta love Syracuse University and the Syracuse Orangemen Football Team, who now are called the Syracuse Orange. I know I think of the Orange as the Orangemen as do many others as all new ideas take time. I have been to the Carrier Dome and Manley Field more than I have been in any college stadium in the country. And, I love College Football and the Syracuse Orangemen.

After many years as an independent, the Orange Football Team joined the Big East in 1991 and then, in 2013, in another change for the better, all of the Syracuse athletic teams joined the Atlantic Coast Conference (ACC). The ACC is part of the National Collegiate Athletic Association (NCAA) Division I conference that is part of the Football Bowl Subdivision (FBS). Syracuse, for all of its great play over the years has one national championship, along with an awful lot of close calls.

Their big championship season was earned under coach Ben Schwartzwalder, a Syracuse coaching immortal during the 1959 season. Currently, The Orange are coached by Dino Babers, who was hired on December 5, 2015, to succeed Scott Shafer. Home games are played at the Carrier Dome, located on the school's beautiful campus in Syracuse. Regardless of what the temperature is outside, the magnificent Carrier Dome facility is always a toasty 69 degrees.

Syracuse opened as an institution in 1870 and it took just nineteen years to begin a football program that became one of the nation's best. They played on what they called the Old Oval Athletic Field. It was deployed by the University from 1898 to 1907. Check it out on the next page:

The Old Oval athletic field, Syracuse University, *circa* 1898–1907

Syracuse played its first football game on November 23, 1889. The score was 0-36 in a game played against Rochester. Things changed for the better, and quite rapidly from 1890 on. In 1890, for example with First coach Robert Winston, the Orangemen put forth a highly respectable season at 7-4, for a team operating in just its second year.

National success was achieved not too long after this first game in the 1890s and 1900s. With the construction of the "state-of-the-art" Archbold Stadium in 1907, Syracuse rose to national prominence under College Football Hall of Fame coach Frank "Buck" O'Neill. O'Neill could not get enough of Syracuse as he kept leaving and coming back. He always produced great teams. His 1915 squad got itself a Rose Bowl invitation, but the administration declined because the team had already played on the West Coast that season. Times have changed.

The 1920s brought on continued success with teams featuring star end Vic Hanson, one of only two individuals who are members (Amos Alonzo Stagg—not from Syracuse being the other) of both the Basketball Hall of Fame and the College Football Hall of Fame. Hanson later coached the team.

Back then, there were a lot of football teams from schools we heard little about in the national spotlight. From 1891 to 1961, Colgate University was Syracuse's biggest rival. Despite how powerful the Orangemen were, Colgate held the edge during this period, 31–26–5.

From 1937–1945, Ossie Solem served as Syracuse's head coach, compiling a 30–27–6 record. Though a winning record, things had slowed down a bit for the Orange on their path to football glory. Ben Schwartzwalder would change that as he put in 25 years and is responsible for modern Syracuse football for being a mainstay on the US college and university football map.

Ben Schwartzwalder era (1949–1973)

Coach Schwartzwalder with quarterback Dick Easterly at the Los Angeles Coliseum, 1959

When Ben Schwartzwalder took over as coach in 1949, it was a breath of fresh air for the program, which had been neglected and had stagnated during the 1930's and 1940's. Army dominated the national scene at this time as did Notre Dame with Frank Leahy at the helm.

A number of special teams during this war-time period benefitted by service academy personnel in attendance, or their universities were part of a service academy. They prospered while a lot of other one-time fine teams, including basketball great Gonzaga could not find enough players to field a quality football team during the war years. Syracuse was affected in a major way by WWII in 1943 and did not field a team that year.

The Orangemen made their first bowl appearance in the 1953 Orange Bowl under Coach Schwartzwalder, in his fifth year. They followed this in 1957 with an appearance in the Cotton Bowl, and then the 1959 Orange Bowl.

The 1957 Cotton Bowl Classic team featured Hall of Fame running back Jim Brown who my dad and many others believe is the best "living" football player of all time. When Jim Brown passes on in another 75 years, I suspect, the adjective "living" will be deleted and he will be known simply as the best running back of all time. Rumor has it that to stay as fast and as powerful as he wanted to be, Brown chose not to wear hip-pads. Perhaps the lack of those extra inches on his width also helped him slip through smaller openings. However, from having watched Jim Brown on our brand new black and white Admiral TV, during this time period, I have a feeling his record would be the same even if his bones were that big.

In 1959, Syracuse was undefeated. Because the team played the best colleges in the nation, they were awarded their first national championship following this undefeated season and their Cotton Bowl Classic victory over Texas. Though Jim Brown was playing pro football for the Browns that year, a phenomenal sophomore running back named Ernie Davis, assured the championship season for Syracuse and Ben Schwartzwalder. Davis was great. He went on to become the first African American to win the Heisman Trophy, a major milestone in Syracuse football history.

in 1961, Syracuse All-American tackle Ron Luciano, who eventually become a prominent Major League Baseball umpire was a bulwark on the team. Tragedy hit Ernie Davis, who with today's medicine would be alive and offering commentary with Jim Brown. He was slated to play for the Cleveland Browns in the same backfield with Jim Brown.

Can you imagine the agony of the defensive lines with that combo pounding them play after play. Ernie Davis, a great young man, died of leukemia before being able to play one game professionally. Syracuse remained competitive through the 1960s with a series of All American running backs, including the great Floyd Little and one of the best fullbacks ever, Larry Csonka.

Ben Schwartzwalder retired as Syracuse's head coach following the 1973 season, which was Syracuse's third-consecutive losing season. Whether Schwartzwalder had lost his fight, or the Syracuse administration chose not to work hard to receive scholarship athletes is a question for the ages. Ben Schwartzwalder left Syracuse with a proud 153–91–3 record. Regardless, the great one, Ben Schwartzwalder chose to pack it in.

Frank Maloney era (1974–1980)

There was only one Ben Schwartzwalder though many times school administrations think that it was some other magic than the coach, that brought in all the wins. Michigan assistant coach Frank Maloney was hired as Schwartzwalder's replacement. Giving the benefit of the doubt, the best one could say about Maloney's tenure at Syracuse was that it was marked by inconsistency. The fan base turned on him as the Orange failed to achieve the national status they had enjoyed under Schwartzwalder. It is always better to replace a coach who is a bum than a great coach. Maloney learned this lesson.

Maloney had a problem with racial unrest among other things. Many who look at it objectively saw that the administration's lack of financial support for the program was a large part of the blame. Few coaches would have done well in similar circumstances. Maloney's program had a tough go with the limitation of archaic facilities. Archbold Stadium, Syracuse's home field since 1907, had had its best days and it was in need of replacement. Despite adversity, Maloney was able to recruit a number of future NFL stars such as Joe Morris and Pro Football Hall of Fame member Art Monk.

Maloney was the subject of criticism, not only from the fans and alumni, but also from the 1959 national championship team, who had forgotten that Ben Schwartzwalder had losing seasons before he finally left the program. Members of this elite championship team wanted more championships regardless of university resources. They began a campaign calling for Maloney's ouster.

Ironically enough, this call from program alumni came during the 1979 season, which was Coach Maloney's best season at Syracuse. The Orangemen qualified for the Independence Bowl, beating McNeese State. After coaching the Orangemen for seven seasons and presiding over the opening of a new stadium, the Carrier Dome, in 1980, Maloney resigned. When somebody who knows the inside scoop writes a factual article about what really happened to Syracuse for ten years, beginning the last three years of the Schwartzwalder era, in a second edition, we will be pleased to tell the full story.

Dick MacPherson era (1981–1990)

When visiting Syracuse's Carrier Dome on my many bus trips, I always thought Dick MacPherson was a great coach and I thought Don McPherson was his son. I later learned they spelled their names differently.

Dick MacPherson was hired as the head coach in 1981 and after several mediocre seasons, fans wanted MacPherson fired. They coined the phrase, "Sack Mac." Once a team tastes national success as Syracuse did under Schwartzwalder, the alums and the fan base want nothing less. Syracuse is no different than other universities across the country. After losing to Clemson in 2016, I bet we could find a number of feint calls for Alabama's Nick Saban's head out there in the ethosphere.

Fans are fickle once the winning begins. The fans' opinion of Coach MacPherson changed when the program returned suddenly to national prominence in 1987 with an undefeated 11–0 regular season record. Dick was OK then by the fans. That team featured Maxwell Award-winning quarterback Don McPherson and fullback Daryl Johnston. Before the BCS times, luck had a lot to do with whether a great undefeated national team could even get into a national championship bowl game.

And so, the team missed an opportunity to play for the NCAA Division I-A national football championship, but not because they were not good enough. It was because both Oklahoma and Miami also finished undefeated that year and finished higher in the polls.

Consequently, the Orangemen were scheduled to face Southeastern Conference Champion Auburn University in the Sugar Bowl. In a nail-biter, the game ended in a tie. Auburn managed to kick a late field goal rather than trying for a game-winning touchdown.

Dick MacPherson resigned after the 1990 season to accept the position of head coach for the NFL's New England Patriots. MacPherson coached the Patriots in 1991 and 1992 and received strong consideration for Coach of the Year honors in 1991. The Pats were 1-15 in 1990 and with five more wins, McPherson led them to a 6–10 record in his first season.

Things were looking bright but then in his second season the team struggled like in the past, starting four different quarterbacks and the Pats finished a dismal 2-14. MacPherson was subsequently fired at the end of the season. Later, he took a spot as assistant coach with the Denver Broncos and then the Cleveland Browns.

Paul Pasqualoni era (1991–2004)

Syracuse had gotten its mojo going again with McPherson and continued to do well under his successor, Paul Pasqualoni. Coach Pasqualoni had previously been the team's linebackers' coach, as head coach, his teams appeared in 11 bowl games (including three major bowls) and they won 9 of the 11 games. Syracuse also captured or shared three Big East football championships during the Pasqualoni period.

Big name players under Pasqualoni included Donovan McNabb, Marvin Harrison, Dwight Freeney, Keith Bulluck, Rob Moore, Donovin Darius, Qadry Ismail, Kevin Johnson, Rob Konrad, Tebucky Jones, and Marvin Graves.

Coach Pasqualoni

Pasqualoni had good talent and he made the most of it.

For years, every other year, IBM took a trip to Syracuse from Scranton to see the Penn State v Syracuse game at the Carrier Dome. It was great football. Every other year, it was Pitt. In the early 1990's Penn State ended its series with Syracuse and joined the

Big Ten. After I had left IBM, I brought a busload from Scranton every year for many years.

Meanwhile, fewer and fewer independents, such as Penn State, were finding it advantageous to go it alone. Syracuse chose to join the newly formed Big East football conference with traditional rivals University of Pittsburgh, West Virginia University, and national power Miami. In 2004, Miami and Virginia Tech left the Big East to join the Atlantic Coast Conference (ACC). In 2004, Syracuse gave up its nicknames Orangemen and Orangewomen, and settled on being the Syracuse Orange in all sports.

In 2005, Boston College left the Big East for the ACC. Syracuse felt this threatened the stature of the Big East. Syracuse had been originally invited to leave the Big East and join the ACC, but politics entered the fray. The Governor of Virginia pressured the ACC, which then decided to invite Virginia Tech to join the conference, instead. Thus, Syracuse for a number of years reluctantly remained in the Big East.

Syracuse and Pittsburgh together left the Big East on July 1, 2013. They each had to find the cash. Each team paid the Big East $7.5 million to depart on that date. Notre Dame joined the ACC on July 1, 2013, while Louisville left for the ACC on July 1, 2014. The ACC, with Clemson winning the national championship last year has certainly become a super conference.

Syracuse's streak of winning seasons ended in 2002 when they went 4–8. This was followed by consecutive 6–6 seasons. Although the Orange won a share of the Big East title in 2004 and competed in the Champs Sports Bowl, the teams from 2002–2004 were considered mediocre by Syracuse's new standards. This prompted new athletic director Dr. Daryl Gross to fire Pasqualoni after a mostly-successful 14-years at the helm.

Greg Robinson era (2005–2008)

In 2005, Syracuse hired Greg Robinson as the new head coach. He had been the defensive coordinator for Texas. Robinson changed the style of Syracuse football by installing a new West Coast offense scheme. This replaced the option run style of offense previously run by Pasqualoni, and he added new defensive schemes.

Former football head coach Greg Robinson "chases" the last of his players onto the field before the kickoff of his inaugural 2005 season. It was the first game played on the Carrier Dome's new FieldTurf.

The 2005 season started very positively as Syracuse had an upset going over eventual Big East and Sugar Bowl champion West Virginia. They forced five turnovers but did not capitalize. They lost the game L (7-15).

They came right back with a 31–0 blowout over Buffalo and another near upset win to #25 Virginia. Bad luck prevailed as the Orangemen lost 27–24 on a last-second field goal.

The good news was over for the season as the squad lost its final eight games. Syracuse finished the year 1–10, the worst season in school history and they won only 10 games while Robinson was running the program.

The team showed some signs of life with a 4–8 record in 2006 but skidded to 2–10 in 2007. On the positive side, they did get the best of

#18 Louisville in a great road game nail-biter, W (38-35), but finished with only two wins. The team continued to struggle in 2008, and fired Coach Robinson, after a dismal 3–9 season which ended with a loss against Akron on November 29.

The season high point was a 24–23 upset of Notre Dame. Pundits suggest the game that best represented this low period in Robinson's tenure was a 55–13 loss to long-time rival Penn State.

Doug Marrone era (2009–2012)

Less than two weeks after Robinson got his final notification, on December 12, 2008, Doug Marrone, a former Orangeman and offensive coordinator for the NFL's New Orleans Saints, was announced as the replacement for Robinson as SU head coach. Marrone was the first Syracuse alumnus to serve as head football coach since Reaves H. Baysinger in 1948.

It was reported that he had some powerful alums rooting for him. Tim Green and Floyd Little wanted Marrone from the moment the previous coach Greg Robinson was fired, and when interviewed by Green, Marrone was found to have kept a folder of current high-school players in the Syracuse area to get a head start in recruiting. The program seemed to improve immediately in 2009, as the Orange, despite only a marginal improvement in their win-loss record. looked much better on the field. The team record was 4–8 under Marrone for his first year, including a 28–7 loss at number-seven Penn State.

In 2010, the Orange finished the regular season with a winning record for the first time since the 2001 season at 7–5, including road wins against number-19 West Virginia and two-time defending conference champion Cincinnati. The team earned its first bowl bid since 2004 and along with second-ranked Oregon and 10th-ranked Boise State, the five road wins were the best in 2010 of all FBS teams. December 30, 2010, Syracuse defeated Kansas State in the inaugural Pinstripe Bowl at Yankee Stadium. In 2011, the Orange slipped again to 5-8, but came right back to 8-5 in 2012. In 2012, the Orange defeated West Virginia in the 2012 Pinstripe Bowl. This would be Marrone's last season

On January 7, 2013, Marrone left Syracuse, accepting the head-coaching position of the NFL's Buffalo Bills. He was a fine coach.

Scott Shafer era (2013–2015)

Instead of going out with a national search, the day after Marrone's departure, Syracuse promoted defensive coordinator Scott Shafer to head coach. His first season was marked by inconsistent performance from the team.

In his first game at the helm, Coach Shafer nearly guided the team to an upset of Penn State, with the Orange eventually losing 23–17. The Orange got their first win under Shafer in a 54–0 rout of Wagner, and followed it up with another blowout win, beating Tulane 52–17.

<< Coach Shafer

However, the first season under this new coach also produced blowouts the other way with a crushing 14-49 defeat at home to fourth-ranked Clemson, and road losses to unranked Georgia Tech 0-56 and eventual national champions Florida State 3-59. These huge losses were hard to take.

Syracuse faced off against Boston College in the season finale, needing a victory to become bowl eligible. They got it with a great finish. The Orange were down 31–27 with 2:08 remaining. Quarterback Terrell Hunt pulled off a spectacular 75-yard, game-winning drive, capped off with a 25-yard touchdown pass to tight end Josh Parris with six seconds remaining.

This victory gave the Orange a bowl bid for the third time in four years. Syracuse finished the season with a nice 21–17 victory over Minnesota in the 2013 Texas Bowl to finish above 500 at 7–6. The next season, the Orange would make its debut in the ACC.

Things did not go so well in 2014 despite the Orange starting the season 2–0. The season began with a spectacular double-overtime, 27–26 victory over FCS power Villanova, marked by a Syracuse extra point that was called good, but replays later showed that it was just wide left. Nonetheless the Orange got the V. In the next game, the Orange beat Central Michigan W (40-3) but that was the end of the good times. Syracuse lost 9 of its last 10 games to finish the season a disappointing 3–9.

In 2015, fans and media noticed a significant uptick in the team's performance after they started with three wins 3–0. In game four, they played tough with eighth-ranked LSU at home, barely losing 34–24. Then, the Orange, which had been having trouble finishing seasons positively, lost eight of their last nine games, though they played closely with multiple ranked teams. The team finished 4–8, and on November 23, 2015, and after three losing seasons, it was announced that Shafer would be fired after the last game of the 2015 campaign.

Dino Babers Era (2016–present)

This time, in finding a new coach, the administration took its time and chose to look across the country before they committed to anything.

After an extensive search, the University announced that it had hired Bowling Green head coach Dino Babers, as the new Syracuse head football coach. Babers is the first African-American head football coach in Syracuse University history. He brought with him a very exciting, up-tempo offense that he had employed in the past both as a head coach and as an assistant coach.

In Babers' first season in charge, Syracuse started the year at 4–4. The highlight of the first eight games was a 31–17 upset of # 17 Virginia Tech at home. The Orange kept it going after this upset as they beat rival Boston College on the road, 28–20. Their next game was against the #3 Clemson who soon would be National

Champions. DeShaun Watson was unstoppable running the Tigers' offense. Clemson got the best of the Orange to say the least L (0-54).

In the final game of the season, Syracuse lost to ACC rival Pittsburgh by a score of 76–61. The game was the highest scoring in FBS history with a combined score of 137. Syracuse finished 4–8 for the second consecutive year.

In 2017, the Orange started 4-3, including a great win over defending Champion, #2 Clemson. However, as in the past, the team had a tough time finishing. They lost their final five games to finish 4-8 for the third straight year.

Despite two 4-8 records in his brief tenure, Coach Dino Babers thinks he's got the formula ready for 2018. We all hope he is right. Babers stopped looking back and he has his eye right on the prize for 2018. He made what is being called an "unvarnished statement" that is building up a new set of expectations for his third season.

"I think this is the beginning," Babers said. "I really believe that the 2018 season is going to be something that we're going to be talking about here for a long, long time."

Let's start talking now!

Syracuse has a rich tradition of football greats. Let's take a look at the Syracuse College Football Hall of Fame members that we will read about in this book.

Syracuse Orange Hall of Famers

Inductee	Pos.	Class	Career
Biggie "Smalls" Munn	HC	1959	1946
Frank "Buck" O'Neill	HC	1951	1906–1919; 1936
Ben Schwartzwalder	HC	1982	1949–1973
Joe Alexander	G	1954	1917–1920
Larry Csonka	FB	1989	1965–1967
Ernie Davis	HB	1979	1959–1961
Vic Hanson	E	1973	1924–1926
Floyd Little	RB	1983	1964–1966
Jim Brown	RB	1995	1956–1958
Tim Green	DT	2002	1982–1985
Don McPherson	QB	2008	1984–1987
Tad Jones	HC	1958	1909–1910
Howard Jones	HC	1951	1908
Dick MacPherson	HC	2009	1980–1990
Art Monk	WR	2012	1976–1979

Syracuse football athletes in the Pro Football Hall of Fame below:

- Jim Brown – Pro Football Hall of Fame Class of 1971
- Jim Ringo – Pro Football Hall of Fame Class of 1981
- Larry Csonka – Pro Football Hall of Fame Class of 1987
- John Mackey – Pro Football Hall of Fame Class of 1992
- Al Davis – Enshrined as a coach and not a player. Pro Football Hall of Fame Class of 1992
- Art Monk – Pro Football Hall of Fame Class of 2008
- Floyd Little – Pro Football Hall of Fame Class of 2010
- Marvin Harrison – Pro Football Hall of Fame Class of 2016

Chapter 2 Syracuse Launches its First Football Team

Many of these 1890 players also were on the 1889 team.

1889: Just 19+ years from the founding

On Nov. 23, 1889, nearly 20 years after the big meeting that formed Syracuse University, the first Syracuse team, a rag tag group put together by captain John Blake Hillyer, played its first football game. It was the one and only game played that season. The Orangemen were defeated 0-36 in a game played against The University Rochester. There was one problem with the Orangemen that day besides the loss. They were not yet the Orangemen. In fact, for this game, Syracuse wore pink and blue uniforms. Rochester had already played most of its 1889 season, its first and were pretty well accustomed to playing gridiron, rugby-like football as American football was being defined.

There are very few records of this game or how things got going for the football team but more than likely it was because students demanded it after playing hither and yon on the streets of Syracuse for several years in an intramural style.

There are reports that students had been playing the evolving game of American football for some time before this game in November 1889, but this was the first intercollegiate game in Syracuse's long football history. There is also a reported game, though not at an intercollegiate level that was played by a football team from Syracuse University in 1884 against the Medical College of Syracuse.

Syracuse students began playing football long before there were football helmets and protective gear of any kind. In this devastating 0-36 loss to the University of Rochester, the game was painful even without enduring the big loss. There were a few broken bones during the game to match the bruised egos of the Syracuse players who then had to make it home by locomotive, licking their wounds After the lopsided loss. It had to be a tough ride back to Syracuse that night.

Shortly after the first game began the day before Thanksgiving 1889, the rain fell in torrents. The football field was a quagmire. There ae no accounts of how the scoring went after the opening kick-off, but Syracuse University's uniform pants were caked with mud and blood. John Blake Hillyer, who founded the team and served as its captain for two years, was forced to leave the game and watch from the sidelines as he sustained a dislocated elbow. Shortly after Hillyer left the game a fellow player suffered a fractured collarbone. Football with no helmets and no padding was a tough sport for sure pre-1920's.

The more experienced Rochester team was also playing in its first intercollegiate season. The difference was that Rochester had played almost a full season before their ninth game, which was Syracuse. Their record was 4-4 record entering the game. Unlike Syracuse which began play in late November, Rochester had played teams such as Trinity and Amherst and a number of other teams from New York State from September on.

Syracuse knew what to expect but had never played a game before their whipping by Rochester in their first game ever, 0-36. It was demoralizing but it got the program rolling nonetheless. Then,

Hillyer and the rest of the team took the locomotive back to Syracuse and were mentally ready for a much better 1890 season. Rochester played one more game after this—a scoreless tie against Union on November 28. The following year, Syracuse would have a full season with a real coach.

Looking back from the 100th anniversary, as the Syracuse players piled off the train after that ignominious debut on Nov. 23, 1889, they were understandably disappointed. But they weren't crushed. Like so many schools wanting to engage in football at the time, the players and Captain Hillyer were pioneers. They overcame many obstacles to get their program started and the Syracuse Orange Football program of today owes them a huge debt of gratitude.

The university, like many at the time considered football a violent sport. They did not believe that it was in synch with the school's academic mission. Consequently, they offered little financial or moral support. So Hillyer and Co. had to scrape together money to buy uniforms and a football. There was no such thing as equipment. Out of their persistence a football program was born. The Syracuse campus and the college game would never be the same.

In the 1890's besides the Oval field, some games were also played at Star Park where the baseball team *The Syracuse Stars* played for years. These games normally attracted 200 to 700 spectators, some of whom (not kidding) occasionally would wander onto the field to help tackle opposing ball-carriers. The game was rough and tumble and to assure their own safety, referees often turned their backs on the shenanigans of the fans. Coach Winston could handle just one year, and he left after his one year of directing the team. He had done a fine job and his absence was felt immediately. The 1890 team had an 8-3 record. However, in 1891, the Orangemen slipped to 4-6 but soon Syracuse would reconstitute its football team and the future was bright. We'll pick the stories of Syracuse's prowess in football in Chapter 7.

Chapter 3 Seven SU Coaches 1889 to 1902

Coaches #1 to #7

Finishing the 1890's—with a coach)

Year	Coach	Record	Conf
1889	No coach	0–1	Ind
1890	Robert Winston	7-4-0	Ind
1891	William Galbreath	4-7-0	Ind
1892	Jordon C. Wells	0-8-1	Ind
1893	George H. Bond	4-9-1	Ind
1894	George H. Bond	6-5-0	Ind
1895	George O. Redington	6-2-2	Ind
1896	George O. Redington	5-3-2	Ind
1897	Frank E Wade	5-3-1	Ind
1898	Frank E Wade	8-2-1	Ind
1899	Frank E Wade	4-4-0	Ind
1900	Frank Sweetland	7-2-1	Ind
1901	Frank Sweetland	7-1-0	Ind
1900	Frank Sweetland	6-2-1	Ind

Circa 1890 Syracuse Fans Getting Ready to Tailgate

The Oval Field Used until 1907 as SU Home Football Field

Intro to SU 1890's Football

After the 1889 inauguration year with one game at Rochester the Wednesday before Thanksgiving, it seemed like it would be all downhill. SU got the program going with a great coach in 1890 but Head Coach Winston left right after the season. With a new coach, 1891 was a mediocre season. Then, with another new coach, in 1892, Syracuse had what would become known as the worst season in the school's first 100 years of football. The team was shut out eight times and outscored, 218-4, finishing with a 0-8-1 record. That team poorly executed on both sides of the ball, but its offensive ineptitude contrasted starkly with a much improved 1904 club, which averaged an astounding 45 points per game. Syracuse was back in business.

The phenomenal scoring average in 1894 was bolstered by a 144-0 victory against Manhattan College half way through the season. The Orangemen scored more points in that contest alone than they did in 32 of their first 100 seasons.

Eleven years later, with Frank "Buck" O'Neill coaching, defense became the trademark of Orange football. The 1915 team recorded nine shutouts and limited the opposition to a meager total of 16 points and 16 first downs in 12 games. That year, the Orangemen finished 9-1-2 but for its own reasons, turned down a bid to play Washington in the Rose Bowl. The rationale given was that they had already traveled more than 10,000 miles by rail in playing their regular season games. It was no pleasure traveling days on a train for a football game.

Back to 1890

An English boxer named Robert Winston became the school's first football coach in 1890. He was a no-nonsense coach and lorded over the team with an iron fist. Under Winston, in its second year on the intercollegiate scene, SU compiled a nice 7-4 record. Uniforms and equipment were not a priority. That season, during a game at Hamilton College, SU players were mocked for their pink-and-blue uniforms.

Worse than that, the team lost 4-6 away in Clinton, NY. When they returned to Syracuse, they urged the student council to change the school colors. Their plea was taken seriously. Orange became the dominant color from then on, thus sparing subsequent generations from having to chant, "Let's go, Pink!"

Like all football teams that are starting out, the early football years of the new Orangemen were primitive at best. There was no huge alumni pool ready with contributions to buy as much as a pair of socks for a needy player. Players dressed for home games and practices in the basement of the school library and bathed one at a time in an old washtub filled with cold water.

At the 100th anniversary celebration, the pundits wrote: A century from the beginning of SU football, "under the stewardship of peripatetic Coach Dick MacPherson, the football team that had problems getting off the ground is in full flight. SU ranks among the top 20 teams nationally and is rekindling memories of previous successes under legendary coaches such as Ben Schwartzwalder, Buck O'Neill and Chick Meehan."

1889 No coach: Syracuse's football program began in 1889 with its first official intercollegiate game against the University of Rochester on November 23. The soon-to-be Orangemen were defeated 0-36. The team wore their pink and blue uniforms without incident.

1890 Robert Winston Coach # 10

Orange was adopted as the school color and Syracuse athletic teams henceforth were known as "Orange" or "Orangemen". SU defeated Rochester 4-0 on Nov 15, to make up for the 36-0 shellacking from Rochester in SU's first and only game in its first season (1889). The season record was very respectable at 7-4. Bobby Winston was the program's first head coach.

First Football Victory Ever for SU

On September 26, 1890, SU managed to win its first game ever against the Syracuse Athletic Club W (14-0). It was only the second game in the second season in the history of the program. They followed this up with another win against the same club W (32-0) on Oct 2. In the 1890's and for about thirty more years, college teams would play just about any group to get a game.

<< **Coach Bobby Winston**

There were many athletic clubs, such as the Syracuse Athletic Club, and The Scranton Athletic Club, that sponsored athletic teams, especially football at that time. They normally gave the fledgling college teams a good run for their money. Some colleges and universities also played well-formed high-school clubs when the alternative was to not play a game.

On Oct 18, Syracuse faced off against St. John's Military Academy and won their third straight. W (26–6). The first loss came at home on Oct 27 against Union NY L (0-26). This was followed by a home win on Nov 1 against Hamilton in a nail-biter W (14-12). Next up was Union in a game played on Nov 8 at Schenectady. Syracuse was defeated for loss #2 of the year L (0-28).

The following week the big locomotive took the team to Rochester for a rematch from their first game and this time SU prevailed W (4-0). However, when Rochester came to Syracuse the following week on Nov 22, they beat Winston's squad L (0-11). Syracuse then made the trip to Clinton, NY on the day before Thanksgiving Nov 24, and were humiliated about their pink and blue uniforms, and they were also beaten on the field by Hamilton L (4-6). That was the last loss of the season

On Nov. 27, Syracuse beat the athletic association again W (16-14) and followed it up a few days later with another victory over St. John's Military Academy at home W (16-14).

Famous Coaches (From the Past) by SWC75.

This is from a blogger known as SWC75. The idea of including a piece of his post in each new coach's section is fully explained right before the Ben Schwartzwalder Era (Chapter 12) and within the section after the 1948 games of the season. The full blog URL is:

Part I or Part II of https://syracusefan.com/threads/famous-coaches-part-1.60694/, and
https://syracusefan.com/threads/famous-coaches-part-2.60695/

For each coach that SWC75 writes about, we offer his blog piece with the same title as this" Watch for inserts tiled:
Famous Coaches (From the Past) by SWC75

> (This is even longer that my "Facilities" post, so I'm posting it in two parts to make it look a little less intimidating.)
>
> Whenever the SU football program takes a dip, the same suggested cure always makes its appearance on internet boards, radio shows and letters to the editor: The University ought to pony up and hire (fill in name of a famous unemployed coach).

He'll be the answer. I think it's another issue that needs some historical perspective. I thought I'd go over the history of SU head football coaches and see what it can tell us. My intention was to be brief but, well, you know me. I like a good story.

Syracuse' first head football coach was Bobby Winston, an English rugby player and boxer who had immigrated to this country in 1883 and was Syracuse' athletic trainer. The school had played its first football game the previous year, losing 0-36 to Rochester. Winston led the team through its first full season, winning 8 and losing 3. (The schedule, such as it was, included two games against Rochester, both victories, a split with Hamilton, two one-sided losses to Union, two wins over St. John's. later Manlius, Military Academy and ended with three straight wins over the Syracuse athletic club.).

Ken Rappoport, in "The Syracuse Football Story", in a chapter entitled "The Stone Age," quotes a contemporary observer:

"Winston's services were timely. He instilled an enthusiasm and love of the game into the players, which, though it has sometimes dwindled in times of poor support and defeat, has never left the team. His odd English ways and London songs made him a great favorite and, when he left, the team had the principles of the game as played at that time well in hand." He left for other jobs after that and was also the first head coach at the University of Georgia in 1894.

One more note on facilities: "The players dressed in a tiny room in the basement of the school library and after practice bathed one after another in an old wash tube filled with cold water. (Bob Snyder's "Orange Handbook" says that "the players took postgame baths by raising a trapdoor and dropping into icy water beneath the library". At least they had hydrotherapy.

The campus playing field was no better that a stone quarry. The ground was hard as diamonds, uneven in spots and punctuated by boulders the size of watermelons. Stones filled the area. Miniature craters abounded." One player recalled: "We had to spend a day or two raking and picking off the stones, filling up the holes with dirt and sawdust." Syracuse undoubtedly had some of the worst facilities in the nation at that time. They were a mess.

1891 William Galbraith Coach # 2

After Coach Winston left the University, the 1891 Syracuse Orangemen football team in their third season were managed by head coach William Galbraith, coaching his first season with the Orangemen. William Fanton was the team captain.

Stephen Crane, author of the Civil War classic, "Red Badge of Courage," was a member of the SU squad that finished 4-7.

On Sept 26, a tough Cornell team defeated the Orangemen at Cornell. After a few weeks break, and some more practices, Cornell came to Syracuse on Oct 17, and barely beat the Orangemen L (6-12) before 800. On Oct 22, SU played the Syracuse Athletic Assoc. and won the game W (22-0). Two days later on Oct 24, SU lost a close on to St. John's Military Academy L 0–4. Then on Oct 30 at Hamilton in Clinton, NY, the Orangemen lost another L (4–22).

On Nov 7 at Colgate in Hamilton, NY, SU lost to its new rival L (16-22) On Nov 11 in a game at Union in Schenectady, NY, the Orangemen were overpowered L (0–75). Things were not going good after that blowout and the disappointed Orangemen lost for the first time to the Syracuse Athletic Assoc. (L (0–28). This was followed with a nice win at home against Rochester on Nov 21, W (18-6)

On Nov 26, the Orangemen came back to beat the Syracuse Athletic Assoc. in a nice match W 22–10 before 1,000 onlookers. Then, on Nov 28 SU defeated St. John's Military Academy at home W (22–4)

Famous Coaches (From the Past) by SWC75.

Winston was replaced by William Galbraith, who became the first SU head coach to get fired- I think. He had played center for Cornell and doubled as the team manager. Rappoport's book shows Galbraith as the coach for the whole season but "Syracuse

University Football: A Centennial Celebration" by Michael Mullins says that Galbraith was replaced by Jordan Wells after an opening 0-68 loss to Cornell. They didn't waste time in those days. SU's second game was a 6-12 loss to Cornell's "second team", (I assume this was a JV squad). According to Mullins it was coached by William Galbraith! Bum Phillips used to say of Don Shula: "He can take his'un and beat your'un or he can take your'un and beat his'un". Like most coaches, Galbraith needed to have better material than his opponent. That was Galbraith's only year as a collegiate head coach.

1892 Jordan C. Wells Coach # 3

The 1892 Syracuse Orangemen football team was led by head coach Jordan C. Wells, in his first season with the Orangemen. This was the fourth season in school history for football and it would be the worst in Syracuse's history of sporting a football team. Here we are in 2018, and this was the only season that Syracuse was ever winless.

Syracuse began the year again Sept 28, against Cornell in Ithaca, NY, and were subjected to a major blowout L (0-58). On Oct 12, it was the Syracuse Athletic Assoc. L (0–24). Then again on Oct 21, it was the Syracuse Athletic Assoc. L (4–18). These were the only points SU scored all season long.

On Oct 29, it was Union at home L (0–52) On Nov 5, it was Hamilton at home L (0–12). On Nov 9, it was the Syracuse Athletic Assoc. The Orangemen played them to a scoreless tie T (0-0). Next SU traveled to Rochester NY L (0–22). Again, came the Syracuse Athletic Assoc. for another loss L0-4). Then, on Nov 23, St. John's Military Academy at home L (0–28). It was a tough year. A year such as this would thankfully never come again.

Famous Coaches (From the Past) by SWC75.

Jordan Wells "coached as well as he could" but 1892 was SU's only winless campaign, (despite all of G-Rob's efforts). That was his only year on the official records as anybody's head coach, although, if

Mullins' account his correct he should be credited with the four victories from the prior year. But it seems a shame to spoil a spotless record, (although the 1892 team did tie Syracuse Athletic club 0-0, one of four games with them). The next year we tried not having a coach and that was actually an improvement, as we went 4-9-1, beating Hamilton, tying Rochester and ending the season with a three-game winning streak over "Syracuse High School", Onondaga Academy and Cazenovia. Those Lakers are tough to beat!

1893 George H. Bond Coach # 4

Officially, SU had no coach this year but George H Bond, captain of the team served as captain and coach. "Without a coach," the Orange finished the season with a 4-9-1 record with wins against Syracuse High School, Hamilton, Onondaga Academy and Cazenovia.

The 1893 Syracuse Orangemen football team competed in their fifth season of intercollegiate football. They were led by stand-in head coach and team captain George H. Bond in his first of "two" years as head coach of the Orangemen. This season was a big improvement over 1892 but nobody was making big smiles yet. In fact, the beginning of this season for the first six games were as winless as 1892. It was frustrating for the team and the fans.

Here are the six quick losses to begin the season:
Sept 21 Syracuse Athletic Assoc home L (0–22)
Sept 27 Cornell home L (0–44)
Oct 7   St. John's Military Acad. L (16–24)
Oct 14   Syracuse Athletic Assoc. home L 0–28
Oct 21   St. John's Military Acad. Home L 4–18
Oct 26   at Colgate L (0–58)

It was getting so nobody thought the Orangemen would win again. On Oct 31, the Orangemen played Syracuse High School and finally won a game W (20–0). Then, on Nov 4, the Orangemen played Hamilton in Clinton, NY for a close win W (16–14).

Union was always tough and on Nov 11 in Union pitched a blowout shutout L (0–66). On Nov 15 at Syracuse Athletic Assoc. field, SU lost L (4–28) with just 75 fans in the stands. On Nov 18, at Home SU tied Rochester T (10-10). Then, after a locomotive to Rochester on Nov 30, SU was defeated L (0-6). Two late season games were scheduled, and they added to the win column. On Dec 2, Onondaga Academy at home W 30–0 and Dec 9 Cazenovia at home W 24–0.

Things were getting better, but nobody was passing out cigars yet. Coach Winston had spoiled everybody for wins.

Famous Coaches (From the Past) by SWC75.

At this point James Roscoe Day became Chancellor. He was a big man who loved sports and football; Under him the first athletic department was organized, a gymnasium built and a special training table for athletes established. (We catch up to other schools eventually.) Also, George Bond, one of Winston's players, became our fourth coach and led the team to a 6-5 record. "Fighting against defeat and hoping against hope, (we) knew that the dawn of better days was breaking." One of his players said that "the father of Syracuse football was George Bond. He was an uncanny diagnostician of the offense, a great teacher, mean as the devil on the football field but a fine chap off." But that was also his only year as a college head coach.

1894 George H. Bond Coach # 4

The 1894 Syracuse Orangemen football team competed in their sixth season of intercollegiate football. They were led by George H. Bond in his second as official head coach of the Orangemen. Robert Adams was the team captain. The team record was above five hundred with a record of 6-5. This season was another big improvement over 1892 and there were some who were smiling that the bad days might be over.

<<George Hopkins Bond (August 10, 1873 – May 8, 1954) was an American football player, coach, and lawyer. He served as the head football coach at Syracuse University for one season in 1894, compiling a record of 6–5. He was captain of the team in 1893 and served as its head coach, unofficially.

Bond was born in Syracuse, New York on August 10, 1873. He graduated from Syracuse University with a bachelor's degree in philosophy in 1894 and from Syracuse University College of Law in 1897. Bond was a senior partner in the law firm of Bond, Schoeneck & King until his resignation in 1953. In 1937 he served as president of the New York State Bar Association. He was also an organizer and president of the New York State Association of District Attorneys.

Bond was the fourth coach in SU football history; in 1893, the team played without a formal coach after Jordan C. Wells couldn't muster a win the prior year. The team entrusted Bond and he led it on a school-record winning streak with victories over Cazenovia, St. John's Military Academy, Rochester and Hamilton. The streak began and ended with shutouts while the Orange also set a mark for points scored in a season, with 188.

Even teams that previously had whooped Syracuse had a more difficult time this year. For example, on Sept 26 at Cornell in Ithaca, NY, the Orangemen narrowed the margin but still did not score L (0–39). On Sept 29, SU defeated Hobart at home W 18–4. On Oct 6, the feast day of St Bruno (also Brian), SU fell to Hamilton College at Hamilton L (8-32). On Oct 13, Syracuse had recovered from the opening day pasting by Cornell enough to shut them out at home W (22-0). This was a very good sign for the program to beat Cornell.

The Syracuse Athletic Assoc. was getting tougher and on Oct 20, Syracuse suffered its third loss of the season L (6–10). SU then beat

Cazenovia on Nov 3 W 20–0. They followed this on Nov 6 with a win v St. John's Military Acad. W (20–12) and a win on Nov 10 at the University of Rochester W 28–18. Feeling pretty good about itself, the Orangemen pounded Hamilton at Syracuse W (50–0). Union no longer had its way with Syracuse, but they won the game on Nov 21 at home L (10-20). Syracuse let down on the last game of the year and were beaten on Nov 24 by St. John's Military Academy L 6–22

1895 George O. Redington Coach # 5

The 1895 Syracuse Orangemen football team competed in their seventh season of intercollegiate football. They were led by George O. Redington in his first of two years as head coach of the Orangemen. Robert Adams was again the team captain. The team record was the best ever with a record of 6-2-2. This season was another big improvement over 1892 and there were some who were smiling hard knowing the bad days from 1892 were over.

<<< George O Redington

The Orange secured its first real home field as SU went from playing in parks throughout the city of Syracuse to playing at The Oval, which was a space located behind the Hall of Languages. The Orange recorded its first victory against rival Colgate, by what appears to be an unusual score of 4-0. However, in 1895, a touchdown was worth just four points.

Syracuse even began to play away tough games quite well. In the away opener at Cornell on Sept 26, played in Ithaca, NY, SU came really close but could not score and lost the game L (0–8). Even Scranton, PA got in the act. This coal town was huge back then and big in mining with a lot of tough players. On Oct 5, at

Scranton Athletic Assoc, the Orange prevailed in a tough match W (12–0).

On Oct 10, the Orangemen had clearly regained their moxie a the finally beat what was once their easiest foe, the Syracuse Athletic Assoc. at home W 24–0. On Oct 19, SU traveled out of state to Maryland and played Williams in Williamstown MA but did not have enough for the win L (10–28). This was SU's first opponent from outside of New York State. On Oct 26, SU played to a tie with St. John's Military Academy at home T (6–6).

Finishing up a fine season with no more losses, SU beat Hobart at home W (46-0) on Nov2. On Nov 9, in a squeaker, with a TD worth just four points, they shut-out Colgate at home W (4-0). Then they finished a fine season with another win on Nov 13 against the Syracuse Athletic Assoc. W 18-0, followed by a home win v Rochester on Nov 16 W (30-0). After such a fine season, they capped it off with a hard-fought tie on Nov 23 at St. John's Military Acad. T (4–4).

Famous Coaches (From the Past) by SWC75.

Another former Winston player was George Redington, who would coach the team for the next two seasons, winning 11, losing 5 and tying 4 (there were lots of ties in those low-scoring days). He was noted for being very strict about training rules and keeping schedules. He was the first SU coach to last two full seasons. But like Galbraith, Wells, and Bond, those were his only seasons as a collegiate head coach. He had spent the 1896 commuting from his New York City law office to coach the team, (no mean feat in those days), and decided to stick with the law.

1896 George O. Redington Coach # 5

The 1896 Syracuse Orangemen football team competed in their eighth season of intercollegiate football. They were led by George O. Redington in his second of two years as head coach of the Orangemen. Robert Adams was again the team captain. The team record was great with a record of 5-3-2. This season found fans no longer thinking about the big disappointment from 1892. Syracuse was on its way to greatness. Wunderbar!

1896 Syracuse Football Team

This year, SU played the Clyde Athletic Association at home on Nov 26 as another great association that wanted to kick the pants off college teams. They did not but SU finished the season with a tie because the Athletic Associations were getting stronger, having picked up a lot of college graduates who knew how to play great football.

On Sept 29, a tough Syracuse HS team was defeated by SU W (24-0). Still not able to begin a season with a win v Cornell at Ithaca, the Orangemen want down in the season opener again L (0-22). Elmira got itself an Athletic Association in 1896 and they played a close game Oct 10m v SU but lost W (20-6). Williams then beat SU at home on Oct 17, L (6-24). In a road trip to Hamilton, NY on Oct 24, SU lost to Colgate L (0-6).

Never forgetting the 1889 first loss to Rochester, Syracuse hammered them om Cot 27 W (62-4). On Oct 31, it was the Syracuse Athletic Assoc. and SU prevailed W (26-0). Then, on Nov

7 at Buffalo at the Buffalo Baseball Park, SU played to a tie T (6–6). Rebounding again, on Nov 14, SU whooped St. John's Military Acad. At home W 40–0, and after an OK season, on Nov 26 at Clyde Athletic Assoc., they tied in the season finale, T (10–10)

Famous Coaches (From the Past) by SWC75.

Redington was followed by Frank Wade, who became our first three-year coach, going 17-9-2. He was our first coach who had been a head football coach anywhere else before getting the job here, having spent one-year coaching DePauw in Indiana to a 3-3-1 record. He was attending law school here. He was credited with upgrading the athletes in the program: "Not only were they smarter about the game: they were also faster and in better condition." I wonder if he did what we would now call "recruiting"? His great accomplishment was considered to be a near-upset of Army in 1899. Wade then began a long career as a lawyer and businessman in the Syracuse area and Syracuse began a new century.

1897 Frank E. Wade Coach # 6

The 1897 Syracuse Orangemen football team competed in their ninth season of intercollegiate football. They were led by Frank E. Wade in his first of three years as head coach of the Orangemen. Robert Adams was again the team captain. The team record was great with a record of 5-3-1.

A major rule changed occurred in 1807 as a touchdown, which had previously been worth four points was upgraded to five points.

On Sept 25, SU defeated Cazenovia in the home opener W 36–0. On Oct 2 at Cornell, SU was shut out L (0–16). Then, the Orangemen came back on Oct 7 against Hobart at home for another win W (20-6). Next was a tie against rival Colgate on Oct 16 in Hamilton, NY T (6-6)

The Colgate "Hoodoo" was born when a newspaper reporter sympathetic to the Red Raiders' cause, tackled an SU player who was on his way to scoring the winning touchdown. The game ended in a 6-6 tie.

Syracuse then blew out Union on Oct 23 at home W (40-0). This was followed by a win against neighboring Cortland at home W (24-0). The following week Rochester came to town and were defeated by the Orangemen W (36-0). The season ended in two disappointing losses against Buffalo. The first was a shutout on Nov 6 at Buffalo's Baseball Park L (0–16) before 800 fans and the second was at home on Nov 13 L (0-10).

1898 Frank E. Wade Coach # 6

The 1898 Syracuse Orangemen football team competed in their tenth season of intercollegiate football. They were led by Frank E. Wade in his second of three years as head coach of the Orangemen. Morgan Wilcox was the team captain. The team record was great posting a record of 8-2-1. They outscored opponents 192-69. It was a fine season indeed.

Syracuse had a tough first game this season against Cornell on Sept 21 in Ithaca, NY were shut out by the Big Red L (0-28). On Sept 21, SU came right back and shut-out Rochester at home W (35-0). Cornell then came to Syracuse on Oct 5 and shut out the Orangemen again L (0-28). This would be the last loss of the season.

On Oct 12 at Hobart in Geneva, NY, SU prevailed W 46–5. Travelling to Cleveland Ohio on Oct 22 to play the Case School of Science, SU won its third game of the season in a shutout W (10-0). At home on Oct 26, the Syracuse Athletic Assoc. fell to the Orangemen W 28–0. Then, on Oct 29, the Orangemen traveled way up NY state to Ogdensburg, right across the St. Lawrence from Brockville Canada, and the Orangemen came home with the win (17–6). The next game was on Nov 5 at Ohio Field in New York against NYU for another victory W (17-0)

On Nov 9 SU beat the Syracuse Athletic Assoc. W (28–0). Then on Nov 12, Syracuse traveled down through Scranton, and Wilkes-Barre PA to Kingston for a victory of a tough prep school, Wyoming

Seminary W (11-0). On Nov 19, SU finished the season with a tie at home against Trinity T (0-0).

1899 Frank E. Wade Coach # 6

The 1899 Syracuse Orangemen football team competed in their eleventh season of intercollegiate football. They were led by Frank E. Wade in his third of three years as head coach of the Orangemen. Carl Dorr was the team captain. The team finished with a season record of 4-4-0.

The Orangemen played just eight games in 1899, cutting back by about three games from its average season. The team, regardless of the coach, had settled into a negative tradition of losing its opener to Cornell and this year was more of the same. The game was played in Ithaca, NY on Sept 27 L (0-17). On Oct 7, Syracuse shut out the Syracuse Athletic Assoc. at home W 6–0. This was followed on Oct 14 by another home win against NYU W (10-5).

On Oct 28, Syracuse lost at home to Williams L (0-6) and the following week on Nov 4, lost to Buffalo at home L (0-16) On Nov 11 at Rochester, the Orangemen pitched a shutout W (23-0). Then, on Nov 18, at Army's "The Plain" at West Point NY, Syracuse fell in a close match L (6–12). The Orangemen wrapped up the season on Nov 22 at Dickinson in Carlisle, PA NY with a nice victory W (18–7)

Famous Coaches (From the Past) by SWC75.

Our first 20th century coach was Edwin R. Sweetland, still another Cornellian who had played for Pop Warner there and coached Hamilton College, (Mullins reports it as Colgate, which is in Hamilton, New York). At Syracuse he stressed speed. His 1900 team averaged 163 pounds per man. "Syracuse, light almost to frailty, compensated for a clear lack of brute force and achieved success through the sheer rapidity of its play." Mullins calls Sweetland "a Vince Lombardi type: tough, aggressive, intelligent, a disciplinarian". (We have had a Vince Lombardi type here, after all.) He was the first Syracuse coach who made coaching a profession: he was also the University's crew coach and later became Kentucky's first basketball coach.

The team was also accused of dirty play and brawls with Cornell and NYU caused an interruption in those series. At the same time, Syracuse upgraded its schedule and was now playing the top teams in the East, giving their records more meaning. Sweetland's teams were up to the task, going 20-5-2 in his three years here. Sweetland wanted more money and returned to Hamilton. From there he went to Ohio State, then came back to coach Colgate, moved on to Kentucky, (one observer said his team "fought like Wildcats", which became their official nickname), then Miami of Ohio, West Virginia and Tulane, finally winding up at Alfred, finishing his mercurial career in 1918 with an even 100 football wins vs. 41 losses and 10 ties. He retired to become a farmer and part-time lawyer.

1900 Edwin Sweetland Coach # 7

From the 1899-1904 Alumni Record: "On Sept. 4 Coach Sweetland began his work with the football team. An excellent showing was made this Fall. As a football coach Mr. Sweetland is a genius. St. Lawrence was defeated by a score of 70 too, New York University 12 too, Amherst, 5 too, Dickinson 6 too, Rochester 68 to 5. and the game with Brown was a tie, 6 to 6. The Cornell game resulted in a score of 6 to o in favor of Cornell. It was the last game with that College to the present time."

<< Coach Sweetland<<

Edwin Sweetland was a Cornell grad, hired as head football coach and to start the crew program. He later coached against SU as the head coach at Colgate

After a mediocre 1899 football season, the 1900 Syracuse Orangemen football team rebounded in their twelfth season of intercollegiate football. They were led by Edwin Sweetland in his first of three seasons as head coach of the Orangemen. Haden Patten was the team captain. The team finished with a season record of 7-2-1. Sweetland had two more fine seasons for SU before he moved on. He was a great coach and under his direction Syracuse became a powerhouse.

SU went back to a ten-game season for 1900. On Sept 22 at home SU shut-out Cortland W (35–0). The following week, SU traveled to Ithaca to play Cornell and just about pulled it off this time. L (0-6). On Oct 6, SU beat St. Lawrence W (70-0). On Oct 13, the Orangemen beat NYU in Geneva, NY W (12–0).

In the early days of football, the Ivy League schools were especially strong. Syracuse decided to test Princeton on Oct 17 at University Field New Brunswick, NJ, and suffered a blowout from the Tigers L (0-43. SU came right back and beat Amherst at home on Oct 20. On Nov3, at Oberlin Ohio, SU shut out Oberlin W 6–0. On Nov 10, it was Dickinson at home W (6-0). Then on Nov 17, the Orangemen laid a big hurt on Rochester at home W 68–5. SU finished the season with a tie, on Nov 24 against another IVY League school, Brown in Providence, RI T (6–6).

1901 Edwin Sweetland Coach # 7

The 1901 Syracuse Orangemen football team were again playing great football in their thirteenth season of intercollegiate football. They were led by Edwin Sweetland in his second of three seasons as head coach of the Orangemen. Lynn Wycoff was the team captain. The team finished with a season record of 7-1-0. Sweetland had two more fine seasons for SU before he moved on. If it were not for a close loss (0-5) to Lafayette, Syracuse would have had its first undefeated season. Sweetland was a genius and a fine football coach.

In the home opener on Sept 21, Cortland came to Syracuse and were shut-out W (35–0)/ Next, on Sept 28, RPI played at the Oval and Syracuse prevailed in a shutout W (26-0). On Oct 5, it was at Brown in Providence, RI. The Orangemen won again, W (20–0) before 500 fans. On Oct 12 in a home contest at the Oval, SU lost to Lafayette L (0–5) before 3,000, Clarkson came down from the North Country to take a shutout beating from the Orangemen on Oct 19, W (27–0).

In another home game on Oct 26 SU beat Amherst at Syracuse, W (28–17) before 5,000. In a road trip on Nov 9 at Columbia's South Field in NYC, Syracuse hung on for the win W (11–5) On Nov 20, Vermont was shutout by the Orangemen W (38–0) before 1,000 fans.

1902 Edwin Sweetland Coach # 7

The 1902 Syracuse Orangemen football team competed well in their fourteenth season of intercollegiate football. They were led by Edwin Sweetland in his third of three seasons as head coach of the Orangemen. Ancil D. Brown was the team captain. The team finished with a season record of 6-2-1.

As I slowly go through each and every season of each and every team when I write Great Coaches books, I get to take notice of the records of all the coaches. It is a labor of love. I love writing about wins, however, much more than I like wiring about losses. Having a long-time affinity for Syracuse, having lived in Utica as a 21-23year old and having run many bus trips to the Carrier Dome in my day, I root for Syracuse. As I encounter 1902, for example, I am rooting for Syracuse to win it all and then as I research further I find they lost two and had a tie. For me, it's like being at the games. So, now what I know the record and I am about to write the game summaries, I sure wish Edwin Sweetland, one of the great coaches of Syracuse had another few more years. But, I am most appreciative for all the good work that he did as football was becoming more accepted in the USA.

On Sept 20, 1902, in the home opener, Syracuse shut out Cortland W 21–0. On Sept 27 at home the Orangemen pitched another shutout—this time against the Onondaga Indians W (34–0). The Onondagas were a tough and gritty bunch of football players from the turn of the last century who loved their education and they loved the game of football. Below is a picture of the 1902 team. They also played Syracuse in 1903. Onondaga, is a big name in the areas outside Syracuse. Like the Carlton Indians from PA who had the famous Jim Thorpe on their squad, these folks were tough football players.

Chapter 3 Seven SU Coaches 1989-1902   67

The Onondaga Indians – A Tough Team

On Oct 4 at home Syracuse beat Clarkson W (34–0). On Oct 11, SU pitched another shutout against Colgate at home on the Oval, W 23–0. On Oct 18, SU shut out Amherst W (15–0). Testing the Ivy League again, on Oct 25, Syracuse traveled to Yale at Yale Field in New Haven, CT to put up a good fight but lose the game in a shutout L 0–24. Williams came down from Massachusetts on Nov1 and Syracuse just got the win with little to spare W (26–17).

One of the toughest teams in the nation until the 1950's was Army. Syracuse made the trip across NY state to play on Nov 15 at Army at The Plain in West Point, NY. It was a lopsided loss L (0–46). Army often decimated opponents. On Nov 27 at Columbia's South Field in NYC, SU played Columbia to a hard-earned tie T (6–6).

Chapter 4 Six SU Coaches 1903 to 1915

Coaches # 8 to #13

Year	Coach	Record	Conf
1903	Ancil D. Brown	5-4-0	Ind
1904	Charles P. Hutchins	6-3-0	Ind
1905	Charles P. Hutchins	8-3-0	Ind
1906	Frank "Buck" O'Neill	6-3-0	Ind
1907	Frank "Buck" O'Neill	5-3-1	Ind
1908	Howard Jones	6-3-1	Ind
1909	Tad Jones	4-5-1	Ind
1910	Tad Jones	5-4-1	Ind
1911	C. Def. Cummings	5-3-2	Ind
1912	C. Def. Cummings	4-5-0	Ind
1913	Frank "Buck" O'Neill	6-4-0	Ind
1914	Frank "Buck" O'Neill	5-3-2	Ind
1915	Frank "Buck" O'Neill	9-1-2	Ind

Syracuse Football Team Practice in Snow at New Archbold Field

1903 Ancil D. Brown Coach # 8

The 1903 Syracuse Orangemen football team competed in their fifteenth season of intercollegiate football. They were led by Ancil D. Brown, his first and only season as head coach of the Orangemen. Brown had been the captain on the 1902 Syracuse football team. Nobody in those days was paid a lot for bringing new football teams into being. Frank H. O'Neill was the team captain. He would soon become one of SU's revered coaches. The team finished with a season record of 5-4-0.

The season home opener on Sept 19 against Cortland resulted in a nice W (23–0) shutout for the Orangemen before 2,000. On Sept 26, Syracuse shut out the Onondaga Indians on the Oval W (35–0). On Oct 3, SU defeated Clarkson at home W (34-0). RPI came to Syracuse on Oct 10 and were shut out W (33-0). With a nice 4-0 record going, it looked like a great season until Oct 17 at home Colgate squeaked a win out against the Orange L (5-10).

Famous Coaches (From the Past) by SWC75.

SU anticipated something the Chicago Cubs would do decades later and used two coaches who alternated, game by game, in 1903. Unlike the Cubs' experiment Jason Parrish and Ancil Brown led the team to a winning record at 5-4. But neither of them were head coaches in any other year. They were replaced by Dr. Charles P. Hutchins, who must have had the right prescription, because the team outscored nine opponents 405-57, including a school record 144-0 win over Manhattan College, (whose facilities were not very good). They stopped the game after 32 minutes. We had 25 touchdowns. They had no first downs. (I'm hoping the Florida State game will be closer.) Hutchins was 14-6 in his two years here, before moving on to coach Wisconsin for two years. He went on to become athletic director at Indiana.

<< Coach Charles P. Hutchins

In the sixth home game of the season, on Oct 24, Syracuse lost to Williams from Massachusetts L (5-17) before 2500. On Oct 31, SU got back its moxie in another home game against Niagara W (47-0). Then, the Orangemen traveled to New Haven Connecticut to the Yale Field where they were beaten by another Ivy League team, Yale, L (0–30) before 5,000. On Nov 4, the Orangemen lost a close match at Brown on Nov 14, in Providence, RI L (5–12) before 3800 fans.

1904 Charles P. Hutchins Coach # 9

Charles Pelton Hutchins (September 10, 1872 – December 28, 1938) was an American football coach. He served as the head football coach at Dickinson College (1902–1903), Syracuse University (1904–1905), and University of Wisconsin–Madison (1906–1907), compiling a career college football record of 31–16–1. From 1904 to 1905, he coached at Syracuse, tallying a 14–6 record. From 1906 to 1907, he coached at Wisconsin, where he compiled an 8–1–1 record. Hutchins was also the athletic director at Indiana University Bloomington from 1911 to 1913.

The 1904 Syracuse Orangemen football team competed in their sixteenth season of intercollegiate football. They were led by Charles P. Hutchins in his first of two seasons as head coach of the Orangemen. This was the ninth different coach in the 16 years since the program was started in 1898. For such constant change in coaching, Syracuse was doing quite well compared to other startups across the nation. Robert Park was the captain on the 1904 Syracuse football team. The team finished with a season record of 6-3-0.

The home opener was played on Sept 24 against Cortland's Red Dragons at the Oval in Syracuse, NY. SU shut out Cortland W (27–0) before 600 fans On Oct1, SU defeated Clarkson in a major blowout at home W (69–0). Colgate came over to play at the Oval from Hamilton, NY on Oct 8 in a rival match and defeated the Orange L (0–11). Traveling to Yale again for another chance, the Orangemen played better than the year before and almost pulled it off on Oct 15, but were defeated despite the close score at Yale Field in New Haven, CT L (9–17)

On Oct 22 SU defeated Niagara at home in a blowout W (52–4). On Oct 29, still feeling mighty after the prior week's blowout, SU did a bigger number against Allegheny at Yale Field in New Haven, CT W (69–0). On Nov 5, SU collected a huge blowout win of W (144-0) at Syracuse. On Nov 12 at Lehigh in Bethlehem, PA, SU prevailed W 30-4. On Nov 19, SU lost at Army to the powerful Cadets in The Plain at West Point, NY (L 5–21).

1905 Charles P. Hutchins Coach # 9

The 1905 Syracuse Orangemen football team competed in their seventeenth season of intercollegiate football. They were led by Charles P. Hutchins in his second of two seasons as head coach of the Orangemen. David Tucker was the captain on the 1905 Syracuse football team. The team finished with a season record of 8-3-0.

In the season home opener on Sept 22, SU took on a new opponent, Alfred University at home, and shut them out W (52–0). On Sept 27, SU defeated Hobart at home W (24–0) In another home game, on Sept 30, the Orangemen defeated Rochester W (16–0). It was back to Yale again on Oct 7 for another unsuccessful try in a game played in Yale Field New Haven, CT L (0–16). Th next road trip was on Oct 14 to Clinton, NY v Hamilton College W (27-0). On Oct 14, SU defeated Hamilton's neighbor Colgate at home in a close match W (11-5).

Next home game was on Oct 28, in which SU defeated Lehigh before 3000 fans W (17-0). Still struggling against Ivy League teams. SU lost to Brown in Providence, RI on Nov 4 L (0–27). On Nov 11, at home, SU beat Holy Cross W (16-4). RPI was next and the Orangemen gave them a big shellacking on Nov 18 W (62-0). Still without a win against Army, SU tried again on Nov 25 at The Plain in West Point, NY but failed L (0–17). This ended the 1905 season.

1906 Frank "Buck" O'Neill Coach # 10

The 1906 Syracuse Orangemen football team competed in their eighteenth season of intercollegiate football. They were led by Frank "Buck" O'Neill in his first of two seasons (on this tour – O'Neill would be back) as head coach of the Orangemen. James Stimson was the captain on the 1906 Syracuse football team. The team finished with a season record of 5-3-1.

The season opener on Sept 22 pitted Hobart against Syracuse at home. The Orangemen grabbed the victory W (28-6) before 800 at

the Oval. On Sept 27 SU defeated Rochester at home in a shutout W (38-0). On Oct 6, Syracuse faced a powerful Yale team at Yale Field in New Haven, CT and lost in a blowout L (0–51). After playing Yale, on Oct 13, SU traveled to Clinton NY to play Hamilton College and pitched a fine shutout W (37-0). At home the next week against Colgate, who happen to be from Hamilton, NY, the SU offense never fired up and the team was defeated narrowly L (0-5). Five points was one touchdown in 1906.

On Nov 3 vs. Carlisle at Buffalo, NY, Syracuse lost a close game L (4–9) before 8,000. On Nov 10, at home SU walloped Niagara W (46–0). Then, after traveling to Lafayette in Easton, PA, the Orange brought home a victory W (12-4). Finishing up a fine season, the Buck O'Neill boys came through with a huge victory against Army played on The Plain in West Point, NY W (4–0)

Famous Coaches (From the Past) by SWC75.

Charles Hutchins was replaced by the first Syracuse coach who would wind up in the Hall of Fame. Frank "Buck" O'Neill had coached at Colgate for three years, going 18-8-2. He was another coaching lawyer, (I'll bet those guys knew the rulebook), and took some years off to tend to his law practice in New York City. He was head coach at SU from 1906-07, 1913-1915 and 1917-19 "and his name was synonymous with Syracuse through that era. Of high intelligence and executive capacity, he was forceful, rigorous and adamant in his system, method and discipline. He knew and loved this great game and was impatient with indifferent, incapable or stupid play or players."

He was a Syracuse native, working in a butcher's shop in Manlius that supplied meat for the St. John's Military Academy. He delivered it and became intrigued by football practice. He volunteered to help out the scrubs when they were short a man and filled his derby hat with straw as protection against concussions, (does the NFL know about this?). He was invited to attend the academy and play football for the team, worked hard in class and became an honor student. He went to Williams College. He played football for them and became team captain.

Colgate hired him in 1902 and he coached them while coaching and playing for a professional team representing the Syracuse Athletic Club, which won something called "The World Series of Football", (a year before the Baseball World Series began), in Madison Square Garden, the first indoor football games ever played. The field was 70 by 35 yards, (Manley Field House's field is bigger). They beat something called "the New York Team", (which was from Philadelphia: it consisted of baseball players from the Phillies and Athletics trying to stay in shape during the off-season: they called themselves that to draw more fans in the Big Apple), 5-0, (a touchdown was worth 5 points then). Syracuse could have made it to 6 points but Pop Warner, who was playing for Syracuse, along with his brother and a couple of Carlisle Indians, missed an extra point. Syracuse then beat the Knickerbockers 36-0 and then a team from New Jersey, the Orange Athletic Club, by the same score.

O'Neill and the coaches who followed him benefited from the opening in 1907 of John D. Archbold's gift to SU, a huge, (by 1907 standards), concrete and steel football stadium named after the benefactor. O'Neill guided Syracuse to a 52-19-6 record, including the 9-1-2 team of 1915 that was invited to the second Rose Bowl, (the first having been held after the 1901 season, to be replaced for 14 years by chariots races), but had to turn it down for financial reasons. And he coached the team that in 1919, crushed Warner's Pittsburgh team that had won 34 straight games against collegiate teams, 24-3. He then became the coach at Columbia, which was much closer to his law offices, from 1920-22, finishing with an 81-42-8 record. He was elected to the College Football Hall of Fame in 1951, primarily for his record at Syracuse.

1907 Frank "Buck" O'Neill Coach # 10

The 1907 Syracuse Orangemen football team competed in their nineteenth season of intercollegiate football. They were led by Frank "Buck" O'Neill in his second of two seasons (on his first tour – O'Neill would be back) as head coach of the Orangemen. Ford Park was the captain on the 1907 Syracuse football team. The team finished with a season record of 6-3-0.

On Sept 25 Syracuse hosted Hobart in its brand new Archbold Stadium before 2000 fans. The Orangemen won their season home opener in their state of the art stadium with a nice shutout W (28–0). Sept 28. See Chapter 3 for information about Archbold Stadium.

On Sept 28, at Archbold Stadium, Syracuse defeated Rochester W (40–6). On Oct 5, SU made their annual trek to Yale Field In New Haven, CT and were shut out by Yale L (0–11). Still licking their wounds from the close Yale defeat, on Oct 12 vs. Carlisle in

Buffalo, NY, the Orangemen suffered another loss. L (6–14). On Oct 19 at Archbold Stadium on the Syracuse campus in Syracuse NY, SU defeated Williams W 9–0 before 6,000 fans.

1, Simpson, Mgr.; 2, Hartman; 3, Stein; 4, Cadigan; 5, Waugh; 6, Dudley; 7, Bisgood, Asst. Mgr.; 8, Sullivan; 9, Reynolds; 10, Fisher; 11, Horr, Capt.; 12, Clarke; 13, Banks; 14, Darby; 15, Barry; 16, Hinkey.   Ryder, Photo.
SYRACUSE (N. Y.) UNIVERSITY.

On Oct 26 Hamilton played SU at Archbold Stadium and were shut out by the Orangemen W (22–0). On Nov 2, Syracuse played Bucknell for the first time. This game was at Archbold Stadium and the Orange grabbed the victory W (20–6). On Nov 16 Lafayette played Syracuse to a tie at Archbold Stadium T 4–4. In the season finale, Army was up for the task after losing the prior year to the Orange. On Nov 23, the Cadets defeated the Orangemen at The Plain in West Point, NY L (4–23). The Orangemen did not lose a game at Archbold Stadium in 1907, their first year playing in this great facility.

Famous Coaches (From the Past) by SWC75.

During this first O'Neill, interregnum the team was coached, successively, by a pair of brothers who would wind up in the Hall of Fame with O'Neill. The 1908 coach [described above] was Howard Jones, who had just finished playing for Yale for three years during which the Elis never lost a game. He directed Syracuse to a 6-3-1 record. This was the year Pop Warner fooled the Orange by stitching a football-shaped decoration on his player's jerseys and bamboozled the Syracuse players in a 0-12 Carlisle win. They the Indians played Harvard. Coach Percy Haughton had the footballs painted Crimson and Harvard won 17-0. But Jones scored a huge victory over Michigan, 28-4, the team rushing for 400 yards to 75 for the Wolverines.

Howard Jones moved onto Ohio State the next year, then went into private business. He coached Yale for a year in 1913. His great fame began when he became the coach at Iowa (1916-23), Duke for one year, (1924), and Southern California (1925-40). He turned the latter school into the national power they have been ever since. His overall record was 194-65-21. Jones was elected to the Hall of Fame in 1951, (both he and O'Neill were part of the first class, which had 54 inductees).

Howard then turned the job over to his brother, Thomas, Albert Dwight, "TAD" Jones. He had been a star quarterback for Yale in 1906-07. This was his head coaching debut, but he didn't have as much success as his brother. His 1909 team had a losing record for the first time since 1909. His 1910 team got back above the line at 5-4-1 but was a very dull team that outscored ten opponents by a combined 53-42. He didn't coach another team until he got the Yale job in 1916. With a break for the war, he coached them until 1927, going 69-24-6 overall and getting elected to the Hall in 1958.

1908 Howard Jones Coach # 11

The 1908 Syracuse Orangemen football team competed in their twentieth season of intercollegiate football. They were led by Howard Jones in his first and only season as head coach of the Orangemen. Marquis Horr was the captain on the 1908 Syracuse football team. The team finished with a season record of 6-3-1.

<< Coach Howard Jones

This year's home opener was on Sep 23 with a nice blowout over Hobart W (51-0) The Syracuse offense was clicking, and the defense was strong again on Sep 26 at Archbold Stadium as SU defeated Hamilton W (18-0). The win streak would end on Oct 3 at Yale in New Haven CT with a close match against the Bulldogs L (0-5). The Carlisle Indians, always tough beat SU the following week on Oct 10 L (0-12) making the Syracuse record 2-2 for the season.

On Oct 17 at Archbold, SU defeated Rochester W (23-12). After a trip to the Ivy League to play Princeton, SU returned home with a hard-fought scoreless tie T (0-0). On Oct 31, SU shut out Williams W (23-0) at Archbold. Colgate then gave the Orangemen their final loss of the season on Oct 31, in a close match L (0-6) On Nov 14, Syracuse shut out Tufts at Archbold W 28 0. For the first time, Syracuse played Michigan. The game was at Archbold and the Orangemen got the best of a very experienced Michigan team W (28-4).

1909 Tad Jones Coach # 12

The 1909 Syracuse Orangemen football team competed in their twenty-first season of intercollegiate football. They were led by Tad Jones in his first of two seasons as head coach of the Orangemen. Herbert Barry was the captain on the 1909 Syracuse football team. The team finished with a season record of 4-5-1.

<<< Coach Tad Jones

Being a Pennsylvanian, I was surprised as I read some of the archives about this season and others. SU had played the very tough Carlisle Indians but some of the accounts such as Wikipedia have the Carlisle Indians playing out of Buffalo, NY. So, I looked for a Carlisle College in Buffalo and there is none.

The Carlisle Indians football team is the one and only and they represented the Carlisle Indian Industrial School in intercollegiate football competition. They were great and well feared as being tough and willing to do what it took to win a game. Their campus was in Carlisle Pennsylvania, not Buffalo NY as some would suggest.

Their program was active from 1893 until 1917, when it was discontinued. During the program's 25 years, the Indians compiled a tough-to-beat 167–88–13 record and 0.647 winning percentage, which makes this group of great men over 25 years to be the most successful defunct major college football program. Teams had to play their best to beat this crew.

At the turn of the 20th century, the college leading the football gridiron in the US was not Harvard or Yale – it was a little-known powerhouse called the Carlisle Indian Industrial School. During the early 20th century, Carlisle was a national football powerhouse. Hey, they were good enough that they got to play national powerhouse Syracuse. They regularly competed against other major programs such as the Ivy League schools. Several notable players and coaches were associated with the team, including Pop Warner and Jim Thorpe, a native American, and an All-American hero in many sports as well as the Olympics. To beat Carlisle was to beat a great team.

The season home opener on Sept 25 featured Syracuse v Hamilton at Archbold Stadium. SU grabbed a nice shutout win W (20–0). Many of the NY teams with smaller stadiums permitted SU to have home games in the larger and nicer Archbold to help more fans see the games. Yale, on the other hand would not play Syracuse unless it was a Yale home game. And, so, again on Oct 2, the Orangemen went off to the Yale Field in New Haven, CT and came back with a loss L (0–15). At Archbold on Oct 9, SU defeated Rochester W (17-0)

Still not ready to beat the Carlisle Indians, especially away, Syracuse licked its wounds coming back home with a loss after a close-in brawl on Oct 16 losing L (11-14). On Oct 23 at Archbold, SU got the best of Niagara W 9–0. On Oct 30, after beating Michigan in the first encounter at Archbold, the Orangemen had to go to Ferry Field, not yet the Big House, but in Detroit Michigan to play the Wolverines. It was a make-up day for Michigan as they had promised themselves never to take Syracuse lightly again. SU lost big that day in a blowout L (0-43).

On Nov 6, at Archbold, SU lost to Bucknell in a close match, L (0-5). For want of an extra point on a five-point TD, on Nov 13, at Archbold, SU lost to Colgate L (5-6). On a losing streak with a new coach, the Orangemen kept the losing streak going against another new team on Nov 20, v Illinois at Archbold Stadium in Syracuse, L (8–17). The best SU could do to wrap up what had become a poor season was to squeak out a tie Fordham in New York, NY T (5–5)

1910 Tad Jones Coach # 12

The 1910 Syracuse Orangemen football team competed in their twenty-second season of intercollegiate football. They were led by Tad Jones in his second of two seasons as head coach of the Orangemen. Harry Hartman was the captain on the 1910 Syracuse football team. The team finished with a season record of 5-4-1.

On Sept 25 in the home opener SU could not take down St. Bonaventure at Archbold Stadium in Syracuse NY and were forced to settle for a scoreless tie T (0–0). On Oct1, Syracuse made the annual trek to Yale in New Haven CT and were barely defeated L

(6–12). On Oct 8 at Archbold, SU defeated Rochester by a slim margin W (6–0). Then, on Oct 15, the powerful Carlisle Indians were ready to take home a big win at Archbold Stadium on the campus in Syracuse, NY, but they were surprised and did not score against the Orangemen who won W 14–0 before 10,000 fans.

On the road again on Oct 19 at Illinois Field in Champaign, IL, the Orangemen endured a close loss to the Fighting Illini, L (0–3). On Oct 22 SU engaged Hobart at their complex in Geneva, NY, and walked away with a close win W (12–5). Knowing Michigan would be tough and that they were coming to town on Oct 29, Syracuse was ready but that was not enough at Archbold Stadium on campus in Syracuse, NY, as SU could not score and lost the game against Michigan L 0–11 before a record crowd of 11,000.

On Nov 5 Vermont played Syracuse at Archbold Stadium but were beaten back in a close game W (3–0). In a NY rival game on Nov 12, a determined Colgate crew came to Archbold Stadium ready to win. They played tough and took home the win L (6–11). In the season finale, on Nov 24, Coach Jones took a chance and went outside the state again to the country's midsection and they played against Saint Louis at St. Louis, MO, and walked away with a very close win after a hard-fought game, W (6–0).

Famous Coaches (From the Past) by SWC75.

The Jones Brothers were replaced by Deforest Cummings. The highlight of his two-year run, (9-8-2) was a 12-11 win over Carlisle's greatest team, coached by Warner and with Jim Thorpe at his peak in 1911. Those two teams were the only ones ever coached by Cummings. O'Neill came back for the next three years after the two years of Cummings.

1911 Charles Deforest Cummings # 13

The 1911 Syracuse Orangemen football team competed in their twenty-third season of intercollegiate football. They were led by C. Def Cummings in his first of two seasons as head coach of the

Orangemen. Preston Fogg was the captain on the 1911 Syracuse football team. The team finished with a season record of 5-3-2.

On Sept 30, the Archbold Stadium home opener in Syracuse, NY, the Orangemen defeated Hobart W 6–0. Off to Yale for an annual defeat, which in time would eventually be a victory, on Oct 7 at Yale Field in New Haven, CT, SU lost again by a little bit. L 0–12. It was a loss nonetheless and no matter how good Yale was at the time it was very annoying to Syracuse fans.

On Oct 14, away at Rochester in Rochester, NY, the Orangemen hung on to win W (6–5). Then, on Oct 21, Lafayette, another great academic and athletic school came to Archbold Stadium in Syracuse, NY, and defeated the Orange L (0–10) before. The days of the stands filling up at Archbold were in front of the University at this time.

<< **Coach Cummings**
On Oct 28, Springfield (from MA) came to Archbold Stadium and beat the Orangemen by a slight margin – the margin of victory L (5–9). On Nov 4 at Michigan's Ferry Field in Ann Arbor, Michigan, SU tied the home team T (6–6) in a tough contest. On Nov 11, SU invited Vermont to play at Archbold Stadium and prevailed against the out-of-staters, W 16–0. The Carlisle Indians, tough on their weakest days came back on Nov 5 to Archbold Stadium in Syracuse, NY and lost by one point to Syracuse W (12–11) In a first time ever match, on Nov 25, SU took on Ohio State in Ohio Field, Columbus, OH and came home with the victory, W 6–0. In the season finale, in the second game ever

against St. Louis played on Nov 30 at Saint Louis, St. Louis, MO, the teams squared off for a season ending tie T (6–6)

1912 Charles Deforest Cummings # 13

The 1912 Syracuse Orangemen football team competed in their twenty-fourth season of intercollegiate football. They were led by C. Def Cummings in his second of two seasons as head coach of the Orangemen. Rudolph Propst was the captain on the 1912 Syracuse football team. Team finished with a losing season record of 4-5-0.

In the SU home opener on Sept 28 at Archbold Stadium in Syracuse, NY, the Orangemen defeated Hobart W (12–0). After traveling to Yale, the following week, Oct 5, in a game played at Yale Field in New Haven, CT, Syracuse took a shutout loss L (0–21). In these early years tough Yale Teams rarely gave up any points to the Orangemen. On Oct 12 at Archbold, the Carlisle Indians beat the Orange in a shutout L (0–33).

The worst game of the year was the following week on Oct 19 at Princeton's University Field in NJ as the Orange were walloped L (0-62). On Oct 26, SU got its moxie back and defeated Michigan at Archbold Stadium W (18-7)

On Nov 2 at Archbold, Syracuse defeated Rochester W (28–0). Then, on Nov 9 at Lafayette's March Field in Easton, PA, the Orange beat the Tigers W (30–7). On Nov 16, at home, Syracuse lost to Colgate in a close match L (0-7). On Nov 23, Syracuse lost to Army at The Plain in West Point, NY L 7–23. The army team had quite a few notables on the squad such as to-be General Dwight D. Eisenhower, and to-be General Dwight D. Eisenhower. I thought you'd like the picture below:

Part of the 1912 West Point football team.
Cadet Eisenhower 3rd from left; Cadet Omar Bradley 2nd from right

1913 Frank "Buck" O'Neill Coach # 10

The 1913 Syracuse Orangemen football team competed in their twenty-fifth season of intercollegiate football. They were led again by Frank "Buck" O'Neill in the first of three years in his second tour of duty as head coach of the Orangemen. O'Neill was one of the best Army coaches. Martin Hilfinger was the captain on the 19132 Syracuse football team. The team finished with a winning season record of 6-4-0.

In the home opener on Sept 27 at Archbold Stadium on the campus of Syracuse University in Syracuse, NY, the Orangemen toppled Hobart W (41–0). On Oct 4 Hamilton was defeated by SU at Archbold Stadium W (18–0). On Oct 11, SU p traveled to Rochester and won in a close shutout W (6–0). The next week, Oct 18, SU lost to Princeton at Princeton's University Field in Princeton, NJ L (0–13).

On Oct 25, Western Reserve rolled into Archbold Stadium in Syracuse, NY and were shut out by Syracuse W 36–0. On Nov 1, the Orangemen made the trip to Ferry Field in Ann Arbor, MI and were soundly defeated by the Wolverines L 7–43. The following week, Nov 8 NYU was blown out of Archbold Stadium W (48–0). Then Colgate beat the Orangemen on Nov 15 at home   L (13–35). On

Nov 22, the tough Carlisle Indians beat the Orange at Archbold L (27–35) before 5,000 fans. SU finished the season with a big win on Nov 27 at St. Louis in St. Louis, MO W 75–0, before 10,000 fans.

1914 Frank "Buck" O'Neill Coach # 10

The 1914 Syracuse Orangemen football team competed in their twenty-sixth season of intercollegiate football. They were led again by Frank "Buck" O'Neill in the second of three years in his second tour of duty as head coach of the Orangemen. 'Neill was one of the best Army coaches. James Schufelt was the captain on the 1914 Syracuse football team. The team finished with another winning season record of 5-3-2.

The season home opener was On Sept 26 featuring Hobart at Stadium on the campus of Syracuse University in Syracuse, NY. The Orangemen dominated the game W (37–0). Next game was on Oct 3 when Hamilton was defeated by SU at Archbold in a blowout W (81–0). After two wins, SU suffered its first defeat on Oct 10, at the hands of Princeton in a game played at University Field, Princeton, NJ -- L (7–12). On Oct 17, SU grabbed win # 3 from Rochester at Archbold Stadium W (19–0).

<<< **Buck O'Neill** later in life. After being beaten badly in 2013, Buck O'Neill's Orangemen were ready on Oct 24 to gain some respect back against Michigan. In this game, the Orangemen made amends at home in Archbold Stadium with a nice win W (W 20–6) before 10,000 fans. O'Neill had the Orangemen on a roll and on Oct 31, they won again v the Carlisle Indians from Carlisle PA. W (24–3).

In the first game ever against Rutgers, aka the State University of New Jersey, on Nov 7, Syracuse played the Scarlet Knights at home to a tie T (14–14) On Nov 14, SU pitched another tie against Colgate at home but this one was scoreless T (0-0) before a packed house of 17,000 fans. On Nov 21, back to the Ivy League at Dartmouth in Hanover, NH, the Orangemen were shut out L (0–40). Working against Jesse Harper, ND Head Football Coach and Knute Rockne, Assistant, Buck O'Neill's team hung in and made it a real game on Nov 26 at Notre Dame's Cartier Field in South Bend, IN L (0–20).

1915 Frank "Buck" O'Neill Coach # 10

The 1915 Syracuse Orangemen football team competed in their twenty-seventh season of intercollegiate football. They were led again by Frank "Buck" O'Neill in his third second of three years in his second tour of duty as head coach of the Orangemen. If you are counting at home folks, at this point O'Neill had coached five years, and this was the most of any coach to that date. This would be a great season for the Orangemen. 'Neill was one of the best Army coaches. The team finished with another winning season record of 9-1-2

For the first year ever, Syracuse was in the running for the national championship with a 9-1-2 record. Cornell, however finished 9-0, and in a season full of contenders, they were the consensus choice for the 1915 mythical national championship and would have run away with #1 had there been an AP poll that season.

The games of the 1915 Season

On Sept 25, in a rare occurrence, Syracuse played its season home opener against a group of Syracuse Alumni that had formed a "pick-up" team. The current Syracuse varsity beat the old-timers W (43-0) at Archbold Stadium on campus in Syracuse NY.

On Oct 2, 1915 at Archbold. SU defeated Bucknell W (6-0). The next week at Princeton, Syracuse lost a squeaker L (0-3). O'Neill's squad came right back the next week at home and shellacked Rochester W (82-0). On Oct 23, at Brown Syracuse won in a tight match W (6-0). In a big game on Oct 30, Syracuse traveled to Ann Arbor Michigan and beat the wolverines in a tight match W (14-7).

On Nov6, at home against Mt. Union, Syracuse pitched a big blowout-shutout W (73-0). They grabbed another shutout the following week from Colgate on Nov 13 at Archbold Stadium W (38-0). On Nov 20, the Orangemen tied Dartmouth T (0-0) and then on Thanksgiving they tied Montana at Montana T (6-6). On Wed, Dec 1, Buck's boys shut-out Oregon State W (28-0) and on a Monday, Dec 6 at Occidental, they brought home a nice shutout W (35-0). This great season 9-1-2 was SU's best ever at the time. Just a field goal prevented the Orangemen from being undefeated.

Chapter 5 Five SU Coaches 1916 to 1929

Bringing excellence to an already great record

Year	Coach	Record	Conf
1916	William Hollenback	5-4-0	Ind
1917	Frank "Buck" O'Neill	8-1-1	Ind
1918	Frank "Buck" O'Neill	5-1-1	Ind
1919	Frank "Buck" O'Neill	8-3-3	Ind
1920	Chick Meehan	6-2-1	Ind
1921	Chick Meehan	7-2-0	Ind
1922	Chick Meehan	6-1-2	Ind
1923	Chick Meehan	8-1-0	Ind
1924	Chick Meehan	8-2-1	Ind
1925	Pete Reynolds	8-1-1	Ind
1926	Pete Reynolds	7-2-1	Ind
1927	Lew Andreas	5-3-2	Ind
1928	Lew Andreas	4-4-1	Ind
1929	Lew Andreas	6-3-0	Ind

There was not one losing season from 1916 to 1929

1923 SU Football Team – great picture with no attributions

Famous Coaches (From the Past) by SWC75.

Bill Hollenbeck, a former Penn all-American who had coached at Missouri and Penn State, going unbeaten in Happy Valley in 1911-12. He was beatable in Syracuse, going 5-4 before retiring from coaching, preferring business and politics. He's in the Hall of Fame but as a player, not a coach. Perhaps if he'd kept at it...

1916 William Hollenback Coach # 14

The 1916 Syracuse Orangemen football team competed in their twenty-eighth season of intercollegiate football. They were led by William Hollenback in his first and only year as head coach of the Orangemen. Harold M. "Babe" White was the team captain. The team finished with another winning season record of 5-4

<<< **William Hollenback**, picture from 1910

All games but two were played at Archbold Stadium on the SU campus in Syracuse NY. Michigan and Tufts were played on the road.

On Sept 30 in the season home opener, the Syracuse Alumni decided to try the varsity one more time but were defeated by the current Orangemen in a blow-out W (57-0). On Oct 7, SU defeated Ohio in a blowout W (73-0). On Oct 14, in another blowout, SU defeated Franklin & Marshall W (60-0). The first loss came against Pit in a shutout L (0-30). After traveling to Ann Arbor on Oct 21, the Orangemen went home disappointed with a one-point loss to the Michigan Wolverines L 13-14). On the road again on Nov 4 in Springfield Mass, SU lost a tough match to Dartmouth L (10-15),

On Nov 11, SU shut out Susquehanna U from Selinsgrove PA W (42-0). The following week on Nov 18, the Orangemen were shut out L (0-15) by Colgate. In the season finale, on Nov 25 # Tufts, the Orangemen found enough steam to win in a close match W (20-13)

Famous Coaches (From the Past) by SWC75.

O'Neill returned for the third time, greatly assisted by Chick Meehan, his quarterback in 1917 and his assistant coach in 1918-19. When O'Neill took the Columbia job.

1917 Frank "Buck" O'Neill Coach # 10

The 1917 Syracuse Orangemen football team competed in their twenty-ninth season of intercollegiate football. They were led by Frank "Buck" O'Neill in his third tour as head coach of the Syracuse Orangemen. This was his first year of three in his third tour, making this his sixth season overall. O'Neill was SU's best coach at this point and they kept bringing him back and he kept winning. The team finished with another great winning season record of 8-1-1.

< Coach Buck O'Neil Pic from 1901

William Hollenback was a fine and respected coach by all parties at the time, but he was no Buck O'Neill. The only thing Buck never brought in to Syracuse was an undefeated season. But, with time like all the great immortals, he would have done so.

As the War approached, more and more men were opting the service over college. The US was gearing up for a major conflict.

The Impact of World War I on College Football

At the beginning of the 1917 football season more Americans were concerned about World War I than were concerned about football or any sport. The country was at war and were in it in a big way. Until the draft, the volunteers for duty were less than 100,000 and as the country was preparing for war, this, plus the small army that existed, simply could not do.

The Selective Service Act or Selective Draft Act (Pub.L. 6512, 40 Stat. 76), was enacted on May 18, 1917. It authorized the United States federal government to raise a national army for service in World War I through conscription. It was envisioned in December 1916 and brought to President Woodrow Wilson's attention shortly after the break in relations with Germany in February 1917.

The Act itself was drafted by then-Captain (later Brigadier General) Hugh S. Johnson after the United States entered World War I by declaring war on Germany. The Act was canceled with the end of the war on November 11, 1918. The Act was upheld as constitutional by the United States Supreme Court in 1918.

The draft was a major impetus for many to volunteer. By the end of World War, I, some two million men had volunteered for various branches of the armed services, and some 2.8 million had been drafted.

On Sep 29, 1917, SU played the 47th Infantry Division Team, and like most service teams, they were no slouches. They held the Orangemen to zero and they scored zero in a scoreless tie T (0-0). Syracuse was yet to be affected by the war, but the SU team always gave the service the priority and so on Oct 6, 1917, they played the 47th Infantry again and this time, they beat them W (19-0). Nobody laid down for the service teams and in fact, they played tougher against them as it helped both teams. Everybody was concerned about the war and we all wanted America, if Wilson chose to engage the US, to be victorious. Football was good practice for military personnel and it was a lot of fun for the Orangemen.

Moving through their schedule, next was on Oct 13, v Rutgers at home. SU prevailed W (14-10). Then on Oct 20, at Pitt, SU took a big shutout defeat L (0-28) in a game played in Pittsburgh, PA. On Oct 27, SU beat Tufts in a blowout win W (58-0).

On Nov 3, the Orangemen traveled to Brown for a nice but very close win W (6-0). Then, on Nov 10, 1917, SU faced Bucknell in a one-way advantage match for Syracuse W (42-0). Colgate came to Archbold to win on Nov 17 but left with a solid defeat provided by its arch rival SU W (27-7).

Then back to Michigan to play the other team from that State on Nov 24. SU won the match v Michigan State W (21-7). Syracuse had been making a point through many coaches to play the best teams in the country and on Nov 29, another great team invited the Orangemen to play in Nebraska against Nebraska, which was and is one of the finest teams in the nation. SU came home this year with the tough win in 1917, W (10-9).

1918 Frank "Buck" O'Neill Coach # 10

The 1918 Syracuse Orangemen football team competed in their thirtieth season of intercollegiate football. They were led by Frank "Buck" O'Neill in his third tour as head coach of the Syracuse Orangemen. This was his second year of three in his third tour, making this his seventh season overall at the helm. O'Neill was SU's best coach at this point and they kept bringing him back and he kept winning. The team finished with another great winning season record of 5-1-1.

As the war was still in full bloom at the beginning of the season. And the Spanish Flu was in the air, Syracuse began its season late on Oct. 26

On Oct 26, 1918 on a Saturday, after sitting idle practicing and practicing from August through most of October, the Orangemen got their chance to play football again. This game was against the Navy Transport. SU got the W (13- 0). The teams were willing to play anytime, anywhere to get in some games. Some teams canceled their 1918 seasons because they were impacted in one way or another by the war.

On Nov 3, 1918, Syracuse played a Sunday game at Dartmouth, a very tough team and they came away with a nice win W (34-6) Buck O'Neill was a great coach and got all he could out of his players. Brown, another great Ivy League team that had dominated in the past were walloped on Sunday Nov 10 at home in Archbold W (53-0). The Orangemen were off and running. Maybe they were reading their own press clippings, because they failed on Nov 16 at Michigan in a game played at Ferry Field in Ann Arbor, MI against Michigan L (0-15).

The Orangemen were tough, but they were clearly beaten by a team that played tougher on Nov 16. That was the last failure of this season, but it was devastating in its impact on the championship.

On Thanksgiving Day, Nov 28, 1918, SU gave the hometown folks a reason to put more gravy on the turkey with a great shutout win against Columbia W (20-0). Doing anything to have a season, SU played two days later on Saturday Nov 30, 1918 against the best football team in New Jersey, Rutgers. It was a great shutout win W (21-0).

Despite only playing six games in a season when the National Champion played just five games and lost one. It was that one unexplainable loss to Michigan that kept SU out of contention for the mythical national championship. The Orangemen were mentioned but they were dismissed;

The best sports writeup by a pundit explaining the scenario goes like this:

"Michigan went 5-0 and defeated a powerful 5-1 Syracuse team 15-0, and they are the only other team I will be considering for the 1918 mythical national championship (MNC). The 1918 football season barely qualified as a football season at all, and there were plenty of teams that may well have been equal to or better than Pittsburgh or Michigan, but what sets Pitt and Michigan apart from the rest is that each defeated another MNC contending team."

There is a lot of irony in that the 1918 NCAA football season had no clear-cut champion. Syracuse was considered but dismissed. The

NCAA schedule was also affected by the war, which ended right before the season ended that there was little season left to be played. The official NCAA Division I Football Records Book list Michigan and Pittsburgh as national champions.

The highest profile game for all those good enough to even sniff the championship air as the pundits were making the determinations. was a highly pundit publicized War Charities benefit that was staged at Forbes Field in Pittsburgh in front of many of the nation's top sports writers, including Walter Camp.

The game pitted John Heisman's undefeated, unscored upon, and defending national champion Georgia Tech Yellow Jackets against "Pop" Warner's Pittsburgh Panthers who were sitting on a 30-game win streak. Yes, this is the same Heisman that the trophy is named after. In this game, Pitt defeated Heisman's vaunted Georgia Tech team 32-0.

The Spanish flu pandemic of 1918 saw the implementation of quarantines that eliminated much of that year's college football season. Pittsburgh dominated the Yellow Jackets in this game and would have had a clean title if it were not for this. Would you count this:

The Cleveland Naval Reserves were great and tough like most service teams continue to be. They literally came out of nowhere to ruin a clean National Championship for Pitt with the help, some say of some slanted officiating. The final game of the season for Pitt at Cleveland Naval Reserve resulted in "Pop" Warner's first loss at Pitt. It is one of the most controversial losses in school history. Could Warner have really lost this game or was some unknown chicanery involved. Warner was never known as a complainer.

Warner, along with some reporters covering the game, insisted Pitt was robbed by the officials who, claiming the official timekeeper's watch was broken, arbitrarily ended the first half before Pitt was able to score and then allowed the Reserves extra time in the fourth quarter to pull ahead 10–9 before calling an end to the game.

Now, that does not sound fair, does it? Judy Harlan, formerly of Georgia Tech, and Moon Ducote, formerly of Auburn starred for the Cleveland Naval Reserves. Ducote kicked the winning field goal. Warner declared him "the greatest football player I ever saw." Harlan stated: "I intercepted a pass and returned it to midfield in the fourth quarter. I felt I at least had evened up some of the losses we had at Tech."

History normally proves the complaining team wrong. Not this time with Pittsburgh. As Spalding's football guide put it at the time, they were "universally conceded to be the champion team of the country," and if there had been an AP poll in 1918, Pitt would have easily finished out as the highest ranked college team.

Though this is an SU book, Syracuse vied for the same National Championship as Pitt did in 1918. The Cleveland Military, a dirt tough team got credit for the win v Pop Warner's team, but Pitt got the national championship in the opinions of the most important authoritative people in the game at the time--even though Pitt had to share the title with Michigan.

To repeat, this highly controversial loss ended the Pitt season and snapped a 32-game Pitt winning streak, but the Panthers had outscored opponents 140–16 in that short season and thus were retroactively selected as the national champion by the Helms Athletic Foundation and Houlgate System and as a co-national champion with Michigan by the National Championship Foundation.

1919 Frank "Buck" O'Neill Coach # 10

The 1919 Syracuse Orangemen football team competed in their thirty-first season of intercollegiate football. They were led by Frank "Buck" O'Neill in his third tour as head coach of the Syracuse Orangemen. This was his third year of three in his third tour, making this his eighth season overall at the helm. O'Neill was SU's best coach at this point and for the longest time SU kept bringing him back and he kept winning for them. This O'Neill team finished with another great winning season record of 8-3-0. After the war and the flu were gone from America. Football went back to normalcy.

In the 1919 season home opener at Archbold Stadium in the center of the campus of Syracuse University in Syracuse NY, all the flurry of the war years was over. From now on, for twenty more years, until WW II, it would be all football. And, so, on **Sep 27,** in this year, the Syracuse Alumni had been bolstered by returning great service players and they put up a fine battle against the varsity but lost anyway because they had no visible offense W (10-0).

On Oct 4, Syracuse whooped Vermont at home at Archbold Stadium in a shutout W (27-0). A still very tough Army team invited Syracuse again to the Plain in West Point, NY and SU escaped with a less than TD loss but a loss nonetheless against a tough advantaged army Cadet Squad W (7-3). National Champion Pitt had lost enough of their big guns that the Orangemen knocked them off the national stage with a finishing blow on Oct 18, W (24-3) in a fine, hard-played game.

Working through the season, on Oct 25, SU unexplainably lost to Washington & Jefferson L (0-13). They then came back and beat an ivy leagues fine football power, on Nov 1, at Brown W (13-0) > the wins kept coming after the unexplainable loss on a Tuesday. Nov 4, 1919 v Rutgers W (14-0). Then there was Bucknell on Nov 8 with a close win W (9-0). Not so big on offense this year, on Nov 19, SU beat Colgate, W (13-7) From here, it was at Indiana on Nov 22 and a loss in a close one, L (6-12). On Nov 27, in a season ender, the game was decided by a field goal against Nebraska in a loss L (0-3)

Famous Coaches (From the Past) by SWC75.

After being his QB and then Assistant coach to Buck O'Neill, Chick Meehan took over as coach at Syracuse after this O'Neill stint, and coached some of our best teams in 1920-24. His Syracuse coaching record was 35-8-4, including a 1923 team that was ranked #1 in the country by James Howell:

http://www.jhowell.net/cf/cf1923.htm

I call that team our "other" national champion.

Meehan opted to move to New York City and coach NYU, briefly turning them into a national power, and Manhattan, (who had improved its facilities). He retired in 1937 with a laudable 115-44-14 record. He was famous for saying: 'We learn practically nothing from a victory. All our information comes from a defeat. A winner forgets most of his mistakes.'" But he was never elected to the Hall of Fame, probably because of his involvement in a scheme to sell steel on the black market during the Korean War.

1920 Chick Meehan Coach # 15

The 1920 Syracuse Orangemen football team competed in their thirty-second season of intercollegiate football. They were led by Chick Meehan in his first season of five as head coach of the Syracuse Orangemen. This SU team finished with another great winning season record of 6-2-1. Coach Meehan is recognized as one of the greatest coaches of the Orange though he put in just five seasons. He was a keeper but he moved on nonetheless after five years.

COACH MEEHAN

<< **Coach Chick Meehan**

On Sep 25, SU defeated Hobart in the home opener at Archbold Stadium, on the campus of Syracuse University in Syracuse, NY W (55-7) Then on Oct 2, at home again SU blew out Vermont, W, 49, 0. Oct 9, at home, Syracuse pitched another blowout against Johns Hopkins W (45- 0). The perfect season ended the following week at home on Oct 16, when the Orangemen played Pitt to a tie T (7- 7).

On Oct 23, at Dartmouth, Syracuse prevailed W (10-0). Then, on Oct 30, at Holy Cross, the Orangemen experienced their first defeat of the season against Holy Cross L (0- 3). The following Saturday, on Nov 6, SU beat Washington & Jefferson W (14-0). The second loss of the season came on Nov-13 against Maryland L (7- 10). Syracuse then wrapped up its season on Nov 20 with a nice win at Colgate W (14-0)

1921 Chick Meehan Coach # 15

The 1921 Syracuse Orangemen football team competed in their thirty-third season of intercollegiate football. They were led by Chick Meehan in his second season of five as head coach of the Syracuse Orangemen. This SU team finished with another fine winning season record of 7-2-0.

Syracuse played its season home opener on Sept 24, 1921 at Archbold Stadium on the campus of Syracuse University and shut-out Hobart, W (35-0). On Oct 1, SU defeated Ohio, W (38-0) Then, on Oct 8 the Orangemen took on and defeated Maryland, W(42-0). On Oct 15, Syracuse beat (Ivy League) Brown, W, (28-0). As its program grew in strength with great coaches, no longer did SU have to take second fiddle to schools from the Ivy League.

SU played its first away game on Oct 22, against Pop Warner's always-strong Pitt team. Warner was in his seventh season at Pitt and he mentored his team on the way to defeating Syracuse L (0-35) in Pittsburgh, PA. Syracuse lost its second game of the season in a row on Oct 29 against Washington & Jefferson, L (10-17). On Nov 21, the Orangemen traveled to Montreal Canada to defeat McGill University W (13-0). Then, on Nov 12, SU defeated Colgate W (14-0) and they wrapped up the season with a win on Nov 19 at Dartmouth in New York, NY W (14-7).

1922 Chick Meehan Coach # 15

The 1922 Syracuse Orangemen football team competed in their thirty-fourth season of intercollegiate football. They were led by Chick Meehan in his third season of five as head coach of the Syracuse Orangemen. This SU team finished with another fine winning season record of 6-1-2.

Syracuse played its season home opener on Sept 23, 1922 at Archbold Stadium on the campus of Syracuse University and defeated Hobart, W (28-7.). All games were played at Archbold field this years except for Brown and Penn State. On Sept 30, Syracuse defeated Muhlenberg, W (47-0) Then on Oct 7, 1922, Syracuse shut out New York University (NYU) W (34-0). On Oct 14, the Orangemen traveled to Providence Rhode Island to fight Brown University to a scoreless tie T (0-0). For its first loss of the season, Syracuse were defeated by Pitt in a nail biter L (14- 21).

Then, on Oct 28, the Orangemen played on a neutral field game against Penn State in the NYC Polo Grounds and fought the Nittany Lions to a scoreless tie T (0-0) It was their second scoreless tie of the season. Then, Syracuse played perennial great Nebraska at home and fought for a tough victory against the Cornhuskers W (9-6)

On Nov 11, McGill from Canada were shut out at home by the Orangemen W (32-0). In the season finale, Syracuse defeated Colgate at home W (14-7)

1923 Chick Meehan Coach # 15

The 1923 Syracuse Orangemen football team competed in their thirty-fourth season of intercollegiate football. They were led by Chick Meehan in his fourth season of five as head coach of the Syracuse Orangemen. This SU team finished with the best record of Meehan's tenure 8-1-0. Again, SU just missed having its first undefeated season.

Games of the 1923 season

Syracuse played its season home opener on Sept 29, 1923 at Archbold Stadium on the campus of Syracuse University and defeated Hobart in a shutout, W (33-0). On Oct 6, SU defeated William & Mary, in a blowout, W (61-3). In their first ever matchup against Alabama at home on Oct 13, Syracuse shut out the Crimson Tide W (23-0)). Then on Oct 20, at Yankee Stadium in the Bronx, NY, Syracuse survived Pop Warner's Panthers W (-03). Next up at home was Springfield and the Orangemen made quick work of them W (44-0).

On Nov 3, at home against Penn State, SU shut out the Nittany Lions in a close match W (10-0). Next at home on Nov 10, the Orangemen defeated Boston University, W (49-0). SO far, the Orangemen were undefeated this season until they faced their nemesis Colgate at home and were defeated by the Raiders L (7-16). This would be the only loss of Chick Meehan's otherwise perfect season with the Orangemen. The following week, Meehan's squad took on Nebraska at Nebraska and defeated the Cornhuskers by a close shutout W (7-0).

The loss to Colgate not only kept SU out of contention for the mythical national championship, it kept them from consideration for the top twenty-five, but it did wonders for Colgate which at least was mentioned in pundit write-ups as a potential top-25 team. "Colgate (6-2-1) beat 8-1 Syracuse, and would have been ranked in a top 25," even with two losses. However, the tie really was what hurt their 1923 record.

1924 Chick Meehan Coach # 15

The 1924 Syracuse Orangemen football team competed in their thirty-sixth season of intercollegiate football. They were led by Chick Meehan in his fifth and last season of five as head coach of the Syracuse Orangemen. This SU team finished with a fine record of 8-2-1.

Syracuse played its season home opener on Sept 27, 1924 at Archbold Stadium on the campus of Syracuse University and defeated Hobart in a shutout, W (35-0). On Oct 4, my Wedding Anniversary, SU defeated Mercer at Archbold Stadium, W (26-0). On Oct 11, the Orangemen defeated William & Mary, at home, W (24-7). On Oct 18 at Archbold Stadium, SU beat Boston College, W (10-0). Then on Oct 25 at New Beaver Field in State College, PA, Syracuse defeated the Nittany Lions, W (10-6).

On Nov, at home SU tied Pitt T (7-7). This was followed by the first loss of the season at home against West Virginia Wesleyan, L (3-7). On Nov 15, the Orangemen beat Niagara, W (23-6). On Nov 22, SU defeated Colgate at home W (7-3). On Thanksgiving Day, Nov 27, at Baker Field in Manhattan, New York, NY, Syracuse beat Columbia in a nail-biter W (9-6). Then in the season finale, the Orangemen sustained their second loss of the season to USC, after traveling to the Los Angeles Memorial Coliseum in Los Angeles, CA, on December 6, 1924, L (0-16).

Famous Coaches (From the Past) by SWC75.

Pete Reynolds took over for one year and did a good job, going 8-1-1. As in 1923, the only loss was to Colgate. It was the beginning of the "HooDoo", when we were unable to beat Colgate for 13 consecutive years, including three where that was the only game we lost, (and that doesn't include '23). Reynolds was back again the next year, going 7-2-1. Vic Hanson was his big star. That was also the year of the "Massacre of the Plains", a big brawl after a game at West Point against Army that terminated the series until 1955. Reynolds was at the end of a long coaching career that began in 1909.

His previous stops had been at Hobart, Hamilton and Bucknell. He was from Illinois and he also coached at Knox College in 1935-37. Most sources don't list that period but if that's true, Pete's overall coaching record was 77-58-14. He settled in Oneida, New York, where he died in 1951.

1925 Pete Reynolds Coach # 16

The 1925 Syracuse Orangemen football team competed in their thirty-seventh season of intercollegiate football. They were led by Pete Reynolds in his first of two as head coach of the Syracuse Orangemen. This SU team finished with a fine record of 8-1-1 – almost undefeated.

Syracuse played its season home opener on Sept 26, 1925 at Archbold Stadium on the campus of Syracuse University and defeated Hobart in a shutout, W (32-0). On Oct 3, SU handed Vermont a defat at Archbold Stadium W (26-0). The next week on Oct 10, Syracuse got win #3, a shutout, under their new coach against William & Mary W (33-0). Win number four was through the next door at Indiana on Oct 17 W (14-0). For SU win number five, Providence did not survive the big blowout shutout on Oct 24 at home W (48-0).

On October 31, for win #6, Syracuse fired all its bricks and put down the Nittany Lions of Penn State at home. W (7-0). Looking for seven, on Oct 31, the Orangemen tied Wesleyan W (7-0). Still without a loss, on Nov 14 nemesis Colgate came in and stopped all the rhymes and beat the Orange in a fair tough game, L (7-0). On Nov 21, SU shut out Niagara at home in Archbold Stadium, W (17 0). In the season finale on Turkey Day at Columbia in New York City, the Orangemen grabbed another victory W (16-5). it was a fine season for new coach Pete Reynolds. But those folks from Colgate, they just would not go away easily.

Chris Island wrote a piece about this one-time rivalry several years ago for the Daily orange and it captures the essence of how serious these two teams took each other.

> "All it took was a pact, and then nothing more than a verbal agreement, to try and stop the insanity of it all. It became too dangerous, too raucous. The store owners grew tired of having to board up the windows, and the Syracuse hotels no longer wanted to have to move furniture out of the lobby to avoid having it destroyed.
>
> All this trouble for a football game between Syracuse and Colgate.
>
> The memories will rush back into the minds of alumni who were once a part of the storied past Syracuse-Colgate rivalry weekends, when those weekends were at their peak. Alumni will remember the pep rallies, the poster contests, the — fairly — innocent kidnappings of students, the scalping, and maybe even the games, themselves.

'There were huge displays outside the fraternities and sororities,' said former Colgate player, coach and athletic director Fred Dunlap. 'They all always said, 'Beat Colgate,' and the game always had a sell-out crowd.'

These were just a part of the unending, all-encompassing events of those long-forgotten weekends that have lost their excitement and draw.

Over the first 20 games the Orangemen and Raiders met, Colgate went 13-5-2. From 1925 to 1937, the Raiders took 11 more games from the Orangemen.

But starting in 1951, Syracuse began to take control of the series. Eventually, it became too much for Colgate — and the towns of Hamilton, N.Y., and Syracuse — to bear, and the series was cancelled for 20 years. But before the cancellation, SU expected to defeat the Raiders every year."

In 1925, Colgate surely had destroyed SU's chance at a shot at the National Championship—again. Of course, the tie to Ohio Wesleyan did not help matters either. And so, in all the discussions by the pundits about mythical national champions and the runners up, Syracuse was mentioned as tying and losing to Colgate, but not as a contender for top honors. Dartmouth was crowned mythical national champion in the pundit post-voting.

When the mythical dust settled, writers hailed Dartmouth as the national champions. Grantland Rice: "In the midst of all the noise and excitement, football's main banner for the waning year goes to the peace and far-away restfulness of Dartmouth, the college on the hill."

Dartmouth was invited to the Rose Bowl to play 10-0-1 Washington, but they were already widely considered the national champions, and the players didn't want to give up their Christmas holidays, so they voted to reject the offer. That was critical for Alabama, who would not have emerged decades later as the consensus national champion among retroactive selectors without that game. Only in college football could a championship be given, and a championship be taken away. One thing for sure, Colgate had made sure that the Orangemen were not in consideration. Grrrrrrr!!!

1926 Pete Reynolds Coach # 16

The 1926 Syracuse Orangemen football team competed in their thirty-eighth season of intercollegiate football. They were led by Pete Reynolds in his second of two as head coach of the Syracuse Orangemen. This SU team finished with a fine record of 7-2-1.

Syracuse played its season home opener on Sept 25, 1926 at Archbold Stadium on the campus of Syracuse University and defeated Hobart in a shutout, W (18-0). On Oct 2, SU handed Vermont a blowout defeat at Archbold Stadium W (64-0). The next week on Oct 10, Syracuse got win #3, a shutout, against William & Mary W (35-0).

With three wins under their belt, the Orangemen looked forward to tangling with a tough Amery team, but the Cadets prevailed and beat Syracuse in a tough match L (21-27). The Orangemen traveled to New Beaver Field in State College to face the Nittany Lions of Penn State and they carried home all the marbles in a nice game W (10-0).

On Oct 30, SU beat Johns Hopkins at home W (31-0). On Nov 6, the Orangemen lost in a first-time match against Georgetown L (7-13). On Nov 13, nemesis Colgate was at the front door again and they plaid the Orangemen to a tie T (10-10). On Nov 20, SU defeated Niagara W (12-6) at Archbold Stadium. Then, the Orange traveled to New York City to face Columbia and the squad prevailed W (19-12)

Famous Coaches (From the Past) by SWC75.

Pete Reynolds was replaced by Lew Andreas, more famous as a long-time basketball coach, (it was his school record for victories that Jim Boeheim broke), and athletic director. He hired Vic Hanson to be his assistant. Andreas sort of stumbled along for three years at 15-10-3 before handing the reigns to Hanson.

1927 Lew Andreas Coach # 17

The 1927 Syracuse Orangemen football team competed in their thirty-ninth season of intercollegiate football. They were led by Lew Andreas in his first of three seasons as head coach of the Syracuse Orangemen. This SU squad finished with a fine record of 5-3-2.

Syracuse played its season home opener on Sept 26, 1927 at Archbold Stadium on the campus of Syracuse University and defeated Hobart in a shutout, W (13-0). Hobart was playing much better football. On Oct13, SU handed William & Mary a shutout shut defeat at Archbold Stadium W (18-0). The next week on Oct 8, Syracuse got win #3, against Johns Hopkins (21-6). On Oct 15, at home, SU defeated Georgetown W (19-6). In a first, Penn State defeated Syracuse on Oct 22 at Archbold Field L (6-9).

After a fine start, and just one loss, in its trip to Nebraska on Oct 29, the Cornhuskers finally won their first game against Syracuse and it was a shutout L (0-21). On Oct 5, Ohio Wesleyan, a proven tough squad tied the Orangemen at Archbold Stadium T (6-6). Those nasty guys from Colgate played Syracuse at Archbold on Nov 12, and the tough play resulted in a tie T (12-12). Niagara was next at Archbold and SU prevailed in a lose match W (13-6). In a rare defeat, Syracuse traveled to Columbia in NYC and were defeated in a close match L (7-14).

1928 Lew Andreas Coach # 17

The 1928 Syracuse Orangemen football team competed in their fortieth season of intercollegiate football. They were led by Lew Andreas in his second of three seasons as head coach of the Syracuse Orangemen. This SU squad finished with a so-so record of 4-4-1.

Syracuse played its season home opener on Sept 29, 1928 at Archbold Stadium on the campus of Syracuse University and defeated Hobart in a close match W (14-6). Hobart continued to play better football and this year scored on the Orangemen. On Oct 6, SU handed William & Mary a shutout defeat at Archbold Stadium W (32-0). The next week on Oct 13, Syracuse got win #3, a blowout against Johns Hopkins (58-0). On Oct 20, at Nebraska, SU lost to the Cornhuskers in a nail-biter L (6-7) On Oct 26, at Penn State tied the Orangemen in a tough battle T (6-6). Then, on Nov 3, at Pitt, SU lost in a shutout L (0-18).

Still having trouble with Ohio Wesleyan, on Nov 10, L (0- 6). On Nov 17, the Orangemen took a tough loss from Colgate L (6-30). Springing back from last year's defeat at home. SU beat Columbia at home in NYC on Nov 29 W (14-6).

1929 Lew Andreas Coach # 17

The 1929 Syracuse Orangemen football team competed in their forty-first season of intercollegiate football. They were led by Lew Andreas in his third and last of three seasons as head coach of the Syracuse Orangemen. This SU squad finished with nice record of 6-3-0.

Syracuse played its season home opener on Sept 28, 1929 at Archbold Stadium on the campus of Syracuse University and defeated Hobart in a blowout W (77-0. On Oct 5, SU handed St. Lawrence a shutout defeat at Archbold Stadium W (55-0). The next week on Oct 12 Syracuse lost against Nebraska at home (6-13). On Oct 19, at home in Archbold Stadium, SU whooped John Hoskins in a major blowout W (85-6). On Oct 29, Black Tuesday, the Stock Market crashed. On Nov 2, at Archbold Field, Penn State beat the Orangemen in a low scoring nail-biter L (4-6).

Then, on Nov 9, at Niagara, SU won the game in a shutout L (20-0. Colgate came into Archbold Field like they owned it on Nov 16 and defeated the Orangemen in a shutout L (0-21). SU went to Columbia in NYC on Thanksgiving, Nov 28, again, and took the close game in a shutout W (6-0).

Chapter 6 Vic Hanson 1930 to 1936

Victor Hanson, Coach # 18

Year	Coach	Record	Conf
1930	Vic Hanson	5-2-2	Ind
1931	Vic Hanson	7-1-1	Ind
1932	Vic Hanson	4-4-1	Ind
1933	Vic Hanson	4-4-0	Ind
1934	Vic Hanson	6-2-0	Ind
1935	Vic Hanson	6-1-1	Ind
1936	Vic Hanson	1-7-0	Ind

Head Football Coach Victor Hanson and Fiancée Dorothy Burns Circa 1931

Famous Coaches (From the Past) by SWC75.

Vic Hanson did somewhat better than his predecessor Pete Reynolds, going 7-1-1 in 1931 and 6-1-1 in 1935. But he couldn't beat Colgate and when the 1936 team fell to 1-7, the old hero was fired. Syracuse was the only head football coaching job Andreas or Hanson ever held. Both were alums of the school.

1930 Victor Hanson Coach # 18

The 1930 Syracuse Orangemen football team competed in their forty-second season of intercollegiate football. They were led by Victor Hanson in his first of seven seasons as head coach of the Syracuse Orangemen. This SU squad finished with nice record of 5-2-2.

Syracuse played its season home opener on Sept 27 at Archbold Stadium on the campus of Syracuse University and defeated Rensselaer (RPI) in a blowout W (55-0. On Oct 5, SU handed Hobart a shutout defeat at Archbold Stadium W (49-0). The next week on Oct 12 Syracuse shut out Rutgers at home W (27-0). On Oct 18, at home in Archbold Stadium, SU lost to Pitt in a shutout L (0-14). On Oct 25, at Archbold Field, SU beat St. Lawrence W (34-6).

Then, on Nov 1, at home, SU tied the game against Brown University from Providence RI T (16-16). On Nov 8, at Penn State in State College PA, the Nittany Lions and the Orangemen finished in a scoreless tie T (0-0). On Nov 15, SU lost big to Colgate at home L (7-36). SU then traveled to Columbia in NYC on Thanksgiving, Nov 27, again, and beat the Lions W (19-7)

1931 Victor Hanson Coach # 18

The 1931 Syracuse Orangemen football team competed in their forty-third season of intercollegiate football. They were led by Victor Hanson in his second of seven seasons as head coach of the Syracuse Orangemen. This SU squad finished with nice record of 7-1-1.

Syracuse played its season home opener on Sept 26, 1931 at Archbold Stadium on the campus of Syracuse University and defeated St. Lawrence in a blowout W (46-6. On Oct 3, SU handed Hobart a shutout defeat at Archbold Stadium W (49-0). The next week on Oct 10 Syracuse blew out Ohio Wesleyan at home W (48-7). On Oct 17, at home in Archbold Stadium, SU beat the Florida Gators W (33-12) Then, on Oct 24, the Orangemen defeated Penn State in a one-TD shutout L (7-0).

On Oct 31, at Spartan Stadium, SU beat Michigan State, W (15-10). On Nov 7, SU shut out Western Reserve W (33-0) at home. Undefeated in seven games, the next team up was the typical spoiler. Still having trouble with Colgate who looked at Archbold Stadium as their own field, SU could not get past Colgate on Nov 14, and were defeated by two touchdowns L (7-21). On Nov 21 SU traveled again to Columbia in NYC and this time the teams played to a scoreless tie T (0-0).

1932 Victor Hanson Coach # 18

The 1932 Syracuse Orangemen football team competed in their forty-fourth season of intercollegiate football. They were led by Victor Hanson in his third of seven seasons as head coach of the Syracuse Orangemen. This SU squad finished with a so-so record this year of 4-4-1.

Syracuse played its season home opener on Sept 24, 1932 at Archbold Stadium on the campus of Syracuse University and defeated Clarkson in a close match W (13-6) On Oct 1, SU handed St. Lawrence a shutout-blowout defeat at Archbold Stadium W (54-0). The next week on Oct 8 Syracuse lost to Ohio Wesleyan at home L (12-19) On Oct 15, at home in Archbold Stadium, SU lost to Southern Methodist (SMU) L (6-16) On Oct 22, at New Beaver Stadium, Syracuse beat Penn State W (12-6)

Then, on Oct 29 at home, the Orangemen were defeated by Michigan State L (13-27) On Nov5, Oglethorpe came to Archbold Stadium and left without a victory as the Orangemen beat these new visitors W (27-6) SU still was on a losing trek against Colgate and extended by a game as Colgate defeated the Orangemen L (0-16). In the season finale against Columbia in NYC, the teams played to a hard-fought scoreless tie T (0-0).

1933 Victor Hanson Coach # 18

The 1933 Syracuse Orangemen football team competed in their forty-fifth season of intercollegiate football. They were led by Victor Hanson in his fourth of seven seasons as head coach of the Syracuse Orangemen. This SU squad finished with a so-so record this year of 4-4-0.

Syracuse played its season home opener on Oct 7, 1933 at Archbold Stadium on the campus of Syracuse University and defeated Clarkson in a bow-out match W (52-0) On Oct 14, SU handed Ohio Wesleyan a shutout defeat at Archbold Stadium W (40-0). The next week on Oct 21 for the first time in years, SU played at Cornell and beat the Big Red in a close match W (14-7). On Oct 28, at Spartan Stadium in Michigan, the Spartans beat Syracuse L (3-27).

On Nov 4, at Archbold, SU defeated Penn State W (12-6). Then, on Nov 11, Brown defeated SU at Archbold Stadium L (7-10) Colgate was next up and they were tough as usual beating the Orangemen in a tough match L (3-13). At Columbia on Nov 25, SU lost its season finale L (0-16)

1934 Victor Hanson Coach # 18

The 1934 Syracuse Orangemen football team competed in their forty-sixth season of intercollegiate football. They were led by Victor Hanson in his fifth of seven seasons as head coach of the Syracuse Orangemen. This SU squad finished with a nice record this year of 6-2-0 . The Orangemen were the 28th nationally ranked team this year.

Syracuse played its season home opener on Oct 6, 1934 at Archbold Stadium on the campus of Syracuse University and defeated Clarkson in a shutout W (28-0) On Oct 13, SU handed Cornell a tough defeat at Archbold Stadium W (20-7). The next week on Oct

20, in a tough match, SU prevailed over Ohio Wesleyan W (32-10) On Oct 27, at Brown, SU beat the Bears in Providence RI in a shutout W (33-0).

On Nov 3, at Penn State's New Beaver Field, SU defeated Penn State W (16-0). Then, on Nov 10, The Orange got the best of Michigan State at Archbold Stadium W (10-0). Colgate was next up, and they were like a cog in the wheel of success for SU that could not be undone. They beat the Orangemen in a tough match as usual L (2-13). At Columbia on Nov 25, SU lost its season finale L (0-12)

1935 Victor Hanson Coach # 18

The 1935 Syracuse Orangemen football team competed in their forty-seventh season of intercollegiate football. They were led by Victor Hanson in his sixth of seven seasons as head coach of the Syracuse Orangemen. This SU squad finished with a very nice record this year of 6-1-1.

This was a nice year …the next year was a disaster as if Syracuse had pulled the plug on scholarships. I will investigate this and if I find something, I will show it in the 1936 season. With one less loss in 1935, SU's ranking was almost top 10 nationally but # 14 was not so shabby.

Syracuse played its season home opener on Oct 5, 1935 at Archbold Stadium on the campus of Syracuse University and defeated Clarkson in a shutout W (33-0) On Oct 12, SU handed Cornell a tough defeat at Archbold Stadium W (21-14). The next week on Oct 19, in a tough match, SU prevailed over Ohio Wesleyan W (18-10) On Oct 26, at Brown, SU beat the Bears in Providence RI in a shutout W (19-0).

On Nov 2, at home SU again beat an eager, tough Penn State Team W (7-3) in a nail-biter. Then, on Nov 9, The Orange got the best of Columbia at NYC W (14-12). Colgate was next up, and they were like rocks preventing Syracuse from championships. As much as I hate to say it, they walloped the Orangemen in an easy match for Colgate. L (2-27). Instead of the last game being at Columbia, SU finished the season at Baltimore Maryland on Nov 28, the teams played tough and finished in a scoreless tie L (0-0).

1936 Victor Hanson Coach # 18

The 1936 Syracuse Orangemen football team competed in their forty-eighth season of intercollegiate football. They were led by Victor Hanson in his seventh and last of seven seasons as head coach of the Syracuse Orangemen. This SU squad finished with one of its worst records ever 1-7-0.

I promised that I would investigate what happened this year, and I did. However, information is hard to come by at Syracuse. I contacted the Sports Information Department and I received no response. If an avid Syracuse fan happens to have the information as to why the team did so poorly in 1936, and also why Victor Hanson was replaced by what appears to be a less-capable coach, I will update this book after it is published so that SU fans can know what happened.

In my second research effort, I did find a great write-up about Hanson, commemorating his placement in the hall of fame that I will share below. It comes from http://www.footballfoundation.org/Programs/CollegeFootballHallofFame/SearchDetail.aspx?id=20054

Victor Hanson Great SU Coach – Member Biography

Called by Grantland Rice, "the best all-around athlete Syracuse ever had," Victor Hanson was a three-sport star for the Orangemen. In addition to playing as an All-America end in football, Hanson was an All-American in basketball and good enough in baseball to be signed by the New York Yankees.

Hanson began his collegiate career in 1924 as the only sophomore on the varsity. A teammate on that 1924 team was future Hall of Fame coach Lynn Waldorf. During three varsity seasons Syracuse posted a 23-5-3 record. Hanson, playing end, called the plays for the offense.

He captained the football, basketball and baseball teams. After graduation he played one year in baseball's minor leagues. He returned to Syracuse as an assistant coach in 1928 and 1929. In 1930, at the age of 27, Hanson was named head football coach. In seven seasons he posted a 33-21-5 record. He later became a prominent insurance counselor. Hanson was elected to the Basketball Hall of Fame in 1960 and the College Football Hall of Fame in 1973. He was born July 30, 1903 and died April 10, 1982.

Games of the 1936 Season

Syracuse played its season home opener on Oct 3, 1936 at Archbold Stadium on the campus of Syracuse University and defeated Clarkson in a shutout W (31-0). This would be the only win of the year. On Oct 10, SU lost to Baldwin-Wallace L (0-19). The next week on Oct 17, in a tough match, SU lost at Cornell L (7-20) On Oct 24, at Brown, SU was shut out by Maryland at home L (0-20).

On Oct 31, at State College, PA, Penn State beat the Orangemen L (0-18). Then, on Nov 7, The Orange lost in a nail-biter at Indiana L (7-9). On Nov 14, at Columbia, Syracuse lost their sixth game in a row L (0-17). Colgate was next up in the season finale and again, the Raiders were like rocks preventing Syracuse from a chance of victory. The Orange lost their seventh game in a row capping a miserable season L (0-13)

Chapter 7 Ossie Solem 1937 to 1948

Ossie Solem, Coach # 19
Biggie Munn Coach # 20
Reaves Baysinger Coach #21

Year	Coach	Record	Conf
1937	Ossie Solem	5-2-1	Ind
1938	Ossie Solem	5-3-0	Ind
1939	Ossie Solem	3-3-2	Ind
1940	Ossie Solem	3-4-1	Ind
1941	Ossie Solem	5-2-1	Ind
1942	Ossie Solem	6-3-0	Ind
1943	No team due to World War II		
1944	Ossie Solem	2-4-1	Ind
1945	Ossie Solem	1-6-0	Ind
1946	Clarence Biggie Munn	4-5-0	Ind
1947	Reaves Baysinger	3-6-1	Ind
1948	Reaves Baysinger	1-6-0	Ind

Two other coaches are highlighted in this chapter – Clarence "Biggie" Munn, and Reaves Baysinger.

Crowd in downtown Syracuse, World War II victory parade, September 1945.

Famous Coaches (From the Past) by SWC75.

Hanson was replaced by possibly the most prominent coach at the time of hiring we've ever had, (Bill Hollenbeck might be the exception, but he only lasted that one year and then retired). Ossie Solem has played for Dr. Henry Williams at Minnesota when they were a major national power. Then he went into pro football, coaching a team called the Minneapolis Marines that went on to join the NFL.

By that time, Solem had switched to college coach as well as being an athletic director at Luther College in Iowa, (1920), Drake, (1921-31) and Iowa, (1932-36). Drake was a fairly prominent program at that time and his teams went 7-0-0 in 1922 and 7-1-0 in 1928. Wikipedia, in its article on the Drake Bulldogs, says that they "shared the national championship in some national polls. They were invited to the White House for their accomplishments."

I've checked the various selectors who list rankings for each year online and I couldn't find anyone who rated that team higher than 16th. Usually they are around #30. They were what we would now call a good "mid-major". But it still got Solem some national recognition. Drake was a founding member of the Missouri Valley Conference in 1928 and won its first four championships. .

Solem moved on to Iowa in 1932. The Hawkeyes had just been temporarily suspended by the Big Ten due an athletic department slush fund scandal that dated back to the Howards Jones Era. (They were paying players! Horrors!) Even after the suspension, Solem had a hard time filling out his Big Ten schedule because all the members would rather play Notre Dame. The Depression also hit the University hard and they weren't able to pay Solem his full salary.

Nonetheless, he soldiered on to a 15-21-4 record over five seasons. The period was not without its high points. In 1933 they surprised with a 5-3 record and quarterback Joe Laws was Big Ten MVP. But his greatest player was Ozzie Simmons, "The Ebony Eel" who was named second team All-American in 1934 and first team in 1935. Solem was also able to recruit a strong freshman class in 1936 that included Nile Kinnick, who would win the 1939 Heisman Trophy.

But Solem had a run-in with Simmons, whose teammates resented his notoriety and maybe also his color. They decided not to have a captain of the team his senior year to avoid voting for him. Some even refused to block for him. The coach accused him of "laying down" in a 0-52 loss to Minnesota, even though Simmons played the game with an injured leg. Simmons left the team saying "I've taken too much abuse this season because of Iowa's poor showing. I've taken more punishment than I did in my sophomore year and Solem has been screaming at me. He doesn't scream at the other players, just me." (There was bullying in those days, as well.)

Solem replied "Other players on the team were berated for their play in the Minnesota game but they took it without a word. I made one criticism of Simmons and he couldn't take it." They later made up and Simmons said, "He probably could have been tougher (on the players), but he was the finest gentleman I've ever been around."

Nonetheless, Solem left Iowa to come east and coach Syracuse for the 1937 season. He assembled perhaps the finest football staff ever with two protégés who had also played for Minnesota assisting him, Clarence "Biggie" Munn and Bud Wilkinson. One of their players was Hugh "Duffy" Daughtery, who gave this scouting report for himself:

"He may be small, but he sure is slow."

Duffy joined Solem's staff on graduation. Wilkinson, of course, went on to become coach at Oklahoma, turning them into a dominant program while Munn and then Daugherty coached Michigan State to nearly equal prominence. Despite the quality of the coaching, there were plenty of ups and downs during Solem's tenure, (1937-45), during which he went 30-27-6.

The high points were winning what Grantland Rice called the greatest game he had seen against powerful Cornell in 1938, 19-17, finally breaking the HooDoo against Colgate later the same year, 7-0 and upsetting national power Wisconsin 27-20 in 1941 using the controversial "reverse center" formation which was subsequently banned. (Amos Alonzo Stagg commented that "a time of war was not the time to be showing your backside to the enemy"). The most prominent players were Marty Glickman and Wilmeth Sidat-Singh.

Solem moved on after the war to coach at Springfield College in Massachusetts, (Wikipedia, for some reason, lists it as "YMCA" the first seven years but it was the college). In 1956 his team went 8-0-1 thanks, in part to a center/linebacker named Dick MacPherson, who captained Solem's last team in 1957.

Solem was 44-7-3 coaching the Minneapolis pro team and then 162-117-20 in a 37-season college coaching career, (SU did not field a team in 1943). He had also gone 37-31 in four seasons as the Drake basketball coach. I had thought he was in the Hall of Fame but, in fact, he is not, although his three famous assistants are.

About Coach Ossie Solem

Oscar Martin "Ossie" Solem (December 13, 1891 – October 26, 1970) was an American football player, coach of football and basketball, and college athletics administrator. He served as the head football coach at Luther College in Decorah, Iowa (1920), Drake University (1921–1931), the University of Iowa (1932–1936), Syracuse University (1937–1945), and Springfield College (1946–1957), compiling a career college football record of 162–117–20.

From 1913 until 1920, Solem was the head coach of the Minneapolis Marines, prior to that team's entry into the National Football League (NFL). During his time with the Marines, Solem introduced the team to the single-wing formation, developed by the famed coach, Pop Warner, and used by the University of Minnesota, where Solem had played football. Solem was also the head basketball coach at Drake University for four seasons, from 1921 to 1925, tallying a mark of 37–31. For Syracuse, he was a fine coach, and if it were not for the frustration of fielding a team in the WWII years, Ben Schwartzwalder may not have been needed.

1937 Ossie Solem Coach # 19

The 1937 Syracuse Orangemen football team competed in their forty-ninth season of intercollegiate football. They were led by Ossie

Solem in his first of eight seasons as head coach of the Syracuse Orangemen. This SU squad finished with a fine record of 5-2-1.

Syracuse played its season home opener on Friday Oct 1, 1937 at Archbold Stadium on the campus of Syracuse University and defeated Clarkson W (26-6). This would be the first of five wins this year. On Oct 9, SU beat St. Lawrence in-a shutout W (40-0). The next week on Oct 16, at Cornell, in a tough match, SU defeated the Big Red W (14-6) On Oct 23, at Maryland in a game played in Baltimore, Maryland defeated the Orangemen L (0-13).

On Oct 31, at home, SU beat the Nittany Lions of Penn State W (19-13) 0-18). Then, on Nov 6, at home, the Orange defeated Western Reserve W (27-6). The Orangemen then traveled to Columbia in NYC on Nov 13 and tied the Lions T (6-6) Colgate was next up in the season finale on Nov 20, and again, though this time in a very close match, the Raiders defeated the Orangemen L (0-7).

1938 Ossie Solem Coach # 19

The 1938 Syracuse Orangemen football team competed in their fiftieth season of intercollegiate football. They were led by Ossie Solem in his second of eight seasons as head coach of the Syracuse Orangemen. This SU squad finished with a fine record of 5-3-0.

Syracuse played its season home opener on Friday, Sept 30, 1938 at Archbold Stadium on the campus of Syracuse University and shut out Clarkson W (27-0). This would be the first of five wins this year.

On Oct 8, SU beat Maryland in a shutout W (40-0). The next week on Oct 15, at Cornell, in a tough match, SU defeated the Big Red W (19-17) On Oct 22, at Michigan State the Spartans defeated the Orangemen L (12-19.

On Oct 31, at Penn State, SU lost to the Nittany Lions of Penn State L (6-33). Then, on Nov 5, at home, after ten losses in a row, the Orange finally defeated nemesis Colgate W (7-0) The Orangemen then lost to Duke at home L (0-21). The next week, on Nov 19, the Orange traveled to Columbia in NYC in the season finale and beat the Lions T (13-12).

1939 Ossie Solem Coach # 19

The 1939 Syracuse Orangemen football team competed in their fifty-first season of intercollegiate football. They were led by Ossie Solem in his third of eight seasons as head coach of the Syracuse Orangemen. This SU squad finished with a so-so record of 3-3-2.

Syracuse played its season home opener on Friday, Sept 29, 1939 at Archbold Stadium on the campus of Syracuse University and shut out Clarkson W (12-0). This would be the first of just three wins this year. On Oct 7, SU lost at Cornell L (6-19). The next week on Oct 14, at Georgetown, the teams played to a tie T (13-13) On Oct 21, at Duke, the Blue Devils overpowered the Orangemen L (6-33).

On Oct 28, at home, Penn State and SU played to a tie T (6-6). The Orangemen then lost in a lopsided game at Duke L (6-33). On Nov 4, at home SU lost a close match to Michigan State L (3-14). Then, on Nov 18, at home, the Orange beat nemesis Colgate for the second year in a row and by the same score, W (7-0.). About two weeks later, on Nov 30, the Orange traveled to Maryland in the season finale and beat the Terrapins W (10-7).

1940 Ossie Solem Coach # 19

The 1940 Syracuse Orangemen football team competed in their fifty-second season of intercollegiate football. They were led by Ossie

Solem in his fourth of eight seasons as head coach of the Syracuse Orangemen. This SU squad finished with a losing record of 3-4-1.

Syracuse played its season home opener on Friday, Sept 27, 1940 at Archbold Stadium on the campus of Syracuse University and shut out Clarkson W (33-0). This would be the first of just three wins this year. On Oct 5, SU was shut-out at Archbold Stadium by Northwestern L (0-40). The next week on Oct 14, at NYU in the Bronx, NY, SU got its moxie back, W (47-13). On Oct 19, at Cornell, the Red Raiders overpowered the Orangemen L (6-33).

On Oct 26, at Columbia, SU defeated the Lions in a close match W (3-0). On Nov 2, at home SU lost by a bigger score against Georgetown L (6-28). Then, on Nov 9, at home Syracuse & Penn State played to an unlucky tie T (13-13). Then, on Nov 16, after two victories in a row SU lost to nemesis Colgate L (6-7.

1941 Ossie Solem Coach # 19

The 1941 Syracuse Orangemen football team competed in their fifty-third season of intercollegiate football. They were led by Ossie Solem in his fifth of eight seasons as head coach of the Syracuse Orangemen. This SU squad finished with a fine record of 5-2-1.

Syracuse played its season home opener on Friday, Sept 26, 1941 at Archbold Stadium on the campus of Syracuse University and shut out Clarkson W (39-0). This would be the first of five wins this year. On Oct 4, SU was shut-out at Cornell by the Red Raiders L (0-6). The next week on Oct 11, at home against Holy Cross, the Orangemen pitched a close shutout W (6-0). On Oct 18 at NYU in the Bronx, NY, SU threw another shutout W (31-0). On Oct 25, at home, SU defeated the Scarlet Knights of Rutgers in a big win W (49-7).

On Nov 1 at Wisconsin, SU squeaked by the Badgers for the win -- W (27-20). On November 8 at State college, PA, Syracuse lost to Penn State L (19-34) On Nov 15, SU tied Colgate T (19-19) in its season finale.

1942 Ossie Solem Coach # 19

The 1942 Syracuse Orangemen football team competed in their fifty-fourth season of intercollegiate football. They were led by Ossie Solem in his sixth of eight seasons as head coach of the Syracuse Orangemen. This SU squad finished with a fine record of 6-3-0. This was the most wins that SU would get in its eight seasons under Coach Solem.

Syracuse played its season home opener on Friday, Sept 25, 1942 at Archbold Stadium on the campus of Syracuse University and blew-Out Clarkson W (58-6). This would be the first of six wins for SU this year. On Oct 3, SU shut-out Boston University at Archbold Stadium W (25-0). On Oct 9, at home, SU beat Western Reserve W (13-0). The next week on Oct 17, at Holy Cross, the Orangemen pitched a shutout W (19-0). On Oct 18, at home, SU just got past Cornell in a close match W (12-7)

On Oct 31, at home, SU lost to a military team, North Carolina Pre-Flight, L (0-9) The military was in full bloom again with the beginning of WWII in 1939. On Nov 1 at Wisconsin, SU squeaked by the Badgers for the win --W (27-20). On November 7 at State college, PA, Syracuse lost to Penn State L (13-18). On Nov 14, at home, SU lost to nemesis Colgate L (0-14). On Nov 21 @ Rutgers, SU defeated the Scarlet Knights W (12-7). In the season finale.

1943 Season cancelled due to World War II

1944 Ossie Solem Coach # 19

The 1944 Syracuse Orangemen football team competed in their fifty-fifth season of intercollegiate football. They were led by Ossie Solem in his seventh of eight seasons as head coach of the Syracuse Orangemen. This SU squad finished with a poor record of 2-4-1 After the year off for the war, it was a difficult task for college teams to rebuild as many of their best players were in the service of our nation.

The military teams, especially Army, were knocking them all out across the country and the people of America were cheering for their armed services. It was tough being Syracuse this year and the next. Ironically, for Coach Solem, this happened after his most productive season, 1942.

The war played havoc on college teams across the country and teams such as Gonzaga gave up on football for good after the war. So, also with Clarkson, who puttered around for a while but were not ready to play SU in 1945. Clarkson students still like football and they still have homecoming games but not at a Division I level as Syracuse.

Clarkson has not fielded a school sponsored football team since 1951, The Club football notion is alive and well as students form clubs and play intercollegiate football but not NCAA football. The new teams are charter members of the Yankee Collegiate Football Conference, a collection of seven tackle-football club teams across New England and New York.

My alma mater King's College from Wilkes-Barre, PA, with one of my best friends, RIP, Frank Kurilla as a star player, and with Eddie Brominski, as their dedicated unpaid coach, won the Club Football Championship in 1968 in a game at IONA, NY, which I attended. Club Football was and is great for students. The Friday SU games with Clarkson ended in 1942.

Syracuse thus played its season home opener on a Saturday, Sept 23, 1944 at Archbold Stadium on the campus of Syracuse University and lost big to Cornell L (6-39). On Oct 7, at Columbia, SU lost to the Lions, L (2-26). On Oct 14, at home, SU beat Lafayette for its first win of two this season. The next week on Oct 21, at Temple in Philadelphia, the teams played hard to achieve a tie T (7-7).

On Oct 28, at Boston College SU lost a close game to the Eagles L (12-19). On November 4 at home, Syracuse lost to Penn State in a blowout L (0-41). Then, as a sweet finish to an otherwise dismal season. on Nov 18, at home, SU finally put a good whooping on nemesis Colgate W (43-13), who were still struggling with the war taking all the players. For SU, this was a great season finale.

1945 Ossie Solem Coach # 19

The 1945 Syracuse Orangemen football team competed in their fifty-sixth season of intercollegiate football. They were led by Ossie Solem in his eighth and last of eight mostly fine seasons as head coach of the Syracuse Orangemen. This SU squad finished with another poor record of 1-6-0. After 1943, a year off for the war, SU had not yet come back to full strength as many of their best players were in the service of our nation. Coach Solem looked at it as his fault and he resigned after the completion of the season. He moved on to Springfield and finished off a nice career there.

Syracuse played its season opener on a Monday, Sept 24, 1945 at Archbold Stadium on the campus of Syracuse University and lost to Cornell L (14-26). On Friday, Sept 28, at Temple, SU lost to the Owls in a nail-biter, L (6-7) On Oct 6, at Columbia in NY, the Orangemen lost L (0-32) On Oct 21, at home, SU beat West Virginia for its only win of the season. The games for the most part were not blowouts, but victories were almost impossible to achieve. Coach Solem was a good coach, nonetheless.

On Oct 27, at Home, SU lost a close game to Dartmouth, L (0-8). the Eagles L (12-19). On Nov 3, at Penn State, Syracuse was shut-out by the Nittany Lions. L (0-26). In the season finale against major nemesis Colgate, for want of an extra point SU lost the game L (6-7). It was disheartening for Coach Solem for sure.

Famous Coaches (From the Past) by SWC75.

Biggie Munn took over as head coach in 1946 after Solem had a 1-6 season the previous year. [Syracuse could not stomach losing seasons.] Munn had been assisting Fritz Crisler at Michigan. He improved the team's record to 4-5 but left for Michigan State with most of his staff, an offer "that comes once in a lifetime". It sounds reminiscent of Doug Marrone [explored later in this essay].

State was a large public school that was ambitious to build up its program and try to gain entrance into the Big Ten, which had become the Big Nine when Chicago gave up the sport. Syracuse was not so ambitious. Munn built the Spartans into a national power, winning 28 games in a row from 1950-53, the national championship in 1952 and the Rose Bowl in '53, the first year they were eligible for it. Munn then became athletic director and appointed Daugherty as his successor. Duffy won the Rose bowl with his 1955 team and the coach's version of the national title in 1965. Munn was elected to the Hall of Fame in 1959 and Daugherty in 1984

[Think of all the great coaches that mentored at Syracuse. They were the best of the best. SU officials seemed to take all the talent for granted.]

1946 Clarence "Biggie" Munn Coach # 20

The 1946 Syracuse Orangemen football team competed in their fifty-seventh season of intercollegiate football. They were led by "Biggie Munn in his first and last of one losing season as head coach of the Syracuse Orangemen.

<< Biggie Munn.

This SU squad finished with a so-so record of 4-5-0 but it was a big improvement from the 1-6-0 season in 1945. I can't keep making excuses for 1943, the year off for the war, but SU still had not yet come back to full strength as many of their best players were in the service of our nation or just getting out of the service. Nonetheless the alumni and fans continued to expect victories from their favorite team.

I have not figured out yet why games were being played on Mondays and Fridays as well as Saturdays during the war but now that the war was over, all games this season were played on Saturdays, which to this day is college football day in America. Especially as we move from the War Years in which the survival of our country was assured by brave men, football players some, but not all. With the disrespect to the flag shown by the NFL in 2017, many college football lovers in 2017 were wishing college football were played on Sunday's also. Many were ready to let pro-football come to a graceful end while helping college players excel in a sport played for sport and for the school--Syracuse in our case.

The Orangemen played their season opener on a Saturday, back to normal, Sept 28, 1946 at Archbold Stadium on the campus of Syracuse University and the Orangemen whooped Boston University W (41-6). On Oct 5 at Dartmouth, SU lost to the Big Green in a tough match, L (14-20). On Oct 12 at home Penn State beat Syracuse in a fair contest L (0-9). Then, on Oct 19, at Holy Cross, SU beat Holy Cross W (21-12). Then, on Oct 26, at West Virginia, SU lost in a shutout, L (0-13).

On Nov 2, at home v Temple, the Orangemen got it together to beat the Owls W (28-7). Next at Cornell, the Orangemen kept their sights on the prize and beat Cornell W (14-7) Still trying to figure out nemesis Colgate, this would not be the year for SU to break free from the spell and they were beaten in a fair game L (7-25. SU liked to finish off its seasons at Columbia, a team that had never come to Syracuse to play a football game. This year after the trip to New York for the game, The Orange had to endure an embarrassing licking L (21-59) One might ask, "where was the 'D'?"

Famous Coaches (From the Past) by SWC75.

Next up was Reaves "Ribs" Baysinger, an old SU football hero from the 20's who had been coaching the freshman team. Les Dye: "His success didn't carry on for reasons beyond my knowledge. And then, consequently football kind of petered out at Syracuse in terms of popularity." Dye felt that things might have been different in Munn had stayed. "He was considerably more aggressive in his recruiting tactics than Baysinger when he was head coach.

Baysinger went 3-6 his first year, although he managed to beat Colgate, 7-0. The next year may have been SU's worst team ever. The beat Niagara in their opening game, 13-9, thanks to a fumble at the goal line in the final seconds. Niagara gave up football after that season, the joke going that they decided to give it up since they couldn't beat Syracuse. Then came eight losses in a row by a combined 76-235. That was it for "Ribs".

SU fans had a solution: bring in a famous coach. They were shocked when Lew Andreas chose the head coach at Muhlenberg to be the next coach at Syracuse. In the words of that Muhlenberg coach: "The alumni wanted a big-name coach…and got a long-name coach."

1947 Reaves Baysinger Coach # 21

Coach Reaves Baysinger was the 21st coach for the Syracuse Orange. He was born February 22, 1902 and passed away at 92 years of age on December 4, 1994. He was the head football coach at Syracuse from 1947 to 1948. Despite his strong ties to the university he only produced a 4-14(.222) record. On a higher note, in 1927, he coached the freshman basketball team== undefeated 23-0 record.

Baysinger played college football as a guard and end at Syracuse. During his senior season, he was an honorable mention all-American. He also played basketball as a point guard, and baseball as an outfielder. Baysinger played one game in the NFL as a member of the Rochester Jeffersons in 1924.

The 1947 Syracuse Orangemen football team competed in their fifty-eighth season of intercollegiate football. They were led by Reaves Baysinger in his first of two very poor seasons head coach of the Syracuse Orangemen. This SU squad finished with a so-so record of 3-6-0. It was a worst season than that turned in by "Biggie" in his one season at the helm.

Nonetheless, Baysinger would get another shot at the apple in 1948, though his record was not worthy of such as shot. I'd love to see the coach's salary records for this period.

Anything was a big improvement from the 1-6-0 season in 1945 or so it seemed. No more excuses for 1943 would be accepted by the very tolerant SU faithful. Instead, it was obvious something other than the weather was the problem. The SU administration was simply making poor choices for coaches as other teams with whom SU competed were doing better than Syracuse That is the major measurement.

Not everybody can lose all games in any season as somebody is better than somebody else them—enough to beat them. SU had a tough time at this time being better than anybody and beating anybody. Why? Typically, that is the coach's fault or the administration's fault, for being tight on the purse strings on coach's salary and / or scholarships. SU fans were not ready for excuses. They were looking for results. After such a great fifty some years, it was no wonder why.

The Orangemen played their season opener again on a Friday, on Sept 26, 1947 at Archbold Stadium on the campus of Syracuse University and the Orangemen defeated Niagara University W (14-7). On Oct 4, my wedding anniversary, at Dartmouth, SU lost again to the Big Green L (7-28). On Oct 11 at home, SU beat Temple W (28-12). Then, on Oct 18 at Penn State, SU was shut out in a big way by the Nittany Lions L (0-40).

Then, on Oct 25, at home v Holy Cross, the Orangemen could not bring in the win and in fact, were shut-out L (0-26).

On Nov 1, at Lafayette, SU lost in a close match L (7-14). Next was a tough Cornell team in a game played in Ithaca, NY. Cornell defeated Syracuse L (6-12). Considering fresh air, a win against Colgate, Syracuse got its fresh air on Nov 8 in a nice win against their nemesis W (7-0). Then, it was off to Columbia for the annual encounter. SU were defeated on Nov 22 by nationally ranked # 19 Columbia L (8-28).

1948 Reaves Baysinger Coach # 21

The 1948 Syracuse Orangemen football team competed in their fifty-ninth season of intercollegiate football. They were led by Reaves Baysinger in his second of two very poor seasons as head coach of the Syracuse Orangemen. This SU squad finished with a terrible record of 1-8-0. There was little positive that could be said of the season. Coach Baysinger was gone as soon as it was over.

Soon in this book, Benn Schwartzwalder will be highlighted and we can expect some good results for his 25 years.

Anything was a big improvement from the 1-6-0 season Syracuse experienced in 1945 or so it seemed. Well, 1-8 is definitely worse than that. SU fans were not ready for excuses. They were looking for results. After such a great fifty some years, it was no wonder why.

Games of the 1948 Season

The Orangemen played their season opener again on a Tuesday, (I have no explanation for the day of the week in this case) on Sept 28, 1948 at Archbold Stadium on the campus of Syracuse University and the Orangemen defeated Niagara University W (13-9). SU had clobbered Niagara for years, and this year, some might even say they played expecting to lose.

The 1948 pundits reported that without a Niagara fumble in the final seconds, SU would not have won the game. Niagara had enough of the game and sent their football records to the archives and liquidated the team. They gave up football after 1948, the year I was born.

On Oct 2, at Holy Cross, SU lost again to the Big Green L (7-33). On Oct 8, on a Friday at home, SU lost to Penn State at Archbold, L (14-34) Then, on Saturday Oct 16, at home v Cornell, ranked # 13 at the time, the Orangemen could not bring in the win and in fact, were dominated by Cornell L (7-34).

On Oct 23, at #10 ranked Northwestern, SU lost in a blowout-shutout L (0-48). Next was a game at Boston University, who stood their ground and defeated the Orangemen 1 (7-12)

On Nov 6, at Temple, the Owls got the chance to scob Syracuse of whatever dignity was remaining as this dismal season was coming to a close. Temple got its due L (0-20). All the fresh air was gone from the prior Colgate match as the Orangemen went down again at the hands of Colgate, Nov 13 in a close loss against their favorite nemesis L (13-20) Then, as normal SU seasons went, it was off to Columbia for the annual encounter. SU was defeated on Nov 20 in a very close game but again, no cigar L (28-34)

Pre Schwartzwalder post script

This wraps up the pre-Ben Schwartzwalder portion of the book in which, despite some recent (in this book) poor years such as 1944 to 1948, the team record from day one was still a very impressive 305-194-41. This early record is actually better than the later record from 1949 on of 458-379-8. You see what I see.

The old-time Orangemen have a much better record than the new Orange. Just saying! Before SU can line up the best coaches, the administration must be committed, and the alumni cannot just expect wins—it must squeeze the administration for all it has to produce a great football team. Settle for good but, always plan and commit for greatness and excellence. Otherwise, as has happened in a number of SY years with the wrong coaches, especially in more modern times, complacency sets in and "medsa-medsa" is all that can be achieved when the goals of the Administration are no higher than medsa-medsa.

Sometimes a lot of grit on the part of the students and the teams and the twenty-year old coaches is all you need for success, even without a dedicated university. We saw that from 1899 to 1948. But, eventually that gets old. Especially when equipment and facilities are concerned.

Startup teams are thrilled to have train fare paid by the university to play away games, but student players on established teams have a right to expect the support of the university in all ways. Football is a big deal or SU would not insist on being in Division I. Players in the early years of football are documented to have lost their lives on the gridiron or be maimed when playing their roughest and toughest for the honor of the school.

It stands to reason that once a school chooses to get out of cheap sandlot-style football to play Division I, if the university does not do what it must to support the efforts of all parts of the team, it's time to move to Club Football is saving money is the primary objective instead of school honor. Other teams have dropped football when it was time.

For example, basketball powerhouse Gonzaga dropped football after World War II just like Niagara. Both concentrated on basketball and gave that sport its support. Like in A Christmas Carol, what seems to be happening at Syracuse are not things that must be but are things that will be if nothing changes.

Ben Schwartzwalder, the guy with the long name was just what the many doctors who graduated from Syracuse University had ordered As a writer, I now look forward to moving to a different era for Syracuse University football. Let's enjoy it together.

Chapter 8 Ben Schwartzwalder 1949 to 1973

Ben Schwartzwalder, Coach # 22

Year	Coach	Record	Conf
1949	Ben Schwartzwalder	4-5-0	Ind
1950	Ben Schwartzwalder	5-5-0	Ind
1951	Ben Schwartzwalder	5-4-0	Ind
1952	Ben Schwartzwalder	7-3-0	Ind
1953	Ben Schwartzwalder	5-3-1	Ind
1954	Ben Schwartzwalder	4-4-0	Ind
1955	Ben Schwartzwalder	5-3-0	Ind
1956	Ben Schwartzwalder	7-2-0	Ind
1957	Ben Schwartzwalder	5-3-1	Ind
1958	Ben Schwartzwalder	8-2-0	Ind
1959	Ben Schwartzwalder	11-0-0	Ind
1960	Ben Schwartzwalder	7-2-0	Ind
1961	Ben Schwartzwalder	8-3-0	Ind
1962	Ben Schwartzwalder	5-5-0	Ind
1963	Ben Schwartzwalder	8-2-0	Ind
1964	Ben Schwartzwalder	7-4-0	Ind
1965	Ben Schwartzwalder	7-3-0	Ind
1966	Ben Schwartzwalder	8-3-0	Ind
1967	Ben Schwartzwalder	8-2-0	Ind
1968	Ben Schwartzwalder	6-4-0	Ind
1969	Ben Schwartzwalder	5-5-0	Ind
1970	Ben Schwartzwalder	6-4-0	Ind
1971	Ben Schwartzwalder	5-5-1	Ind
1972	Ben Schwartzwalder	5-6-0	Ind
1973	Ben Schwartzwalder	2-9-0	Ind

Ben Schwartzwalder was carried off the field by SU players following the team's 48-21 thrashing of Penn State in the Carrier Dome on Oct. 17, 1987. Schwartzwalder was the last SU coach to beat the Nittany Lions before the undefeated 1987 Orangemen pulled off the feat.

It gives me great pleasure that in the next half of this book, before we jump and leap and sometimes limp to 2018, that we cover the twenty-five years of Ben Schwartzwalder in this one big chapter.

God bless Ben Schwartzwalder and the Syracuse Orangemen.

1949 Ben Schwartzwalder Coach # 22

For those football aficionados who just are not sure who Ben Schwartzwalder is, you are about to find out. Suffice it to say that he is one of the football immortals, a legend in the game of football. Knute Rockne became the first big time legend after coaching just 13 seasons with Notre Dame. Ben Schwartzwalder gained his immortality after a brilliant 25-year tenure with the Syracuse Orangemen. Ben made a big difference.

I was one-year old when Schwartzwalder took the reins at Syracuse and until I was twenty-six years old, in my fifth year at IBM, the name Schwartzwalder was forever ingrained in my mind as one of the greatest coaches ever. During these first five years of my 23 ½ years with IBM, I spent the first two years in Utica, NY just 46 miles from Syracuse. Syracuse was our Regional Office, so I spent a lot of time in classes as well as at the big IBM data center.

When I asked people in Utica, as a 21-year old Assistant Systems Engineer, where to go for fun, they did not hesitate to tell me that Syracuse was only 46 miles away. Great town and I was back many times for football games. Everybody in Syracuse and even in my home town in Northeastern, PA knew Ben Schwartzwalder. He was a living immortal.

Ben Schwartzwalder was a "little guy" but only in stature. He was tough as nails. Schwartzwalder played center at West Virginia University, despite weighing only 146 pounds. He was also an all-campus wrestler in 1930 in the 155-pound weight class. He was captain of the WV football team in 1933. He loved Syracuse and he loved WV, engaging the Mountaineers in an annual rivalry game from when he took over the SU program in 1949.

Floyd Burdette "Ben" Schwartzwalder was head football coach at Syracuse University from 1949 to 1973, leading the SU team to an impressive record of 153 wins, 91 losses, and 3 ties.

At Syracuse, this immortal coach trained future National Football League stars such as Jim Brown, Larry Csonka, Floyd Little and Ernie Davis, the first African American to win the Heisman Trophy. Ben (Ben was a childhood nickname) Schwartzwalder was born in Point Pleasant, West Virginia, on June 2, 1909. He attended West Virginia University, where he received a bachelor's degree in physical education in 1933 and a master's degree in education in 1935. Schwartzwalder then coached high school football in West Virginia and Ohio until 1941.

During World War II, Schwartzwalder enlisted and served as a paratrooper in the United States Army. As a member of the famed 82nd Airborne, he parachuted onto Normandy Beach on D-Day in 1944. He rose to the rank of major and was awarded a Silver Star, a Bronze Star, a Purple Heart, four battle stars, and a Presidential Unit citation. He retired as a lieutenant colonel.

After the war Schwartzwalder became head football coach at Muhlenberg College in Allentown, Pennsylvania, and compiled a 25-5 record between 1946 and 1948.

Schwartzwalder became head football coach at Syracuse University in 1949. He led the football team to a 1959 National Championship, four Lambert Trophies, and 7 bowl games. He recruited such notable players as Jim Brown, Ernie Davis, Jim Nance, Floyd Little, and Larry Csonka. Schwartzwalder retired after the 1973 season.

In 1959 Schwartzwalder was voted Coach of the Year, and in 1967 he was elected President of the National Football Coaches Association. Inducted into the College Football Hall of Fame in 1982, he is also in the Huntington High School Hall of Fame and West Virginia University Hall of Fame. Schwartzwalder also has a trophy named after him that goes to the winner of the annual Syracuse University-West Virginia University football game. Schwartzwalder and his wife, Ruth ("Reggie") had two daughters, SUsan and Mary.

He died on April 28, 1993, in St. Petersburg, Florida. He was one of a kind. I think you are going to enjoy our recounting of the 25 great Schwartzwalder years.

The 1949 Season

The 1949 Syracuse Orangemen football team competed in their sixtieth season of intercollegiate football. They were led by the soon-to-be immortal, Ben Schwartzwalder in his first of twenty-five seasons as head coach of the Syracuse Orangemen. This SU squad finished this year with a much better record (4-5-0) than the last several years. The team, the fans, and the alumni were expecting big things from their new coach and for the most part they would not be disappointed. The team captain was James Fiaccio

The Orangemen played their season opener on Sept 23, 1949 at Archbold Stadium on the campus of Syracuse University, and the Orangemen lost to Boston University W (21-33). On Oct 1 at home, SU defeated Lafayette in a tough match, W (20-13) before 22,000 fans. On Oct 7 at home Temple beat Syracuse L (14-7). Then, on Oct 15, at Archbold Stadium, SU beat Rutgers W (21-9). On Oct 22, at Fordham in a game played at the Polo Grounds in NYC, Syracuse lost L (21-47).

On Oct 29, at New Beaver Field in University Park, PA, SU was beaten by Penn State L (21-33) before 18,600 fans.
Next at #7 ranked Cornell, on Nov 5, the Orangemen lost at Schoellkopf Field in Ithaca, NY L (7–33) before 33,000 fans. On Nov 12 at home, SU defeated Holy Cross W (47-13). The real test for Ben Schwartzwalder was "could he beat Colgate? On Nov 15, like always at Archbold Stadium in Syracuse, NY, this game however, had an atypical outcome as Syracuse mopped up Colgate W (35–7) before a packed house at 36,232.

1950 Ben Schwartzwalder Coach # 22

The 1950 Syracuse Orangemen football team competed in their sixty-first season of intercollegiate football. They were led by Ben

Schwartzwalder in his second of twenty-five seasons as head coach of the Syracuse Orangemen. This SU squad finished this year with an even 500 record at (5-5-0). The lose all the time years were done. years. The team, the fans, and the alumni were tuning in to the big things that would come from their new coach. The captains this year were elected for each game and they were known as game captains.

The Orangemen played their season opener on Sept 23, 1950 at Archbold Stadium on the campus of Syracuse University, and the Orangemen defeated Rutgers University, W (42-12). On Sept 29, at home, SU lost to Temple at Temple Stadium in Philadelphia, PA by an extra point L (6-7). On Oct 7 at home, Cornell put a mini-licking on the Orangemen L (7-26). Then, on Oct 14, at Archbold Stadium, SU beat Penn State W (27-7). On Oct 21, at Holy Cross Fitton Field in Worcester, Mass, SU prevailed W (34-27).

On Oct 28, at Boston, University, in a game played at Fenway Park, Boston, MA., the Orangemen walked away with the win W (13-7). On Nov 4, at Lafayette's Fisher Field in Easton, PA SU claimed the win W (34-9) before 9,000 fans.

On Nov 10, at John Carroll in Cleveland Stadium in Cleveland, OH the Orangemen took one in the teeth L (16–21) before 16,724 fans. Then on Nov 18, a repeat victory over Colgate would not occur at Archbold Stadium Syracuse, NY in the traditional at-home every year rivalry. Colgate charmed the Orangemen again into losing a tough game L (14–19) before a packed house of 38,000. Instead of Columbia, in the season finale this year it was a tough Fordham team fighting at the Polo Grounds in New York, NY. SU sustained a close loss L (6–13), before 13,832 fans.

1951 Ben Schwartzwalder Coach # 22

The 1951 Syracuse Orangemen football team competed in their sixty-second season of intercollegiate football. They were led by Ben Schwartzwalder in his third of twenty-five seasons as head coach of the Syracuse Orangemen. This SU squad finished this year with the first positive record in seven years (5-4-0). The team, the fans, and the alumni were becoming more and more pleased. The captains this year were Ed Dobrowolski & John Donat.

The Orangemen played their season opener on Sept 23, 1951 at Archbold Stadium on the campus of Syracuse University, and the Orangemen defeated Temple University in a shutout, W (19-0). On Sept 29, at home, SU lost to #20 Cornell at Schoellkopf Field in Ithaca, NY L (14–21) before 25,000. On Oct 6, Lafayette met a brick wall at Archbold Stadium in Syracuse, NY as the Orangemen pitched a blowout shutout W (46–0) before 13,000 fans. On Oct 13 # 7 Illinois entered Archbold Stadium Syracuse, NY to get a piece of the rebounding Orangemen and they got more than their due share L (20–41) before 27,000.

On Oct 20 at Dartmouth Memorial Field in Hanover, NH. The Orangemen were shut out L 0–14 by the Big Green. Before 11,000. On Oct 27 Fordham arrived in Archbold Stadium in Syracuse, NY expecting to beat the Orangemen again but they did not as SU got the big W, W (33–20) before 5,000. On Nov 10 at Penn State's New Beaver Field in University Park, PA in the annual rivalry game, PSU had their way and defeated SU L (13–32) before 15,000.

Colgate always played its home games v Syracuse at Archbold Stadium because it was not far from Hamilton, NY. For years, Colgate provided big lickings to the Syracuse team. At one point, SU had not won a game for thirteen seasons with two-ties mixed in. On this particular Nov 17, with Ben Schwartzwalder at the helm at Archbold Stadium in Syracuse, NY, in this well-publicized rivalry game, Syracuse defeated Colgate against W (9–0) before a packed house of 34,000 excited fans.

On Nov 24, at Boston University in a game played at Fenway Park in Boston, MA, Syracuse got the big win W (26–19) before 10,148 in the Red Sox baseball park

1952 Ben Schwartzwalder Coach # 22

The 1952 Syracuse Orangemen football team competed in their sixty-third season of intercollegiate football. They were led by Ben Schwartzwalder in his fourth of twenty-five seasons as head coach of the Syracuse Orangemen. This SU squad finished this year with a very respectable record of (7-3-0). The team, the fans, and the alumni were very pleased. The captains this year were Richard Beyer & Joe Szombathy

In 1952, Syracuse had jumped the line again from mediocrity to greatness because the team was getting support from the administration and they had a great coach. This was a historically successful season for the Orangemen, which included victories over rivals Penn State and Colgate. Syracuse lost only twice in the regular season: their season opener against the former college all-stars of the Bolling Air Force Base, and to eventual national champions Michigan State.

The Orangemen were quite pleased with themselves and their coach as they finished the regular season with a record of 7–2 and were ranked 14th in the final AP Poll. This was their first ranked finish in school history. The team was awarded its first Lambert Trophy, which signified them as champions of the East.

The Orangemen were invited to the 1953 Orange Bowl, the school's first ever bowl game, where they lost to Alabama The best that I can say about the Alabama game is that at the end of the first quarter, the score was 6-7 in favor of Alabama. This was such a great breakaway year for Ben Schwartzwalder and Syracuse coming from the pits of the 1940's that you'll have to look someplace else than in this positive season summary to find the specifics of the Orange Bowl v Alabama. There would be many more fine seasons for the Orangemen.

The Orangemen played their season opener on Sept 20, 1952 against a military all-star team from Bolling Field at Archbold Stadium in Syracuse, NY before 18,000 fans and could not survive the tough play of the all-stars. L (12–13). On Sept 27, at home, SU defeated Boston University W (34–21). On Oct 3 at Temple at Temple Stadium in Philadelphia, PA , SU beat the Owls W (27–0). On Oct 11, at home v Cornell, the Orangemen defeated the Red Raiders W 26–6 before 23,000 fans. On Oct 18 at #1 ranked Michigan State at Macklin Stadium in East Lansing, MI, despite working hard, SU could not overcome the talent of the Spartans and were defeated L (7-48) before 32,254.

On Oct 25 at home v Holy Cross, SU prevailed W (20–19) before 18,000. On Nov 8 # 15 Penn State arrived to claim a victory v the Orangemen but the strong SU team sent them home with a defeat W (25–7) before 15,000. Then, on Nov 15, an always tough Colgate team now faced a #13 ranked SU team at Archbold Stadium in Syracuse, NY and Colgate went home weeping after the Orangemen got the victory W (20–14) before a packed stadium of 32,000.

On Nov 22 #15 SU played Fordham at Triborough Stadium in New York, NY and came home with the win W (26–13) before 10,000 fans. SU was then ranked #14 and got to play Alabama in the Orange Bowl.

On January 1, 1953, #14 SU paired off against # 9 Alabama at Burdine Stadium in Miami, FL in the Orange Bowl. After the first quarter which was very tight, SU lost its edge and succumbed to an embarrassing Orange Bowl defeat of L (6–61) before 66,280.

1953 Ben Schwartzwalder Coach # 22

The 1953 Syracuse Orangemen football team competed in their sixty-fourth season of intercollegiate football. They were led by Ben Schwartzwalder in his fifth of twenty-five seasons as head coach of the Syracuse Orangemen. This SU squad finished the year with a very respectable record of (5-3-1). The captains were assigned by game and known as game captains.

The Orangemen played their season opener on Sept 26, 1953 against Temple at Archbold Stadium in Syracuse, NY before 18,000 fans and defeated the Owls in a major shutout W (42-0). On Oct 2 at home v Boston University at home , the teams played to a tie T (14014). On Oct 10 at home. SU defeated Fordham W (20–13) before 20,000. On Oct at Penn State's New Beaver Field in University Park, PA, the Orangemen did not survive the Nittany Lions L (14–20) before 21,500 fans. On Oct 24 at # 7 Illinois's Memorial Stadium in Champaign, IL, the Orangemen almost achieved victory but lost despite a fine effort, L (13–20) before 30,076

On October 31 at Holy Cross on Fitton Field in Worcester, MA, SU won the game W (21–0) before 15,000. Then, on Nov 7 at Cornell's Schoellkopf Field in Ithaca, NY, the Orangemen dominated W (26–0). Always worried about Colgate, on Nov 14, at Archbold Stadium in Syracuse, NY, SU prevailed W (34–18) before a packed house of 37,000. In the season finale, on Nov 21, at Villanova in Franklin Field, Philadelphia, PA SU dropped a close on L (13–14). It was a great season and with a little extra luck, it would have been better.

1954 Ben Schwartzwalder Coach # 22

The 1954 Syracuse Orangemen football team competed in their sixty-fifth season of intercollegiate football. They were led by Ben Schwartzwalder in his sixth of twenty-five seasons as head coach of the Syracuse Orangemen. This SU squad finished this year with a medsa record of (4-4-1). The captains this year were assigned by game and known as game captains.

Jim Brown, # 44 All American

The Orangemen played their season opener on Sept 25, 1954 against Villanova at Archbold Stadium in Syracuse, NY before 25,000 fans and defeated the Wildcats W (28-6). On Oct 2, SU lost to #10 Penn State at home (0-13) before 18,000. On Oct 16 at Boston University Field, in Boston, MA the Eagles beat the Orangemen L (19–41). On Oct 23 at Illinois Memorial Stadium in Champaign, IL, the Schwartzwalder squad dropped another L (6–34) before 41,820 fans.

Then, on Oct SU defeated Holy Cross at Archbold Stadium W (25-20 before 20,000. On Nov 6, at Cornell's Schoellkopf Field in Ithaca, NY, the Orangemen were defeated by the Big Red, L (6–14). In the big rivalry game on Nov 13 v Colgate at Archbold Stadium, SU defeated the Red Raiders W (31–12) before 37,000 fans. Notice as the years go by, as we move from the fifties to the sixties to 2018, and beyond, bigger stadiums were built. Interest in college football increased and attendance would eventually reach and surpass 100,000 fans per game in the nation's largest stadiums. On Nov 20 at Fordham in a game played at the Polo Grounds in New York, NY, the Orangemen gained a win in their season finale W (20–7) before 10,423

1955 Ben Schwartzwalder Coach # 22

The 1955 Syracuse Orangemen football team competed in their sixty-sixth season of intercollegiate football. They were led by Ben Schwartzwalder in his seventh of twenty-five seasons as head coach of the Syracuse Orangemen. This SU squad finished this year with a winning record of (5-3-0). The captains this year were assigned by game and known as game captains.

The Orangemen played their season opener on Sept 24, 1955 against Pittsburgh's Panthers at Archbold Stadium in Syracuse, NY before 16,000 fans and were defeated by the Panthers L (12-22). On Oct 8 SU beat Boston University at home W (27–12) Then, for the first time in many years, on Oct 15, SU defeated # 18 Army at Michie Stadium in West Point, NY W (13–0) before 12,500. On October 22 SU lost to #2 Maryland at Archbold Stadium in Syracuse, NY L

(13–34) before a packed house of 32,500. On Oct 29 at #13 Holy Cross in Fitton Field, Worcester, MA, SU prevailed in a blowout win W (49–9).

SU was then ranked at #18 after the Holy Cross win. The following week, on Nov 5 at Penn State. The always tough Nittany Lions beat Syracuse by one point at New Beaver Field in University Park, PA L (20–21) before 30,434. On Nov12, in the traditional rivalry v Colgate at Archbold Stadium, SU kept the streak going with a nice win W (W 26–19) before a packed house of 39,500. On Nov 19, SU p picked up its fifth win in the season finale against #13 West Virginia at Mountaineer Field in Morgantown, WV. W (20-13) Because Ben Schwartzwalder was a WVA graduate, this became a new SU rivalry and was played every year in the Schwartzwalder years.

The Ben Schwartzwalder Trophy is the trophy that was presented annually to the winner of the game. It was introduced in 1993 and is named after former WVU football player and Syracuse head coach Ben Schwartzwalder, who died in April of that year. It was sculpted by Syracuse player Jim Ridlon.

1956 Ben Schwartzwalder Coach # 22

The 1956 Syracuse Orangemen football team competed in their sixty-seventh season of intercollegiate football. They were led by Ben Schwartzwalder in his eighth of twenty-five seasons as head coach of the Syracuse Orangemen. This SU squad finished this year with a fine record of (7-2-0) which included the Bowl game. The captains this year were assigned by game and known as game captains.

Syracuse finished its regular season with a record of 7–1 and were ranked 8th nationally in both final polls. They were awarded the Lambert Trophy, which signified them as champions of the East. Syracuse was invited to the 1957 Cotton Bowl, where the team was defeated by TCU.

This 1956 team was led by unanimous All-American halfback Jim Brown. Brown set school records in average yards-per-carry (6.2), single-season rushing yards (986), single-game rushing touchdowns (6, vs. Colgate), and most points scored in a game (43, vs. Colgate). He was drafted sixth overall in the 1957 NFL Draft and went on to become one of the most celebrated professional athletes of all time.

I remember when my dad bought us our first TV for the family. It was a B/W 1957 Admiral. It had many tubes and a 21-inch picture tube. My dad often told me about Jim Brown as he played for the Cleveland Browns when Paul Brown was the coach in those days. He also said that to maintain his speed, Jim Brown did not wear hip pads. I learned recently that he taped foam rubber inside his football pants to help cushion the blows – a little trivia.

The Orangemen played their season opener on Sept 22, 1956 against Maryland's Byrd Stadium in College Park, MD. Syracuse defeated the Terrapins W (26–12) before 27,000. On September 29 at #10 Pittsburgh #7 Syracuse lost to Pitt in Pitt Stadium, Pittsburgh, PA L (7–14) before 49,287 fans.

Two weeks later, on Oct 13 #20 West Virginia lost to Syracuse at Archbold Stadium on the campus of Syracuse University in Syracuse, NY in the newly christened rivalry game W (27–20) before 25,000. On Oct 20 #13 Syracuse defeated Army at home in

Syracuse, NY W (7–0) before a top crowd of 40,053. On Oct 27, #14 ranked SU defeated Boston University in Nickerson Field in Boston, MA W (21–7).

On Nov 3, #17 ranked Syracuse defeated #12 ranked Penn State at home W (13-9) before 35,475 fans in Archbold Stadium. On Nov 10 #9 Syracuse beat Holy Cross at home W (41–20). Then in one of the worst beatings ever delivered by SU over Colgate, on Nov 17, the Orangemen walloped the Red Raiders W (61-7) at Archbold field before 39, 701. SU finished at 7-1 and then headed off to the Cotton Bowl on November 1 ranked # 8 in the country.

The Cotton Bowl.

On January 1, 1957 #8 SU faced off against #14 TCU in the Cotton Bowl Classic. The game was played in the Cotton Bowl Stadium in Dallas Texas. The Horned Frogs beat the Orangemen in a very exciting game L (27-28) before 68,000 fans.

Syracuse had just one loss. It was to Pittsburgh, who enjoyed a great season but ended up losing in the Gator Bowl). SU was 8th ranked, led by Jim Brown, who would play his last game before becoming an NFL player. Texas Christian had finished 2nd in the Southwest Conference, but was invited to play in the Cotton Bowl due to first place Texas A&M being under NCAA sanctions. This was TCU's fifth Cotton Bowl appearance, having lost their previous four (and not winning since 1937). This was Syracuse's first appearance, along with their first bowl game since the 1953 Orange Bowl, which was not a good story.

Game summary

TCU had two 14-point leads, both near the end of the halves. John Nikkel started the scoring for TCU with a touchdown catch from Chuck Curtis, and in the second quarter, Jim Shofner caught a TD pass to make it 14-0. But Jim Brown got it going and ran for two touchdowns in a span of 6:52 to tie the game at halftime.

Late in the third quarter after Brown fumbled the ball back to TCU, Curtis scored on a touchdown run to give TCU the lead back. After another Brown fumble in the fourth quarter, Jim Swink ran in for a touchdown to give TCU a 28-14 lead with 11:44 to go. But Brown would not be stopped as Syracuse went 49 yards in 13 plays and scored on a Brown run. Brown went up for his third PAT attempt of the day to try and narrow the lead to 7.

But Chico Mendoza blocked the extra point, keeping the score 28-20. But Syracuse had one last drive in them, going 43 yards in 3 plays and with 1:17 left, Jim Ridlon caught a pass from Charles Zimmerman to narrow the lead to 28-27. Syracuse kicked it deep but TCU held on and did not let Syracuse get the ball back, in what would turn out to be TCU's last bowl win until 1998. Jim Brown and Norman Hamilton were named Outstanding Players of the game. What a game. Football is a game of inches and luck for sure.

Syracuse University's Jim Brown runs for some of the 132 yards he gained during the 1957 Cotton Bowl against Texas Christian University in Dallas.

1957 Ben Schwartzwalder Coach # 22

The 1957 Syracuse Orangemen football team competed in their sixty-eighth season of intercollegiate football. They were led by Ben Schwartzwalder in his ninth of twenty-five seasons as head coach of the Syracuse Orangemen. This SU squad finished this year with a winning record of (5-3-1). The captains this year were assigned by game and known as game captains.

The Orangemen played their season and home opener on Sept 28, 1957 against Iowa State at Archbold Stadium on the campus of Syracuse University in Syracuse, NY. The game ended in a tie (7-7). On Oct 5 Boston University at Archbold Stadium, SU got the win W (27–20). On Oct 12 at Cornell's Schoellkopf Field in Ithaca, NY, SU won again, W (34–0) before 25,000 fans. Then on Oct 19 at Nebraska Memorial Stadium in Lincoln, NE. the Orangemen defeated the Cornhuskers W (26–9) before 37,582. On Oct 26 at home in Archbold Stadium, PSU beat the SU L (12–20) before 35,000.

On Nov 2 at Pittsburgh's Pitt Stadium in Pittsburgh, PA, SU got the win against the Panthers, W (24–21) before 35,430. Then on Nov 9 SU lost by one point against Holy Cross at Archbold Stadium L (19-20). On Nov 16, Syracuse beat Colgate again in Archbold Stadium in Syracuse, NY 34–6 before 38,500 fans. On Nov 23 in the new rivalry for the Ben Schwartzwalder Trophy (before the Trophy was given) at West Virginia Mountaineer Field, Morgantown, WV, Syracuse was barely beaten by the Mountaineers.

1958 Ben Schwartzwalder Coach # 22

The 1958 Syracuse Orangemen football team competed in their sixty-ninth season of intercollegiate football. They were led by Ben Schwartzwalder in his tenth of twenty-five seasons as head coach of the Syracuse Orangemen. This SU squad finished this year with a great record of (8-1-0). SU was ranked #9 in the AP and got to play Oklahoma in the Orange Bowl where they were defeated. The captains this year were assigned by game and known as game captains.

Games of the 1958 season

The Orangemen played their season and home opener on Sept 27, 1958 against Boston College at Archbold Stadium on the campus of Syracuse University in Syracuse, NY. SU defeated the Eagles W (24–14) before 15,000. Holy Cross was a major contender in college football in the 1950's and gave SU a run for its money. In a season spoiler on Oct 4 at Holy Cross' Fitton Field in Worcester, MA, Syracuse did not have enough to take this game and lost by just one point L (13–14) before. This would be the only loss of the regular season for Ben Schwartzwalder's Orangemen.

On Oct 11 SU beat Cornell at Archbold Stadium in a shutout / blowout W (55–0). Then, on Oct 18 SU beat Nebraska at home in a shutout W (38-0). On Oct 25 at Penn State's New Beaver Field in University Park, PA in a tough match, the Orangemen defeated the Nittany Lions W (14–6) before 27,000.

On Nov 1, SU beat # 12/10 Pittsburgh at home in a very tight match W (16–13) before 38,000. It was a great game. On Nov 7, now ranked #12, in a game played at Boston University's Nickerson Field in Boston, MA, the Orangemen shut out the Terriers W (42–0). Then, on Nov 15 at home, SU shut out Colgate W (47-0). In the season finale on Nov 22 at West Virginia, now ranked #10/11, in a game played at Mountaineer Field Morgantown, WV, the Orangemen defeated the Mountaineers W 15–12 giving them a berth in the 1959 Orange Bowl. So far SU had bad luck in Bowl Games.

The Orange Bowl

On January 1, 1959, playing # 5 Oklahoma, the #9/10 Syracuse Orangemen were defeated in the Orange Bowl in Miami, FL playing in the Orange Bowl game L (6–21) before 75,281

1959 Ben Schwartzwalder Coach # 22

The 1959 Syracuse Orangemen football team competed in their seventieth season of intercollegiate football. They were led by Ben Schwartzwalder in his eleventh of twenty-five seasons as head coach of the Syracuse Orangemen. This SU squad finished this year with a great record of (11-0-0). SU was ranked #1 in both polls and won the national championship. It was not mythical. It was real. They beat Texas in the Cotton Bowl Classic. Gerhard Schwedes was the team captain for the 1959 championship team.

Games of the 1959 championship season

The Orangemen played their season and home opener on Sept 26, 1959 against Kansas at Archbold Stadium on the campus of Syracuse University in Syracuse, NY. SU defeated the Jayhawks, W (35-21) before 25,000. Big things were coming this year and there was a feeling in the air. Opening day had the most fans in many years. On Oct 3 Maryland was shut out by #20 ranked Syracuse at Archbold Stadium W (29–0). On Oct 10 at Navy at Foreman Field Norfolk, VA in the Oyster Bowl field, SU won W (32–6). Then, on Oct 17 at home SU defeated Holy Cross in a big win W (42–6). Now, undefeated at 4-0, on Oct 24 at home, #6 SU shut out West Virginia W (44–0) before 35,000

On Oct 31 at Pittsburgh, at Pitt Stadium in Pittsburgh, PA SU shut out the Panthers W (35–0) before 25,761 fans. Then, on Nov 7 at #7 Penn State, at New Beaver Field in University Park, PA, #4 Syracuse beat the Nittany Lions W (20–18) in a nail biter before 32,800 fans—closest game of the year.

Best SU game of the year 1959

They called it The Game of the Year of the Day, 1959. The final score was Syracuse 20, Penn State 18. For Ben Schwartzwalder's Syracuse Orangemen, it was one of the 50 best games of all time in all of football. The date was November 7, 1959. The matchup was great as SU was heading for its first National Championship ever. Thus, it was #4 Syracuse at-6-0) at #7 Penn State at 7-0. It was a great matchup, but the teams still had to play to see who at the end of the game, would go home with the victory. Victory was what it was all about on this game day.

Though there was no BCS or FBS back then, the stakes were still high. Two undefeated teams each looking good and the battle was for the mythical national title even though it was a giant mess with few teams playing outside of their respective region. Nonetheless, this game was so big, the winner would become the East's representative in the title race.

This was Schwartzwalder's eleventh season at Syracuse. His slow building process was beginning to bear major fruit at Syracuse. After just one ranked finish in his first seven years, the Orange(men) finished eighth in 1956 and ninth in 1958, and with sophomore Ernie Davis emerging as the perfect complement to Ger Schwedes, Ben had exactly the pieces for the "run, and then run some more" offense.

After dealing with an unexpectedly tough game in the season opener, a 35-21 win over Kansas, SU had caught fire, outscoring Maryland, Navy, Holy Cross, and WVU by a combined 147-12. Whew! Meanwhile, Rip Engle's Nittany Lions were on their way to their best season in five years. The Nittany Lions had already won at Missouri and Army and had handled No. 13 Illinois, 20-9, in Cleveland (of all places). They would go on to take down #4 Alabama in the Liberty Bowl as well. But to earn a possible claim of a national title, they would need to beat the best Syracuse team of all time. Thanks to their spiffy special teams, they nearly did.

This great game story comes from *"50 Best."*:

On Nov 7, 1959, both the #1 and the #2 teams in the country would lose. This meant that the Syracuse / PSU winner would have a sudden claim to the top spot in the polls. The moment was not lost on the crowd of 32,800, the largest to fill Beaver Stadium to date; as many as 10,000 more fans trying to get tickets were turned down. (Penn State was in the process of expanding its stadium. It didn't expand it soon enough.

A year earlier, college football had adopted a two-point conversion option: After scoring a touchdown, you could choose to either attempt a one-point kick or line up with your offense and try to score a two-pointer from the 3. As Syracuse took a commanding 20-6 lead early in the fourth quarter, nobody was thinking about that rule change much. But they would soon enough.

On the ensuing kickoff after Davis' touchdown gave the Orangemen a 20-6 lead, Roger Kochman fielded the ball near the right sideline, weaved toward the middle of the field to meet up with his blockers, cut back to the right at the 30, then outran everyone else to the end zone. PSU missed an attempted two-point conversion, but it was a game again, 20-12.

Moments later, PSU's Andy Stynchula burst through the Syracuse line and blocked Bob Yates' attempted punt. The Nittany Lions recovered at the 1, and Sam Sohczak scored with 4:15 left. Penn State suddenly needed only a two-point conversion to tie the game. PSU faked an option left, and quarterback Richie Lucas handed the ball to Kochman on a counter. He was stuffed on the 1. Syracuse got the ball back and completely took special teams out of the equation by rushing for enough first downs to kill the clock and escape with a 20-18 win.

The box score:

Statistics

	Syracuse	Penn State
First Downs	19	8
Rushing Yardage	287	111
Passing Yardage	61	24
Passes	5-13	3-6
Passes intercepted by	1	0
Punts	4-35	7-13
Fumbles lost	1	0
Yards penalized	45	15

Think about how many times a special teams play has triggered an upset? It almost derailed Syracuse's amazing season here. (A kickoff return touchdown is also what allowed Kansas to stick around for a bit.) The 'Cuse and PSU split the turnover battle, and the

Orangemen won the yardage battle, 348-135. But the double dose of Kochman's return and the blocked punt nearly spoiled everything. It didn't, though. And from this moment forward, Syracuse resumed playing like a title-worthy team. The Orange beat Colgate and Boston U. by a combined 117-0, went out west and destroyed UCLA, 36-8, then took on former #1 Texas in the Cotton Bowl and survived a bitter slugfest, 23-14.

After 1959, Ben Schwartzwalder put together another couple of nice seasons with Ernie Davis, and Davis would famously win the Heisman in 1961 and become the No. 1 pick in the 1962 NFL draft before succumbing to leukemia in 1963.
Penn State, meanwhile, would finished ranked each year from 1959-62 before trailing off a bit in Engle's last few seasons. Assistant Joe Paterno took over in 1966 and the rest is history.

Rest of the 1959 Games before the Cotton Bowl

O Nov 14, SU was #1 and they played Colgate at home in Archbold Stadium and shellacked the Red Raiders in a blowout W (71-0)

On Nov 21at Boston University, still #1 Syracuse played at Nickerson Field in Boston, MA and shut out the Terriors W 46–0 before 22,000. Just one more game for an undefeated regular season. It came on Dec 5at #17 UCLA played at the Los Angeles Memorial Coliseum in Los Angeles, CA. #1 Syracuse beat the Bruins, handily, W 36–8 before 46,436 fans. SU won a berth to the Cotton Bowl.

On Jan 1, 1960 #1 Syracuse paired off against #4 Texas in the Cotton Bowl Classic held at the Cotton Bowl in Dallas, TX. SU was not about to go home disappointed and won the game by nine points W (23–14) before 75,504 fans.

Cotton Bowl January 1960

In January 1960, an undefeated Syracuse team whipped Texas, 23-14, in the Cotton Bowl. But it wasn't especially pretty.

1960 Ben Schwartzwalder Coach # 22

The 1960 Syracuse Orangemen football team competed in their seventy-first season of intercollegiate football. They were led by Ben Schwartzwalder in his twelfth of twenty-five seasons as head coach of the Syracuse Orangemen. This SU squad finished this year with a great record of (7-2-0) after the prior year's national championship of 11-0-0. Al Bemiller, Fred Mautino, & Richard Reimer were the team captains for the 1960 team. SU finished 19th in the nation this year and were not invited to a bowl game. Junior halfback Ernie Davis continued to gain national attention, earning consensus All-American honors while rushing for 877 yards and 8 touchdown

Games of the 1960 season

The Orangemen played their season and home opener on Sept 24, 1960 against Boston University at Archbold Stadium on the campus of Syracuse University in Syracuse, NY. SU defeated the Terriers, W (35-7) before 30,000.

On Oct 1 at # 5 Kansas, #2 SU defeated the Jayhawks at Memorial Stadium in Lawrence, KS W (14–7) before 40,000 fans. On Oct 8 at Holy Cross, in the #1 position of rankings and undefeated at this point, SU defeated the Crusaders at Fitton Field in Worcester, MA W (15–6). Because of the closeness of the game, SU dropped to fourth place. Then, on Oct 15 No. 20 Penn State played # 4 Syracuse at Archbold Stadium and the Orangemen won the close game W (21–15). On Oct 22 at West Virginia, the #3 ranked Orangemen played at Mountaineer Field in Morgantown, WV and shut out the Mountaineers W (45–0.

So far undefeated but when Pitt came by on Oct 29 to play ball at Archbold Stadium v #3 Syracuse, the party unbeaten party was over. SU lost its first game in two years and it would not be the last this year as Pitt got the best of the Orangemen, L (0-10) before 41,872. A tough Army team just happened to be next on the 1960 schedule in a game played on Nov 5 at Yankee Stadium in the Bronx. Then #9 ranked SU lost by a squeaker to the Cadets L (6-9).

Undefeated then seemed *a-long-ways-away*. Colgate was having its own troubles and could no longer compete against Syracuse under Ben Schwartzwalder.

On Nov 12, Colgate was shellacked again by #17 Syracuse at Archbold Stadium Syracuse, NY (Rivalry) W 46–6 23,000. Wrapping up the season, thinking there was a chance for a bowl game, on Nov 18, Syracuse defeated # 14 Miami at the Miami Orange Bowl in Miami, Florida in a tight game W (21-14). Syracuse, finishing for some reason at #19, was not offered a bowl game.

1961 Ben Schwartzwalder Coach # 22

The 1961 Syracuse Orangemen football team competed in their seventy-second season of intercollegiate football. They were led by Ben Schwartzwalder in his thirteenth of twenty-five seasons as head coach of the Syracuse Orangemen. This SU squad finished this year with a great record of (8-3-0). Dick Easterly was the team captain for the 1961 team. SU finished 16/14 in the two national polls this year and were invited to the Liberty Bowl in Philadelphia. Running back Ernie Davis became the first African-American football player to win the Heisman Trophy.

The #10 ranked Orangemen played their season opener on Sept 23, 1961 against Oregon State at Multnomah Stadium, Portland, OR, and SU claimed victory W 19–8 before 35,729. Then on Sept 30, at home, SU, ranked #5 in the nation beat West Virginia W (29-14) in the home opener at Archbold Stadium on the campus of Syracuse University in Syracuse, NY before 25,000 fans.

On Oct 7, #7 SU traveled to Maryland's Byrd Stadium in College Park, MD and lost a nail-biter, L 21–22 before 35,000 against the tough Terrapins. On eth mend from the close defeat at Maryland, on Oct 14 at Nebraska Memorial Stadium in Lincoln, NE, the Orangemen came back W (28–6) before 35,387 fans. Penn State was getting sick of losing to Syracuse and so on Oct 21 at Penn State's brand new Beaver Stadium at University Park, PA, the Nittany Lions shut out Syracuse L (0–14) before 44,390.

On Oct 28 SU beat Holy Cross at home in Archbold Stadium W (34–6) before 31,000 fans. Then, making up for last year's defeat at Pitt. On Nov 4, the Orangemen beat Pitt's Panthers W (28-9) at home before a packed Archbold house of 40,152. On Nov 11, SU p ripped Colgate apart at Archbold Stadium W (51-8) before 25,000. As Colgate was losing its zip as a Division I team, Archbold attendance went down. On Nov 18 at Notre Dame, #10 Syracuse faced off with the Fighting Irish at Notre Dame Stadium in South Bend, IN and lost the close game L (15–17) before 49,246 in the house that Rock Built. On Nov 25 at Boston College's Alumni Stadium in Chestnut Hill, MA, SU beat the Eagles W 28–13 before 17,600

Liberty Bowl

In a minor bowl game, the Liberty Bowl played early on December 16 vs. Miami (FL) at Philadelphia Municipal Stadium, Syracuse beat Miami in a nail-biter W (15-14) in Philadelphia, PA.

1962 Ben Schwartzwalder Coach # 22

The 1962 Syracuse Orangemen football team competed in their seventy-third season of intercollegiate football. They were led by Ben Schwartzwalder in his fourteenth of twenty-five seasons as head coach of the Syracuse Orangemen. The leftovers of the championship squad were gone, and SU faced a comeuppance year with a break-even record of (5-5-0). The best of times had come to a quick halt for one year. Next year there would be a great rebound.

The offense scored 159 points while the defense allowed 110 points. Leon Cholakis was the team captain for the 1962 team. SU finished 16/14 in the two national polls this year and were invited to the Liberty Bowl in Philadelphia. Running back Ernie Davis became the first African-American football player to win the Heisman Trophy.

The Orangemen played their season opener on Sept 22, 1962 against Oklahoma at Oklahoma Memorial Stadium in Norman, OK and lost L (3–7) before 54,000. Then on Sept 29, at Army in the Polo

Grounds of New York, NY, the Orangemen were beaten by the Cadets L (2–9) before 29,500 fans. On Oct 13 SU beat Boston College at home in Archbold Stadium, W (12-0). Penn State had climbed onto the better side of lady luck in playing Syracuse as on Oct 20 at Penn State's first Beaver Stadium (not Beaver Field) at University Park, PA, the Nittany Lions just beat the Orangemen in a tough batch L (19–20) before 46,920.

Then, on Oct 27 at Holy Cross Fitton Field in Worcester, MA, SU defeated a resistant Crusaders team W (30–20) before 20,000 fans. Then on Nov 3, at Pittsburgh's Pitt Stadium in Pittsburgh, PA, the Panthers got the best of the Orangemen L (6–24) before 23,473. On Nov 10, Syracuse beat Navy at home in Archbold Stadium W (34-6) before 40,500. The Service academies drew the biggest home crowds at Syracuse.

On Nov 17, SU beat George Washington at home in Archbold Stadium, W (35–0) before a discriminating crowd of 18,000. On Nov 24 West Virginia beat the Orangemen at Archbold Stadium L (6–17) before 13,000. After a lot of rest, and a lot of lectures by Ben Schwartzwalder, Ben led his team cross country expecting nothing less than a win, which he got on Dec 8 at UCLA in the Los Angeles Memorial Coliseum, Los Angeles, CA W (12–7) before 14,485. There were no excuses for Ben Schwartzwalder. This was a bad year with a lot of almost's but few cigars. He would bring the team back in 1963.

1963 Ben Schwartzwalder Coach # 22

The 1963 Syracuse Orangemen football team competed in their seventy-fourth season of intercollegiate football. They were led by Ben Schwartzwalder in his fifteenth of twenty-five seasons as head coach of the Syracuse Orangemen. SU overcame its straggler year and roared back onto the field with a great team with a great 8-2-0 record.

The offense scored 255 points while the defense allowed 101 points Richard Bowman & James Mazurek were the captains for 1963. SU finished #12 in the two national polls this year and despite their great season, they were not among the media favorites invited to bowl games this year.

The Orangemen played their season and home opener on Sept 21, 1963 against Boston College at home in Archbold Stadium on the Syracuse University Campus in Syracuse NY. SU won the game W (32-21) before 30,000. On Sept 28 at Kansas Memorial Stadium in Lawrence, KS, SU was shut out in a close match L (0–10). On Oct 5 at home, SU shut out Holy Cross in a blowout W (48-0). Then on Oct 11, the Orangemen raveled to UCLA at Los Angeles Memorial Coliseum in Los Angeles and got the win W (29–7) before 22,949. On Oct, at home SU shut out Penn State in a close match W (9-0) before 39,600 fans.

On Oct at home, SU beat Oregon State W (31–8). On Nov 2 at No. 10 Pittsburgh at Pitt Stadium in Pittsburgh, PA, the Orangemen lost in a close one (L 27-35) before 44,090 fans. Then, on Nov 9, at home SU squeaked by West Virginia W (15-13. On Nov 16 at home the #18 Orangemen defeated Richmond in a blowout W (50–0). On Nov 28, at Yankee Stadium in New York, NY Syracuse defeated Notre Dame W (14–7) before a nice crowd of 56,972

1964 Ben Schwartzwalder Coach # 22

The 1964 Syracuse Orangemen football team competed in their seventy-fifth season of intercollegiate football. They were led by Ben Schwartzwalder in his sixteenth of twenty-five seasons as head coach of the Syracuse Orangemen. SU had a winning season record of 7-4-0.

The offense scored 264 points while the defense allowed 157 points Billy Hunter & Richard King were the captains for 1964. SU finished # 38 of 120 teams and they were invited to the Sugar Bowl this year.

The #9 ranked Orangemen played their season opener on Sept 19, 1964 at Boston College's Alumni Stadium in Chestnut Hill, MA and were beaten by the Eagles L (14–21). On Sept 26 SU defeated

Kansas in the home opener in Archbold Stadium on the Syracuse University Campus in Syracuse NY. SU won the game W (38-6) before 28,000. On Oct 3 at Holy Cross in Fitton Field, Worcester, MA, SU defeated the Crusaders W 34–8 before 14,000. Then, back at home on Oct 10, SU defeated UCLA W (39–0) before 35,000.

Then on Oct 17 SU beat the Nittany Lions at Penn State's Beaver Stadium in University Park, PA W (21–14) before 46,900. On Oct 24 at Oregon State's Multnomah Stadium in Portland, OR , #8 SU lost L (13–3) before 24,326. Then on Oct 31 at home SU defeated Pittsburgh W (21–6) before 35,000. On Nov 7 at Army, played in Yankee Stadium New York, NY, the Orangemen beat the Cadets W (27–15) before 37,552. SU won again at home on Nov 14 against Virginia Tech W (20–15) before 24,000. Then on Nov 21, it was off to West Virginia in Morgantown, WV. SU lost by one-point L (27–28) before s sparse crowd of 14,000
Sugar Bowl

Sugar Bowl January 1, 1965

In the Sugar Bowl on January 1, 1965 vs. #7 LSU in Tulane Stadium, New Orleans, LA, the Orangemen could not hold on and lost the game L (10–13) before 65,000. The 1965 Sugar Bowl featured the seven-ranked LSU Tigers, and the unranked Syracuse Orangemen.

1965 Ben Schwartzwalder Coach # 22

The 1965 Syracuse Orangemen football team competed in their seventy-sixth season of intercollegiate football. They were led by Ben Schwartzwalder in his seventeenth of twenty-five seasons as head coach of the Syracuse Orangemen. SU had a winning season record of 7-3-0.

The offense scored 237 points while the defense allowed 146 points Harris Elliott was the captains for 1965. SU finished # 25 of 120 teams. Their record was better than last year's, yet they were not among the media favorites invited to bowl games this year.

The Orangemen played their season opener on Sept 18, 1965 at Navy at the Navy–Marine Corps Memorial Stadium in Annapolis, MD. SU beat Navy W (14–6) before 20,367. On Sept 25 SU lost to Miami (FL) in the home opener in Archbold Stadium on the Syracuse University Campus in Syracuse NY. SU lost this game in a shutout L (0-24) before 32,000. On Oct 2 at Maryland's Byrd Stadium in College Park, MD, SU beat the Terrapins W 24–7 before 35,000. On Oct 9 at UCLA in Los Angeles Memorial Coliseum in Los Angeles, CA, Syracuse could not take out the Bruins L (14–24) before 27,729.

On Oct 16 at home SU beat the Nittany Lions of Penn State in a close match W (28–21) before 39,000. On Oct 23 at home, SU beat Holy Cross W (32–6) before 15,000. Then on Oct 30, it was off to another big stadium for a game against Pitt. The venue was She Stadium in New York, NY. SU won big W (51–13) before 24,590. On Nov 6 at home v Oregon State, SU lost by just one point to the Beavers L (12–13) before 33,000.

Then on Nov 13, it was off to West Virginia's Mountaineer Field in Morgantown, WV, where Syracuse defeated the Mountaineers W (41–19) before 33,500. The last game of the season was at home and it pitted the Orangemen against a scrappy Boston College. SU took the close game by W (21-13) before 20,000.

1966 Ben Schwartzwalder Coach # 22

The 1966 Syracuse Orangemen football team competed in their seventy-seventh season of intercollegiate football. They were led by Ben Schwartzwalder in his eighteenth of twenty-five seasons as head coach of the Syracuse Orangemen. SU had a winning season record of 8-3-0.

The offense scored 266 points while the defense allowed 156 points Floyd Little & Herb Stecker were the captains for 1966. SU finished # 16th in the polls this year. After losing their first two games of the season, Syracuse won the next eight games, finishing the regular season with a record of 8–2 The Orangemen were invited to the Gator Bowl, where they lost to Tennessee.

Games of the 1966 season

The Orangemen lost their season opener on Sept 10, 1966 at Baylor in Floyd Casey Stadium, Waco, TX L (12–35) before 31,000. . On Sept 24 SU lost to UCLA in the home opener in Archbold Stadium on the Syracuse University Campus in Syracuse NY. SU lost this game by the score of L (12-31) before 35,000. On Oct 1 at home against Maryland, SU beat the Terrapins W (28–7) before 25,000. On Oct 8 at home against Navy, Syracuse beat a tough group of Midshipmen W (28-14) On Oct 15 at Boston College in Alumni Stadium in Chestnut Hill, MA, SU shut out the Eagles W (30–0 before 24,500

On Oct 22 at Holy Cross's Fitton Field, Worcester, MA SU beat the Crusaders W (28–6). On Oct 29 Syracuse beat Pittsburgh at home in Archbold Stadium W (33–7) before 30,000. On Nov 5 at Penn State's Beaver Stadium in University Park, PA, the Orangemen prevailed over the Nittany Lions in a close match W (12–10) before 46,314. On Nov 12 at home, Syracuse beat Florida State W (37–21) before 35,405. Wrapping up the regular season at West Virginia Mountaineer Field, Morgantown, WV, on Nov 19, SU beat the Mountaineers W (34–7) before 19,000.

The Gator Bowl December 31, 1966

On December 31, 1966, New Year's Eve, Syracuse squared off in the Gator Bowl against Tennessee at Gator Bowl Stadium in Jacksonville, FL and in another close bowl game, lost by a touchdown, L (12–18) before 60,213

1967 Ben Schwartzwalder Coach # 22

The 1967 Syracuse Orangemen football team competed in their seventy-eighth season of intercollegiate football. They were led by Ben Schwartzwalder in his nineteenth of twenty-five seasons as head coach of the Syracuse Orangemen. SU had a winning season record of 8-2-0. It would be Ben Schwartzwalder's last eight-win season.

The offense scored 210 points while the defense allowed 127 points James Cheyunski & Larry Csonka were the captains for 1967. SU finished # 12th in the polls this year. Losing just two games this season, Syracuse won eight, finishing the regular season with a record of 8–2-0. With such a great record, the Orangemen were passed over and did not receive an invitation to any post-season bowl.

Some highlights: In 1967, Tom Coughlin, who later was the long-time NY Giants Coach, set the school's single-season pass receiving record. Larry Csonka was in his senior season and was named an All-American. He broke many of the school's rushing records, including some previously held by Ernie Davis, Jim Nance, Floyd Little, and Jim Brown.

In his three seasons at Syracuse, Csonka rushed for a school record 2,934 yards, rushed for 100 yards in 14 different games, and averaged 4.9 yards per carry. From 1965 to 1967, he ranked 19th, 9th and 5th in the nation in rushing. He was the Most Valuable Player in the East–West Shrine Game, the Hula Bowl, and the College All-Star Game. He went on to play for Miami in the NFL.

On Sept 23 SU defeated Baylor in the home and season opener in Archbold Stadium on the Syracuse University Campus in Syracuse NY. SU won this game by the score of W (7-0) before 31,000. On Sept 30, at home, SU beat West Virginia W (23–6) before 28,435. Then, on Oct 7 at Maryland at Byrd Stadium in College Park, MD, SU defeated the Terrapins W (7–3). SU was rolling along with a great team and along comes Navy, a tough competitor every year. In a game played on Oct 14 at Navy–Marine Corps Memorial Stadium in Annapolis, MD, Syracuse could not hold on L (14–27). Then, at home on October 21 SU beat California by one touchdown, W (20-14) in a close match. The next week at home again, Penn State beat Syracuse L (20–29) before 41,750.

On Nov 4th at Pittsburgh's Pitt Stadium in Pittsburgh, PA, Syracuse squeaked out another close win W (14–7). On Nov 11, in the annual Holy Cross Game, again SU had its way with the crusaders in a nice victory W (41–7) before 32,000. On Nov 8 at Boston College's

Alumni Stadium in Chestnut Hill, the Orangemen got the win W (32–20) before 16,200. In the final 1967 game,
November 25 at consensus #4 UCLA in a game played at the Los Angeles Memorial Coliseum in Los Angeles, CA, SU played a great game and won W (32–14). Despite a great season and a great finish, there was no bowl game for the Orangemen.

1968 Ben Schwartzwalder Coach # 22

The 1968 Syracuse Orangemen football team competed in their seventy-ninth season of intercollegiate football. They were led by Ben Schwartzwalder in his twentieth of twenty-five seasons as head coach of the Syracuse Orangemen. SU had a winning season record of 6-4-0.

The offense scored 252 points while the defense allowed 154 points Anthony Kyasky was the team captains for 1968. SU finished # 47 of 119. Syracuse finished the regular season with a record of 6-4-0. The Orangemen did not receive an invitation to any post-season bowl games in 1968.

Games of the 1958 Season

The season opener was on Sept 21 at Michigan State's Spartan Stadium in East Lansing, MI. The Spartans defeated the Orangemen L (10–14) before 63,488. On Sept 28 SU defeated Maryland in the home opener in Archbold Stadium on the Syracuse University Campus in Syracuse NY. SU won this game by the score of W (32-14) before 31,000. On Oct 5, at home, SU defeated UCLA W (20–7) before 37,367. On Oct 12 at home, Syracuse beat Pittsburgh at home W (50–17). On Oct 26 at #11 California at California Memorial Stadium in Berkeley, CA the Orangemen were shutout L (0–43) before 52,172

On Nov 2 at Holy Cross's Fitton Field in Worcester, MA, SU dominated the game W (47–0). On Nov 9 SU shut out William & Mary at home W (31–0) before 22,889. On Nov 16, at home, SU defeated Navy W (44–6) before 33,785. On Nov 23 at West Virginia's Mountaineer Field in Morgantown, WV SU lost the game

L (6–23). On Dec 7 at #3 Penn State in Beaver Stadium, University Park, PA, in the traditional rivalry, the Nittany Lions defeated the Orangemen L (12–30) before 38,000

1969 Ben Schwartzwalder Coach # 22

The 1969 Syracuse Orangemen football team competed in their eightieth season of intercollegiate football. They were led by Ben Schwartzwalder in his twenty-first of twenty-five seasons as head coach of the Syracuse Orangemen. SU had a break-even season record of 5-5-0.

The offense scored 169 points while the defense allowed 126 points SU had no one captain but instead used game captains for 1969. SU finished # 55 of 122. The Orangemen did not receive an invitation to any post-season bowl games in 1969.

On Sept 20 SU defeated Iowa State in the home opener in Archbold Stadium on the Syracuse University Campus in Syracuse NY. SU won this game by the score of W (14-13) before 30,491. On Sept 27 at Kansas Memorial Stadium in Lawrence, KS, SU was shut out L (0–13) before 44,500 fans. On Oct 4, my wedding anniversary to-be, at Wisconsin's Camp Randall Stadium in Madison, WI, Syracuse got the win W (43–7) before 45,540. On Oct 11 at Maryland's Byrd Stadium in College Park, MD, the Orangemen won their second in a row W (20–9). Then on October 18 at home, #5 Penn State got the win by one-point L (14–15) before 42,491

On Nov 1at Pittsburgh's Pitt Stadium in Pittsburgh, PA, SU lost again by just one point L (20–21). The next week, on Nov 8. SU shut-out Arizona W (23-0). On Nov 15, at Navy in a game played in the Navy–Marine Corps Memorial Stadium, Annapolis, MD, the Orangemen beat the Cadets W (15–0). On Nov 22 #18 West Virginia came to Archbold Stadium for a win and they got it in another close match for the Orangemen L (10–13). To finish the season, an always tough Boston College team played at Archbold Stadium and they beat the disheartened Syracuse Orangemen L (10–35).

They say when the going gets tough, the tough get going. Well, 1969 was a tough year for SU with so many close games and they could not keep it going even when they had a shot at breaking away. They lost to Pitt and Penn State by one point and later to West Virginia by just three points. It was the difference between a nice 8-2 year and their record of 5-5 for 1969.

1970 Ben Schwartzwalder Coach # 22

The 1970 Syracuse Orangemen football team competed in their eighty-first season of intercollegiate football. They were led by Ben Schwartzwalder in his twenty-second of twenty-five seasons as head coach of the Syracuse Orangemen. SU had a winning season record of 6-4-0.

The offense scored 248 points while the defense allowed 208 points Paul Paolisso, Raymond White & Randolph Zur were the co-captains for 1969. SU finished # 41 of 123. The Orangemen did not receive an invitation to any post-season bowl games in 1970.

After a disappointing year in 1969, Syracuse could not get it going in 1970 and lost its first three games. It was like they could not shake the bad cloud from the prior year. Nonetheless, Ben Schwartzwalder never lost faith. He kept drilling them to become excellent and finally their season turned around.

Games of the 1970 Season

On Sept 19 SU was defeated by # 15 Houston in the season opener at the famed Astrodome in Houston, TX. SU was lackluster in this game and lost decidedly L (15–42) before 40,439. On Sept 26, in the home opener in Archbold Stadium on the Syracuse University Campus in Syracuse NY. SU lost another game. This was against Kansas by a score of W (14-31) On Oct 3, at Illinois Memorial Stadium in Champaign, IL, Syracuse lost its third without a win— this time by a shutout L (0–27). It was time for Ben to come up with his best pep talks and some better plays and he did.

On Oct 10, SU picked up a nice win at home—its first win of the year—against Maryland in Archbold Stadium. The Orangemen beat the Terrapins W (23–7). Feeling like a Ben Schwartzwalder team, on Oct 17, the Orangemen traveled to Penn State's Beaver Stadium in University Park, PA and pulled off their second straight win W (24–7) before 50,540.

Riding the win high, on Oct 24 SU beat Navy at home W (23-8). Next was Pittsburgh, always a tough competitor. In a home game, at Archbold Stadium, Syracuse got its fourth win in a row W (43–13). On Nov 7, at Army playing at Michie Stadium in West Point, NY against an always-tough Cadets, team, SU pulled off another victory W (31–29) before a packed Army house of 41,062. On Nov 14 at West Virginia's Mountaineer Field, Morgantown, WV, the Ben rivalry favored WV L (19–28). Ready again to play at the top of its game, the Orangemen walloped Miami of Florida at home in Archbold Stadium W (56–16) for a great finish to a turnaround season.

1971 Ben Schwartzwalder Coach # 22

The 1971 Syracuse Orangemen football team competed in their eighty-second season of intercollegiate football. They were led by Ben Schwartzwalder in his twenty-third of twenty-five seasons as head coach of the Syracuse Orangemen. SU had a breakeven season record of 5-5-1. Joe Ehrmann & Dan Yochum were team captains for 1971. The Orangemen again did not receive an invitation to any post-season bowl games in 1971.

1971 games of the season

On Sept 18 SU tied Wisconsin T (20-20) in the home opener in Archbold Stadium on the Syracuse University Campus in Syracuse NY. On Sept 25 at Northwestern in Dyche Stadium, Evanston, IL. the Orangemen could not get enough points on the board and lost the game L (6–12) before 27,529. On the road on Oct 2 to Indiana Memorial Stadium in Bloomington, IN, Syracuse picked up a tight shutout win against the Hoosiers W (7–0). On Oct 9 at Maryland's Byrd Stadium, College Park, MD, SU got the victory W (21–13) before 20,100. Then, on Oct 16, when #9 Penn State came to SU's home field of Archbold Stadium in Syracuse, NY for the annual rivalry game the surprise was the Syracuse would be shut-out L (0–31) before 41,382, almost all of whom were rooting for Syracuse.

On October 23, SU blew out Holy Cross at home W (63–21) before a small crowd of 18,308. Then, away on October 30 at Pittsburgh's Pitt Stadium in Pittsburgh, PA, in a rivalry match, the Panthers clawed their way to victory and Syracuse notched in another loss L (21–31). On Nov SU lost to BC (Boston College) at home -- Archbold Stadium, in a tough close match L (3–10). Then, on Nov 13 at Navy in Navy–Marine Corps Memorial Stadium, Annapolis, MD, Syracuse lost to the Midshipmen, L (14–17) in a very close game. On Nov 20, at home, SU defeated West Virginia W (28-24). In the season finale, SU traveled to Miami FL in the Miami Orange Bowl to beat the Hurricanes W (14–0) in the SU season closer before 17,224 fans.

1972 Ben Schwartzwalder Coach # 22

The 1972 Syracuse Orangemen football team competed in their eighty-third season of intercollegiate football. They were led by Ben Schwartzwalder in his twenty-fourth of twenty-five seasons as head coach of the Syracuse Orangemen. SU had a losing season record of 5-6-0. In 1972, SU went back to game captains v individual season captain. The Orangemen again did not receive an invitation to any post-season bowl games in 1972.

On Sept 9 SU beat Temple W (17-10) in the home opener in Archbold Stadium on the Syracuse University Campus in Syracuse NY. On Sept 16 at NC State Parker Stadium in Raleigh, NC Syracuse lost to the Wolfpack L (20–43) before 27,100.

On the road on Sept 23 at Wisconsin Camp Randall Stadium in Madison, WI, Syracuse lost its second game of the season L (7–31) before 67,234. On Sept 30, at home, SU defeated the Maryland Terrapins in a close match, W (16-12)

On Oct 9 at Maryland's Byrd Stadium, College Park, MD, SU got the victory W (21-13) before 20,100. Then, on Oct 16, when #9

Penn State came to SU's home field of Archbold Stadium in Syracuse, NY for the annual rivalry game the surprise was the Syracuse would be shut-out L (0–31) before 41,382, almost all of whom were rooting for Syracuse. On Oct 7 at home Syracuse lost its third game of the season to Indiana L (2–10) 18,444. As the Orangemen kept struggling, attendance was dropping.

On Oct 14, at home, Syracuse beat Navy W (30-14) before 22,187. On Oct 21 at #12 ranked Penn State in a game played at Beaver Stadium in University Park, PA(Rivalry), the Orangemen were shut out by the Nittany Lions L (0–17) before 60,465. On Oct 28 at home, SU defeated Pitt W (10-6).

On Nov 4, at Boston College's Alumni Stadium in Chestnut Hill, MA, BC shut out SUL (0–37) in a runaway. before 21,216. On Nov 11 at home, SU defeated Army W (27-6) before 19,525. On Nov 18 in the season close at West Virginia's Mountaineer Field in Morgantown, WV, the Mountaineers laid a big defeat on the Orangemen in the rivalry game L (12–43) before 31,500

1973 Ben Schwartzwalder Coach # 22

The 1973 Syracuse Orangemen football team competed in their eighty-fourth season of intercollegiate football. They were led by Ben Schwartzwalder in his twenty-fifth and last of twenty-five seasons as head coach of the Syracuse Orangemen. SU had its worst season ever under Coach Ben – 2-9-0. Again, SU did not nominate season captains but instead used game captains. The Orangemen again did not receive an invitation to any post-season bowl games in 1973.

On Sept 15 SU lost to Bowling Green L (14-41 in the home opener in Archbold Stadium on the Syracuse University Campus in Syracuse NY. On Sept 22, at home SU lost to Michigan State L (8-14). On Sept 29, 6 at Washington Husky Stadium, Seattle, WA, Syracuse lost its third game of the season L (7–21) before 54,800

On the road on Oct 6 at Maryland's Byrd Stadium College Park, MD. SU lost its fourth in a row, L (0–38) before 32,800. On Oct 13, at Navy Navy–Marine Corps Memorial Stadium Annapolis, MD SU lost # 5 in a row, L (14–23) before 20,591.

On Oct 20 SU lost #6 in a row at home to #5 Penn State in a blowout L (6-49) before 27,595. On Oct 27 at home SU lost #7 in a row, to Miami (of FL) L (23–34) before 19,369. Then, on November 3 at Pittsburgh Pitt Stadium in Pittsburgh, PA, Syracuse lost its eight in a row L (14–28) 24,932.

On Nov 10 at Holy Cross Fitton Field in Worcester, MA SU picked up its first of just two wins this season with baseball-like score W (5–3) before 16,404. On Nov 17 at home, Syracuse won its second and last win of the season against Boston College W (24-13) before an empty stadium of 11,199. On Nov 24 at home West Virginia spoiled the season finale of a dismal season by beating the Orangemen L (14–24) before 12,917 disappointed fans.

Ben Schwartzwalder leaves Syracuse Football

Please enjoy this submission from:
http://cuse.com/sports/2011/9/28/Schwartzwalder.aspx
It is titled simply, BEN SCHWARTZWALDER (1909-93)

> The game ended, and Ben Schwartzwalder walked to the middle of the field, shook hands, exchanged a few words with his opposing coach, then turned and headed toward the dressing room. It was a scene he had repeated several hundred times but on this particular day, November 24, 1973, it was different. It marked the end of the brilliant coaching career of Floyd (Ben) Schwartzwalder, head man of the Syracuse Orange for the past 25 years. He had retired, after a quarter of a century as the head coach at one school.
>
> Less than a dozen men rank in this category. And less than a handful of men who have entered the coaching profession since Princeton and Rutgers started the madness back in 1869 have recorded as many victories as did this crew-cut, bespectacled quiet little giant out of the hills of West Virginia.

His report card shows 178 wins, 96 losses and three ties during his 28-year tenure as a head coach (three years at Muhlenberg, 25 at Syracuse).

How does one describe Ben Schwartzwalder? What made him tick and what made him one of the giants of the game?

A good starting place is his home state of West Virginia. It is where the seeds of the fierce competitor were nurtured and matured. He didn't starve as a boy growing up, but he knew what it was to want. By the time he was in college, it was apparent that he wasn't going to weigh much more than 150 and grow taller than 5-9. But none of these shortcomings stopped Ben Schwartzwalder from plunging head first into the field of battle. This is where that appetite of desire was whetted and the burning determination to succeed was honed.

Ben enrolled at West Virginia University and went out for football. He was the starting center at 152 pounds for the Mountaineers of coach Greasey Neale. He also wrestled and dodged a young coed who was just as fierce a competitor as he when it came to getting her man. And thus, Ruth Simpson became Mrs. Floyd Schwartzwalder.

Both taught and Ben began coaching in his home state. By 1941, he had earned a name for himself and was offered the head coaching job at Canton McKinley High School in Ohio, one of the top jobs in the Midwest. Ben was clearly on his way to the top. But there was to be a delay.

Shortly after Dec. 7, 1941, Canton McKinley lost a coach and the U.S. Army gained a soldier.

Although in his thirties, Ben decided he was going to be a paratrooper. He served with the 82nd Airborne and was in the first wave of troops that jumped on D-Day in 1944. Dropped far behind enemy lines and miles off target, Ben organized his command immediately and a week later brought a bunch of prisoners to the Allied lines.

He rose to the rank of major and in the process picked up the Silver Star, Bronze Star and Purple Heart, four battle stars and a Presidential Unit Citation. He was personally decorated by Matthew Ridgeway who recalled Ben well. "I never expected to see you here to receive this award," said the commander of the 82nd.

Adversity and Ben were old combatants and Ben usually won.

The war ended, and football again became his life. In 1946, Ben came east and guided Muhlenberg to a 25-5 slate in three years. Meanwhile, up in central New York, Syracuse was struggling for survival. The Orangemen had won but nine games in four years and everyone was unhappy. A call for help went out and, in the end, it was that man who was to win more games than Knute Rockne, Frank Leahy, Bud Wilkinson or Earl Blaik that answered.

The rest is now history. Ben gave Syracuse its finest hours in football. He produced 22 straight years of non-losing football, took the Orange to seven bowls, and won the national championship in 1959. He developed some of the most impressive running backs the game has ever seen - Jim Brown, Ernie Davis, Jim Nance, Floyd Little and Larry Csonka. Orange teams outrushed opponents by more than 22,000 yards under Ben.

The public Ben Schwartzwalder often appeared to be a cross between a wounded bear and a crossed bull. He was basically a shy, quiet individual who never got very close to the press or general public. The private Ben was a very devoted family man who loved to putter around in his garden or who always had time to stop and give a stray dog a reassuring pat on the head or say hello to a youngster. And enthusiasm!! He had the same burning drive in 1973 as he did as a rookie coach back in West Virginia in 1933.

"Sometimes outstanding individuals are never appreciated until they are gone," said Beano Cooke, a former sports information director and now with ABC-TV. "I have a strange feeling that in the years to come, officials, alumni and fans might finally realize what a tremendous asset Ben was. The funny part is that so many people have known this for years, including myself."

Ben always refused to pick a favorite team or make comparisons. The team he was coaching at the time was his favorite simply because of his great love of coaching.

"We football coaches are most fortunate," Ben said as he left office as the president of the American Football Coaches Association. "By doing the best we can do with the job we have, wherever it is, we can serve our nation in its greatest task."

The winner of the annual Syracuse-West Virginia football game receives the Ben Schwartzwalder Trophy. Schwartzwalder coached Syracuse and was a graduate of West Virginia.

Syracuse was never so lucky as to have Ben Schwartzwalder for so long at the helm. The school became accustomed to winning.

Please read his obituary which I have provided below. It offers even additional insights into this great man.

Ben Schwartzwalder Dies at 83; Revitalized Football at Syracuse
By ROBERT McG. THOMAS Jr.
Published: April 29, 1993
Correction Appended

> Ben Schwartzwalder, who recruited a series of acclaimed running backs as he restored Syracuse to football glory during 25 sparkling seasons that included an undefeated campaign in 1959, died yesterday at Northside Hospital in St. Petersburg, Fla. He was 83.
>
> Mr. Schwartzwalder, a resident of Syracuse who maintained a winter home in St. Petersburg, died of a heart attack, his wife said.

When Floyd Burdette Schwartzwalder (Ben was a childhood nickname bestowed by a brother) arrived at Syracuse at the age of 41 in 1949, he was not at all what the alumni had hoped for to revive their football program.

Syracuse, once a national powerhouse, had won all of nine games over the previous four seasons, and Schwartzwalder, a former high school coach whose collegiate career consisted of three seasons at tiny Muhlenberg College in Allentown, Pa., seemed hardly the man to turn things around.

As Schwartzwalder later put it, "The alumni wanted a big-name coach. They got a long-name coach."

Most Victorious Coach

But Schwartzwalder, a decorated World War II paratrooper, simply went to work developing a program that made him the most victorious coach in Syracuse history, with a record of 153-91-3.

Although he later became famous for his recruitment of a long line of talented running backs -- including Jim Brown, Ernie Davis, Jim Nance, Floyd Little and Larry Csonka -- Schwartzwalder's success was founded on an earlier triumph, persuading the Syracuse chancellor, William Pearson Tolley, to increase the number of football scholarships from 12 a year to eventually 25 a year.

As the number of scholarships increased, Schwartzwalder, an honors student during his years playing football and wrestling at the University of West Virginia, did not chafe under the directive that he recruit only academically qualified players. He said good students generally made better athletes, anyway. So did a good coach.

His running offenses, based on an unorthodox unbalanced line, were impenetrable to rival coaches, and his practices, generally conducted at full tilt, were all but unbearable to his players. A Legend in Pajamas

Schwartzwalder became a campus legend for his absent-mindedness (he once wore his pajama bottoms to a morning practice), but it was a foible with an advantage. As his wife once explained, "He simply refuses to clutter up his mind with anything but football."

The concentration paid off. In 1959, the year the Orangemen were voted the nation's top team after capping an 11-0 season with a 23-14 victory over Texas in the Cotton Bowl, Schwartzwalder was named coach of the year.

The offense led the nation, averaging 313.6 rushing yards, 451.5 total yards and 39 points a game, and the defense led the nation in holding opponents to just 96.2 yards a game and only 19.3 rushing yards.

Mr. Schwartzwalder, who retired after the 1973 season, is survived by his wife, Ruth, known as Reggie; two daughters, Mary Scofield of Winesburg, Ohio, and SU san Walker of South Salem. N.Y., and five grandchildren.

Correction: April 30, 1993, Friday an obituary yesterday about Ben Schwartzwalder, the former football coach at Syracuse, misstated his age in some editions. He was 83.

Chapter 9 Frank Maloney 1974 to 1980

Coach Frank Maloney #23

Year	Coach	Record	Conf
1974	Frank Maloney	2-9-0	Ind
1975	Frank Maloney	6-5-0	Ind
1976	Frank Maloney	3-8-0	Ind
1977	Frank Maloney	6-5-0	Ind
1978	Frank Maloney	3-8-0	Ind
1979	Frank Maloney	7-5-0	Ind
1980	Frank Maloney	5-6-0	Ind

Coach Frank Maloney in 1980

Famous Coaches (From the Past) by SWC75.

Maloney had his limitations, (especially in-game adjustments: we had a lot of games where we looked great in the first quarter and went downhill from there). But Frank has never received the credit he deserved for keeping the football program alive while the politicians bickered about building a new stadium and the school slowly awoke to the need to get modern facilities such as a genuine weight room. He somehow managed to recruit some fine players such as Bill Hurley, Art Monk, Joe Morris, Craig Wolfley and Jimmy Collins whose ability in key positions allowed the team to remain competitive and interesting. He produced three winning seasons and actually won a bowl game, albeit a very minor one, (the Independence Bowl over McNeese State).

But there were also seasons of 2-9, 3-8, 3-8 and 5-6 and when the promising 1979 team went into a slump the members of the 1959 team signed a petition asking for Frank to be fired. Also, Jake Crouthamel had become athletic director and new AD's like to bring in their own people. Officially, Frank resigned to spend more time with his family. There was talk he might get the Northwestern job, being from Chicago, (the Wildcats had started on their record winning streak), but it didn't happen. Frank wound up with a long-term job running the ticket office for the Chicago Cubs.

1974 Frank Maloney Coach # 23

The 1974 Syracuse Orangemen football team competed in their eighty-fifth season of intercollegiate football. They were led by Frank Maloney in his first of seven seasons as head coach of the Syracuse Orangemen. SU got back on a winning track this year with a record of 6-5-0. Maloney picked Bob Petchel & John Rafferty as team captains for 1974. The Orangemen again did not receive an invitation to any post-season bowl games in 1974.

On Sept 7 SU beat Oregon State W (23-23) in the home opener in Archbold Stadium on the Syracuse University Campus in Syracuse NY. Frank Maloney's squad won their first game played for the new coach. On Sept 14, at home SU lost to Kent State L (14-20). On Sept 21, at Michigan State Spartan Stadium, East Lansing, MI SU lost to the Spartans L (0–19)before 66,847. On Sept 28, #13 NC State defeated the Orangemen L (22-28*. On Oct 5 at home, Maryland shut out the Orangemen L (0-31). In the second and last win of the season, on Oct 12 at home, Syracuse defeated Navy W (17-9)

On Oct 19 at #11 Penn State at Beaver Stadium in University Park, PA, SU lost to the Nittany Lions L (14–30) before 59,100. On Nov 2, at home, SU lost to Pittsburgh L (13–21) before 25,177 fans. On Nov 9, at West Virginia's Mountaineer Field in Morgantown, WV, Syracuse took a shellacking L (11-39). Then, on the road on Nov 16 at Boston College's Alumni Stadium in Chestnut Hill, MA, the Eagles shut out the Orangemen L0–35) before 18,651. On the road again on Nov 22 at Miami (FL) in the Orange Bowl, Miami, FL, Syracuse was beaten in a close game by the Hurricanes. L (7–14) before 12,208.

1975 Frank Maloney Coach # 23

The 1975 Syracuse Orangemen football team competed in their eighty-sixth season of intercollegiate football. They were led by Frank Maloney in his second of seven seasons as head coach of the Syracuse Orangemen. SU got back on a winning track this year with a record of 6-5-0. Maloney picked Raymond Preston as team captain for 1975. The Orangemen again did not receive an invitation to any post-season bowl games in 1975.

Games of the 1975 Season

On Sept 13 SU beat Villanova W (24-17) in the home opener in Archbold Stadium on the Syracuse University Campus in Syracuse NY before 22,867 fans. On Sept 20, at home SU defeated Iowa W (10-7) On Sept 27, at Tulane in the Louisiana Superdome New Orleans, LA the Orangemen won W (31–13) before 33,200. On Oct 4, at Maryland's Byrd Stadium in College Park, MD, the Terrapins beat the Orangemen L (7–24) before 43,863. Then on Oct11 at Navy, Annapolis, MD, the Midshipmen prevailed L (6–10).

On Oct 18, #9 Penn State beat Syracuse at home L (7–19) before 28,153. On Oct 25 at home, Syracuse defeated Boston College W (22–14). On Nov 1 at home, SU were shut out by Pitt L (0-38). On Nov 15 at Virginia Scott Stadium, Charlottesville, VA Syracuse beat the Wahoo's W (37–0). Then on Nov 22, at home, SU defeated West Virginia by one point W (20–19) before 15,336. Then in the season finale against Rutgers at Rutgers Stadium in Piscataway, NJ, the Orangemen were defeated L (10–21) before 22,000 fans.

1976 Frank Maloney Coach # 23

The 1976 Syracuse Orangemen football team competed in their eighty-seventh season of intercollegiate football. They were led by Frank Maloney in his third of seven seasons as head coach of the Syracuse Orangemen. SU got off track again this year with a losing record of 3-8-0. Maloney picked William Zanovich as team captain for 1976. The Orangemen again did not receive an invitation to any post-season bowl games in 1976.

On Sept 11 SU lost to Bowling Green in the home opener in Archbold Stadium on the Syracuse University Campus in Syracuse NY L (7-22) before 23,859 fans. On Sept 18, while on the road at Kinnick Stadium in Iowa City, IA, SU lost big to Iowa, L (3–41) before 54,129

On Sept 25, at home, Syracuse lost to the Terrapins of Maryland L (28-42) before 21,109, On Oct 2 at home SU defeated Oregon State W (21–3) before 18,591. Then at home on Oct 9, SU defeated Tulane in a nail-biter W (3–0) before 11,223 fans. On Oct 16 at Penn State's Beaver Stadium, University Park, PA, PSU won a nice victory L (3–27) before 61,474.

On Oct 23 at home, SU defeated Temple W (24-16). Then, on Oct 30 at #2 Pittsburgh's Pitt Stadium in Pittsburgh, PA, Syracuse lost L (13–23) before 50,390. On Nov 6 at home SU lost to Navy L (10-27). Then on Nov 13 at Boston College's Alumni Stadium, Chestnut Hill, MA, Syracuse was defeated L (14–28) before 25,433. In the Season Finale, Syracuse lost on Nov 20 at West Virginia's Mountaineer Field in Morgantown, WV L (28–34) before 27,848

1977 Frank Maloney Coach # 23

The 1977 Syracuse Orangemen football team competed in their eighty-eighth season of intercollegiate football. They were led by Frank Maloney in his fourth of seven seasons as head coach of the

Syracuse Orangemen. SU got back on track this year with a winning record of 6-5-0. Rather than picking a team captain for the season, Maloney decided to use game captains. for 1977. The Orangemen again did not receive an invitation to any post-season bowl games in 1977.

On Sept 10 SU lost at Oregon State at Parker Stadium Corvallis, OR L 12–24, before 20,540. On Sept 17, Syracuse lost in a shutout to NC State to in the home opener in Archbold Stadium on the Syracuse University Campus in Syracuse NY before 20,696 fans. On Sept 24, at home SU defeated Washington in a tight match, W (22-0) On Oct 1 at Illinois Memorial Stadium, Champaign, IL, Syracuse defeated the Fighting Illini W (30–20) before 52,015. Then on Oct 8 at Maryland's Byrd Stadium in College Park, MD, the Orangemen were defeated by the Terrapins L (10–24) before 39,100.

Then, on Oct 15 at home against #10 Penn State, the Orangemen were defeated by the Nittany Lions L (24–31) before 27,029. On Oct 22 at #14 Pittsburgh in a rivalry game played at Pitt Stadium, Pittsburgh, PA the Orangemen were defeated by the Panthers L (21–28) before 43,551. On Oct 29 at home, SU barely beat the Wahoos, W (6–3) before 20,859.

On Nov 5 at Navy's Navy–Marine Corps Memorial Stadium in Annapolis, MD, the Orangemen defeated the Midshipmen W (45–34) before 16,709. On Nov 12, at home, SU defeated Boston College W (20-3) before16,409. In the season finale on Nov 19, at home, Syracuse defeated West Virginia W (28-9) before another small crowd of 16,118.

1978 Frank Maloney Coach # 23

The 1978 Syracuse Orangemen football team competed in their eighty-ninth season of intercollegiate football. They were led by Frank Maloney in his fifth of seven seasons as head coach of the Syracuse Orangemen. SU slipped off track again this year with a losing record of 3-8-0. Rather than picking a team captain for the season, Maloney again decided to use game captains. for 1978. The

Orangemen again did not receive an invitation to any post-season bowl games in 1978.

On Sept 9, Syracuse lost in a shutout to Bobby Bowden's Florida State Seminoles in the home opener in Archbold Stadium on the Syracuse University Campus in Syracuse NY L (0-28) before 24,272 fans. On Sept 16, at NC State in a game played at Carter Stadium, Raleigh, NC, the Orangemen lost to the Tar Heels L (19–27). Then, on Sept 23 at Michigan State's Spartan Stadium in East Lansing, MI, the Orangemen lost L (21–49) before 74,571 fans.

On Sept 30 at home, SU lost to Illinois L (14-28) before 20,101. On Oct 7 at West Virginia's Mountaineer Field in Morgantown, WV, Syracuse got its first of three wins for the season W (31–15) before 32,491 fans. On Oct 14 at home SU lost to #10 Maryland L (9-24) before a small crowd of 15,079. On Oct 21 in a rivalry game at #2 ranked Penn State at Beaver Stadium in University Park, PA, SU lost big L (15–45) before 77,827. PSU's Beaver Stadium kept growing.

On Nov 4, at home, another PA team beat the Orangemen in this dismal year. #19 Pittsburgh barely got by the Orangemen L (17-18) before 26,037. On Nov 11 at home against Navy, the Orangemen defeated the Midshipmen W (20-17). This would be the last game the Orangemen played at Archbold Field. In the next game, on Nov 18, SU got a win at Boston College's Alumni Stadium in Chestnut Hill, MA W (37–23) before 15,855. Syracuse lost its final game on Nov 25 at Miami (FL) in the Miami Orange Bowl venue in Miami, FL L (9–21) before 15,739.

1979 Frank Maloney Coach # 23

The 1979 Syracuse Orangemen football team competed in their ninetieth season of intercollegiate football. They were led by Frank Maloney in his sixth of seven seasons as head coach of the Syracuse Orangemen. SU had its best year under Maloney this year with a winning record of 7-5-0. Maloney picked Jim Collins, Bill Hurley & Craig Wolfley to be team captains for 1979. The Orangemen were invited to the 1979 Independence Bowl, where they defeated McNeese State, 31–7.

Due to the ongoing construction of Syracuse's new stadium, the "indoor" Carrier Dome, SU home games in 1979 were played in various locations in New York and New Jersey. SO, SU games were played at Giants Stadium, (Capacity: 80,242); Rich Stadium, (Capacity: 80,020); and Schoellkopf Field, (Capacity: 25,597)

Since the Carrier Dome was built in the exact location of Archbold Stadium, this magnificent concrete structure was torn down before the 1979 season to permit the Carrier Dome's construction.

Games of the 1979 season

In the season opener on Sept 8 against Earle Bruce's Ohio State team in Ohio Stadium, Columbus, OH, SU lost L (8–31) before 86.205. This was the first year Ohio State played after Woody Hayes. On Sept 15, Syracuse beat West Virginia W (24-14) as an SU home game played at Giants Stadium, East Rutherford, NJ before 10,375. On Sept 22 at Northwestern's Dyche Stadium in Evanston, IL, SU got a nice win W (54–21) before 20,121. On Sept 29, in a home game against Washington State, played in Rich Stadium, Orchard Park, NY, SU defeated the Cougars W (52–25) before 10,004.

On Oct 6 at Kansas Memorial Stadium in Lawrence, KS, SU got the win, W (45–27) before 36,720. On Oct 13 at Temple in Veterans Stadium, Philadelphia, PA, the Orangemen lost to the Owls in a blowout L (17–49) before 18,504. On Oct 20, at home played at Giants Stadium in East Rutherford, NJ, the Orangemen lost to the Nittany Lions of Penn State L (7–35) before 53,789. On Oct 27, at home played at Rich Stadium in Orchard Park, NY, SU defeated Miami W (25–15) before 7,729.

Then, on Nov 3 at #12 Pittsburgh's Pitt Stadium, Pittsburgh, PA, the Orangemen were defeated by the Panthers L (21–28) before 43,005 fans. Then, on Nov 10 at Navy in a game played in the Navy–Marine Corps Memorial Stadium, Annapolis, MD, the Orangemen defeated the Midshipmen W (30–14) before 20,385, In the final regular season home game on Nov 17, Boston College beat Syracuse at Schoellkopf Field in Ithaca, NY L (10–27) before 20,245

Independence Bowl Game Dec 15, 1979

On Dec 15, 1979. McNeese State and Syracuse tangled in the 1979 Independence Bowl at State Fair Stadium, Shreveport, LA W (31–7) before 27,234 fans. This was McNeese State's 2nd Southland Conference title in three years. This was Syracuse's first bowl game since 1966.

1980 Frank Maloney Coach # 23

The 1980 Syracuse Orangemen football team competed in their ninety-First season of intercollegiate football. They were led by Frank Maloney in his seventh and last of seven seasons as head coach of the Syracuse Orangemen. SU had a losing season under Maloney this year of 5-6-0 in the team's first season in the Carrier Dome. Maloney picked Jim Collins, Joe Morris & Dave Warner to be team captains for 1980. At the conclusion of the season, head coach Frank Maloney resigned, with a record of 32–46 after seven seasons.

In the season opener on Sept 13 at Earle Bruce's Ohio State team in Ohio Stadium, Columbus, OH, SU lost L (12-31) before 86.205. On Sept 20, at home, Syracuse beat Miami (OH) at the Carrier Dome, on the campus of Syracuse University in Syracuse, NY W (36-24). On Sept 27 at home SU defeated Northwestern W (42–21) before 34,739. On Oct 4, at home on my wedding anniversary, SU defeated Kansas L (8–23) before 43,126 in the new dome. On Oct 11 at home, SU beat Temple W (31–7) before 36,485.

On Oct 18 at #12 Penn State's Beaver Stadium in University Park, PA PSU defeated SU L (7–24) before 84,790. On Oct 25 at home, Syracuse defeated Rutgers W (17–9) before 39,937 fans. On Nov1 at home, SU was defeated by #11 Pitt in a rout L (6–43) before 50,243 fans.

On Nov 8 at home SU was defeated by Navy in a nail-biter L (3–6) before 50,350 fans. On Nov 15, at Boston College's Alumni Stadium, Chestnut Hill, MA the Eagles defeated the Orangemen L (16–27) before 22,000. In the final game of the season on Nov 22, SU finished off well with a win W (20-7) at West Virginia's Mountaineer Field in Morgantown, WV before 34,441 fans.

Chapter 10 Dick Macpherson 1981 to 1990

Coach Dick MacPherson #24

Year	Coach	Record	Conf
1981	Dick MacPherson	4-6-1	Ind
1982	Dick MacPherson	2-9-0	Ind
1983	Dick MacPherson	6-5-0	Ind
1984	Dick MacPherson	6-5-0	Ind
1985	Dick MacPherson	7-5-0	Ind
1986	Dick MacPherson	5-6-0	Ind
1987	Dick MacPherson	11-0-1	Ind
1988	Dick MacPherson	10-2-0	Ind
1989	Dick MacPherson	8-4-0	Ind
1990	Dick MacPherson	7-4-2	Ind

Famous Coaches (From the Past) by SWC75.

AD Crouthamel remembered **Dick MacPherson** who had beaten his Dartmouth teams twice when coaching at Massachusetts. That was before Division 1AA and Dartmouth was considered a major college team while UMASS was a small college team. Before that, he'd been Maryland's defensive backfield coach back in 1966 when SU's Jim Del Gaizo threw a record-tying four TD passes in a 28-7 win. MacPherson also had pro experience as an assistant coach for the

Denver Broncos and Cleveland Browns. In fact, he was the Brown's linebacker coach when Jake hired him to be the new Syracuse coach.

1981 Dick MacPherson Coach # 24

Dick MacPherson, resurrected the declining football program at Syracuse University—the decade you just read about from the Maloney years—and after the "Great Coaches" primer above, you are about to read about how Big Mac returned Syracuse Football to national prominence. MacPherson was head coach of the Syracuse Orangemen between 1981 and 1990. He posted a record of 66-46-4. After the team finished 5-6 in 1986, MacPherson took Syracuse on a magical run in which the Orangemen were 36-10 including an 11-0-1 mark in 1987 that included a berth in the Sugar Bowl and a fling with the national championship.

The 1981 Syracuse Orangemen football team competed in their ninety-second season of intercollegiate football. They were led by Frank Maloney in his first of ten seasons as head coach of the Syracuse Orangemen. SU had a losing season under MacPherson this year of 4-6-1 in the team's second season in the Carrier Dome. Syracuse had developed a culture of losing and it took a few years for MacPherson to turn it around. MacPherson picked Ike Bogosian & Joe Morris to be team captains for 1981.

On Sept 5, in the home and season opener Rutgers defeated Syracuse in a nail-biter L (27-29) at the Carrier Dome, on the campus of Syracuse University in Syracuse, NY before 38,715. On Sept 12 at Temple in Veterans Stadium, Philadelphia, PA SU lost another L (19–31) before 15,091. Then, on Sept 19 at Illinois Memorial Stadium in Champaign, IL, SU suffered their third loss in a row, L (14–17) before 57,579. Back at the Carrier Dome on Sept 26, SU picked up win # 1 v Indiana before 32,060.

Then it was off on Oct 3 to Maryland's Byrd Stadium, College Park, MD, as the Terrapins and Orangemen played to a tie T (17-17) before 32,000. On Oct 17, at home, Syracuse lost to #2 ranked Penn State L (16-41). The following week on Oct 24 , SU played # 2 Pitt at Pitt Stadium in Pittsburgh, PA and were beaten by the Panthers L (10–23) before 50,330. On Oct 31, SU began playing Colgate again and defeated the Red Raiders at home in the Carrier Dome W (47–24) before 40,309

On Nov 7 at Navy in Navy–Marine Corps Memorial Stadium, in Annapolis, MD, the Midshipmen had their way L (23–35) before 23,355. On Nov 14 at home in the Carrier Dome, Syracuse defeated Boston College W (27-24) before 35,623. In the last game of the season on Nov 21, Syracuse pulled off a close win at home against West Virginia in the Carrier Dome W (27–24) before 33,117

1982 Dick MacPherson Coach # 24

The 1982 Syracuse Orangemen football team competed in their ninety-third season of intercollegiate football. They were led by Dick MacPherson in his second of ten seasons as head coach of the Syracuse Orangemen. SU had a losing season of three under MacPherson this year -- 2-9-0 in the team's third season in the Carrier Dome. Syracuse had developed a culture of losing and would break away from this affliction in the next year. MacPherson would turn it around. MacPherson picked Gerry Feehery to be team captain for 1982.

Games of the 1982 Season

On Sept 4, in the season opener at Rutgers in Giants Stadium, East Rutherford, NJ, SU won W (31–8) before 20,890. Then, on Sept 11, SU lost to Temple in a close match L (18-23) in the home opener at the Carrier Dome, on the campus of Syracuse University in Syracuse, NY before 29, 574. On Sept 18 at home, SU was defeated by Illinois in a blowout L (10-47). Then, on Sept 25 at Indiana Memorial Stadium in Bloomington, IN, SU lost a close on L (10–17) before 42,020

On Oct 2 at home Syracuse was beaten by the Maryland Terrapins at the Carrier Dome L (3–26) before 30,214. Then, on Oct 16 at #8 Penn State's Beaver Stadium in University Park, PA, the Nittany Lions bested the Orangemen L (7–28) before 84,762. The next loss came in an outing on Oct 23 at home against #2 ranked Pittsburgh.

The Panthers won the game in a low-scoring shutout L (0–14) before 42,321 at the Carrier Dome. On Oct 30 in another Carrier Dome experience, SU grabbed win # 2 against the Colgate Red Raiders W (49-15)

On Nov 6 at home, SU lost a close match to Navy at the Carrier Dome L (18–20) before 43,443. The following week on Nov 13 at Boston College's Alumni Stadium in Chestnut Hill, MA, Syracuse lost another close game L (13–20). Still in its losing way as the MacPherson injection had not yet taken hold yet, on Nov 20 at #16 West Virginia Mountaineer Field Morgantown, WV SU lost its last game of its worst season under Dick MacPherson L (0–26) before 48,456.

1983 Dick MacPherson Coach # 24

The 1983 Syracuse Orangemen football team competed in their ninety-fourth season of intercollegiate football. They were led by Dick MacPherson in his third of ten seasons as head coach of the Syracuse Orangemen. SU had its first winning season under its newest coach, MacPherson this year–6-5-0 in the team's fourth season in the Carrier Dome.

Before Coach MacPherson, SU had unfortunately gotten accustomed to losing year-in and year-out and this year, after two dismal seasons, the new coach would break them away from this pattern this year. He was the new ingredient that SU needed, and he turned the program and the attitudes around. Nothing in life worth doing is easy and it was not easy, but the positive signs were beginning to show. MacPherson picked Blaise Winter & Brent Ziegler, standout team players to be team captains for 1983.

On Sept 2, in the season opener at Temple, in a game played at Franklin Field in Philadelphia, Syracuse lost L (6–17) before 11,549 fans. Then, on Sept 10, SU beat Kent State W (22-10) in the home opener at the Carrier Dome, on the campus of Syracuse University in Syracuse, NY before 24, 605. On Sept 17 at home, SU beat Northwestern in a shutout W (35-0). On Sept 24, at home, Syracuse defeated Rutgers at the Carrier Dome W (17–13), Moving to October, on the first day of the new month, before 76,382 fans at #1 ranked Nebraska's Memorial Stadium in Lincoln, NE, Syracuse took a shellacking from the Cornhuskers L (7–63).

On Oct 8 at #16 ranked Maryland's Byrd Stadium in College Park, MD, the Terrapins got the best of the Orangemen L (13–34) before 43,700. Then, on Oct 15 at home, Penn State beat Syracuse in the Carrier Dome L (6–17) before a packed crowd of 50,010. On Oct 29, at Pittsburgh's Pitt Stadium in Pittsburgh, PA, in a close rivalry match, the Panthers won against the Orangemen L (10–13) before 52,374.

On Nov 5 at Navy, in the Navy–Marine Corps Memorial Stadium, Annapolis, MD, Syracuse nudged Navy W (14–7) before 22,009. On Nov 12, #13 at home, Syracuse engaged Boston College in the Carrier Dome and defeated the Eagles W (21–10) before 41,225. Finishing up the season with a nice win against rival West Virginia at home in the Carrier Dome, Syracuse took the win W (27–16) before 36,661

1984 Dick MacPherson Coach # 24

The 1984 Syracuse Orangemen football team competed in their ninety-fifth season of intercollegiate football. They were led by Dick MacPherson in his fourth of ten seasons as head coach of the Syracuse Orangemen. SU had its second winning season under its newest coach, MacPherson this year–6-5-0 in the team's fifth season in the Carrier Dome. MacPherson picked Marty Chalk, Jaime Covington, Jim Gorzalski & Jamie Kimmel to be the team captains for 1984.

Games of the 1984 season

On Sept 8, in the season opener at Maryland's Byrd Stadium in College Park, MD Syracuse got the win over the Terrapins W (23–7) before 38,850. On Sept 15 at Northwestern's Dyche Stadium in Evanston, IL, Syracuse pulled out a close victory W (13–12) before 23,199Then, on Sept 22, SU lost to Rutgers L (0-19), the State University of New Jersey, in the home opener at the Carrier Dome, on the campus of Syracuse University in Syracuse, NY before 41,810.

Highlight Syracuse Knocks off #1 Nebraska

On Sept 29 at home, Syracuse knocked off then ranked #1 Nebraska at the Carrier Dome W (17–9) before 47,280.

Yes, Dick Macpherson could show great emotion at the right times

It was September 29, 1984, when a tough Syracuse squad knocked off #1 Nebraska 17-9 in Dick MacPherson's fourth year. The performance helped quell any concerns about MacPherson's job security and catapulted the Orange forward to bigger things ahead under the legendary coach.

It also remarkably reversed a 63-7 result from the season before. The winning score was ultimately a 40-yard touchdown pass from Todd Norley to Mike Siano. Many of the players from that team point to the opening kickoff as the key, when SU linebacker Derek Ward decked Nebraska fullback Tom Rathman and knocked him out of the game. Those were the days, my friend.

There was little reason to believe that the SU football team stood a chance on that September Saturday in the Carrier Dome. Nebraska was the No. 1-ranked team in the country, favored by 25 points, and had defeated SU the year before 63-7. But this game turned out to be the biggest shocker in Orange football history.

Nebraska scored twice: a touchdown in the first quarter and a safety in the final seconds of the game. In between, Orange quarterback Todd Norley threw a spectacular 40-yard pass to Mike Siano, who out-jumped two Huskers at the goal line for a touchdown. Later, with just 1:29 left at the Nebraska 1-yard line, SU fullback Harold Gayden got the ball and carried it straight into the end zone. The game ended with SU's 17-9 victory over Nebraska; its first win against a top-ranked team in the history of its program.

After the momentous upset, fans swarmed onto the field and celebrated for more than an hour, with SU players coming back out for a curtain call. Yes, those were the days, my friend.

Continuing the 1984 Season Games

On Oct 6 at Florida at Florida Field in Gainesville, FL, SU lost to the Gators L (0–16) before 70,189. On Oct 13 at West Virginia's Mountaineer Field in Morgantown, WV, SU lost in this annual rivalry game L (10–20) before 57,741. On Oct 20 at #19 Penn State at Beaver Stadium in University Park, PA, the Orangemen took a defeat L (3–21) before 85,860 fans. On Oct 27 at home v Army at the Carrier Dome, Syracuse defeated the Cadets in a tough match W (27–16) before 41,438

On Nov 3 at home, Syracuse beat Pittsburgh in the Carrier Dome W (13–7) before 46,489. On Nov 10, at home, Syracuse beat Navy at the Carrier Dome in a nice shutout W (29-0) before 44,000. Then in the season close this year on Nov 17, the #13 Boston College Eagles got the best of the Syracuse Orangemen at Sullivan Stadium in Foxborough, MA L (16–24) before 60,890.

1985 Dick MacPherson Coach # 24

The 1985 Syracuse Orangemen football team competed in their ninety-sixth season of intercollegiate football. They were led by Dick MacPherson in his fifth of ten seasons as head coach of the Syracuse Orangemen. SU had its second winning season under its newest coach, MacPherson this year–7-5-0 in the team's sixth season in the Carrier Dome. MacPherson picked Tim Green & Rudy Reed to be the team captains for 1985. Syracuse finished with a 7–4 regular season record and played in the 1985 Cherry Bowl against Maryland, where they lost, 18–35. Throughout their history, SU has had a problem winning bowl games.

Notable players on this year's team included captain Tim Green, who earned unanimous All-American honors at defensive tackle and was a finalist for the Lombardi Award. Green was drafted 17th overall in the 1986 NFL Draft, ending his career at Syracuse as the school's all-time leader in sacks with 45.5, a record that he still owns.

On Sept 14, in the season opener at Mississippi State's Scott Field in Starkville, MS SU lost L (3–30) On Sept 21 in the home opener at the Carrier Dome, on the campus of Syracuse University in Syracuse, NY before 29,822, SU shut out Kent State W (34-0) before 29,822. On Sept 28 at Virginia Tech at Lane Stadium in Blacksburg, VA, SU lost to the Hokies L (14–24) before 33,400 fans. Then, on Oct 5 at home against Louisville in the Carrier Dome, SU blanked the Cardinals W (48–0) before 26,922

On Oct 19 at home, #6 Penn State barely got by the Orangemen L (20–24) before a packed Dome of 50,021. On Oct 26 at home, Syracuse defeated Temple at the Carrier Dome W (29–14) before 45,391. On Nov 2 at Pittsburgh's Pitt Stadium in Pittsburgh, PA, Syracuse beat the panthers in a close match W (12–0) before 25,500

Then, on Nov 9 at Navy in the Navy–Marine Corps Memorial Stadium, Annapolis, MD, Syracuse beat the Midshipmen W (24–20) before 25,049.

On Nov 16 at home, Syracuse beat the Eagles of Boston College in the Carrier Dome W (21–21) before 45,790. Then, on Nov 23 at Rutgers in Rutgers Stadium, Piscataway, NJ, the Orangemen defeated the Scarlet Knights W (31–14) before 19,685 fans. Then, in the final game of the 1985 season on Nov 30 at home in the Carrier Dome, SU lost to West Virginia in a close match in the annual rivalry, L (10–13) before 33,431.

Cherry Bowl 1985

This was the first seven-game win season since before Frank Maloney and it earned the Orangemen a berth in the Pontiac, MI(Cherry Bowl) held on December 21 in the Pontiac Silverdome vs. the #20 Maryland Terrapins, a team no stranger to the Syracuse Orangemen. This game, the Terrapins had the oomph to finish off the Orangemen L (18–35).

1986 Dick MacPherson Coach # 24

The 1986 Syracuse Orangemen football team competed in their ninety-seventh season of intercollegiate football. They were led by Dick MacPherson in his sixth of ten seasons as head coach of the Syracuse Orangemen. SU had its third losing season under McPherson this year–5-6-0 in the team's seventh season in the Carrier Dome. MacPherson picked Pete Ewald, Jim Leible & Tim Pidgeon to be the team captains for 1986. Syracuse finished with an OK record, but it was not good enough for a bowl invitation.

On Sept 6, in the season and home opener at the Carrier Dome, on the campus of Syracuse University in Syracuse, NY before 34,212, SU lost by a TD to Mississippi State L (17-24). On Sept 13 at Army's Michie Stadium in West Point, NY, the Cadets beat the Orangemen L (28–33) before a packed house of 38,822 On Sept 20 at home, SU was defeated by Virginia Tech at the Carrier Dome Syracuse, NY L

(17–26) before 33,400. On Sept 27 at home, Syracuse was beaten by Rutgers at the Carrier Dome L (10–16).

On Oct 4, my wedding anniversary, at home, Syracuse defeated Missouri in a nice match W (41–9) before 41,035. On Oct 18 at #6 Penn State in the rivalry game at Beaver Stadium in University Park, PA, the Nittany Lions defeated Syracuse in a rout L (3–42) before 85,512. On Oct 25 at Temple in a tight game played at Veterans Stadium in Philadelphia, PA, SU barely beat the Owls, W (27–24) 19,422

Nov 1 at home Syracuse defeated Pittsburgh at the Carrier Dome before 34, 114 W (24–20). Again at home at the Carrier Dome the following week on Nov 8 SU squeaked out a nice win against Navy W (31–22) before 36,796 fans. On Nov 15 at Boston College's Alumni Stadium in the rivalry played this year in Chestnut Hill, MA, the Eagles got the best of the Orangemen L (9–27) before 32,000. In the last game of the season SU traveled to West Virginia to take on the Mountaineers in the rivalry game held at Mountaineer Field in Morgantown, WV(Rivalry). SU came home with the win W 34–23 before 40,106 fans.

Despite a tough record this season, Dick MacPherson had found his niche at Syracuse and the word on the street and beyond is that if he wanted more than the four years he put in, ending in 1990, he could have had that and more. Next year is the kind of up and down year SU fans have become accustomed to but regardless of the emotional roller coaster at the end of the season. 1987 would be one of the best in SU history. I can't wait to tell you about it.

1987 Dick MacPherson Coach # 24

The 1987 Syracuse Orangemen football team competed in their ninety-eighth season of intercollegiate football. They were led by Dick MacPherson in his seventh of ten seasons as head coach of the Syracuse Orangemen. SU had its best season under McPherson this year–11-0-1 in the team's eighth season in the Carrier Dome. MacPherson picked Paul Frase, Ted Gregory & QB Don McPherson to be the team captains for 1987. What a year! Syracuse finished with a great record, and got a great bowl invitation but, suffered a season destroying tie against Auburn in the Sugar Bowl in what otherwise was a great game.

On the positive side in such a positive year, the 11 wins by the Orangemen matched the school record set by the national champion 1959 team, and their 4th-ranked finish in the AP Poll was the first ranked finish since 1961. When great things happen, there should be no misgivings but then again there are guys like me and many others who wonder whether SU could have found just one more point somehow in that game.

Games of the 1987 Season

On Sept 5, in the season and home opener at the Carrier Dome, on the campus of Syracuse University in Syracuse, NY before 35,234, SU defeated Maryland in a great opening match W (35-11). The Orangemen were off. On Sept 12 at Rutgers in Rutgers Stadium, Piscataway, New Jersey, SU fought hard for the win against a fine team W (20–3) On Sept 19at home against Miami (OH) in the Carrier Dome, the Orangemen were undaunting in pursuing victory this game and this whole year W (24–10) before 33,838.

On Sept 26, SU traveled to play Virginia Tech at Lane Stadium in Blacksburg, VA and the Orangemen came home with a fine win W (35–21) against the Hokies finest before 33,300.On Oct 3 at Missouri Memorial Stadium in Columbia, Missouri, the Orangemen got the best of the Tigers W (24–13) before 36,773.

Highlight: PSU v Syracuse – A game for the ages

In a number of the prior years in the PSU v SU rivalry, always top-ranked under Joe Paterno, Penn State had been having its way with the Orange prior to 1987. This year would call a pause to the Nittany Lions onslaught over the years on the Orangemen. On Oct 17, another high ranked Penn State team (#10) came into the Carrier Dome ready to rip apart an always struggling but this year a ranked #13 Syracuse squad. Penn State did its best as always but there was so much might on the SU side that it was impossible for the Nittany Lions to not give up 48 points against the Orangemen. The game ended W (48–21) before a max sellout crowd at the Carrier Dome 50,011 fans. It was a great standing room only game

It happened on Oct. 17, 1987

Syracuse's 48-21 home destruction of No. 10 Penn State, the defending national champions, highlighted Syracuse's unbeaten season in 1987. The Orange came in ranked No. 13 and would climb as high as No. 4 before tying Auburn in the Sugar Bowl and finishing without a loss. Syracuse had lost 42-3 at Penn State the previous year. Don McPherson completed 15 of 20 passes for a school-record (at the time) 336 yards. He opened the game with an 80-yard touchdown pass to Rob Moore. It is one of just two unbeaten seasons in school history.

On Oct 24 Colgate played #9 SU at home in the Carrier Dome and were beaten in a blowout W (52-6) before 48,097. Then, on Oct 31 at Pittsburgh, #8 SU defeated the Panthers at Pitt Stadium, Pittsburgh PA W (24–10) before 52,714. An always tough Navy squad pulled out all the stops but could not stop the onslaught of the 1987 #8 Syracuse Orangemen on Nov 7 at Navy at the Navy–Marine Corps Memorial Stadium in Annapolis, Maryland W (34–10).

On Nov 14 Boston College faced # 6 nationally ranked SU at home in the Carrier Dome and were defeated W (45–17) before 49,866. On

Highlight A perfect regular season for Syracuse

Nov 21 #6 SU defeated West Virginia in the Carrier Dome W in the closest game of the regular season W (32–31) before 49,866

This highlight game, one of the best in SU history occurred on Nov. 21, 1987. This is the only Syracuse win over an unranked opponent that would be included in highlight games. This was a critical game in Syracuse history, as well as a 32-31 thriller over West Virginia.

The victory clinched a perfect 1987 regular season and sent the Orange off to face Auburn in the Sugar Bowl. Syracuse trailed by a touchdown with less than two minutes left but got a touchdown connection from Don McPherson to Pat Kelly, then a two-point conversion option run from Michael Owens to win the game. Sadly, Pat Dye wouldn't make the same choice in New Orleans, settling for a tie.

The 1988 Sugar Bowl

On January, 1988, #4 ranked Syracuse took on # 6 ranked Auburn at the Louisiana Superdome in New Orleans, Louisiana in this year's Sugar Bowl. The team's played tough to a tie T (16–16) before 75,495. In eight more years, the rules would change. The rules were changed to their current format in 1996. Instead of ties, on the average, about 32 college games go into overtime every year.

1988 Dick MacPherson Coach # 24

The 1988 Syracuse Orangemen football team competed in their ninety-ninth season of intercollegiate football. They were led by Dick MacPherson in his eighth of ten seasons as head coach of the Syracuse Orangemen. SU had its second-best season under McPherson this year–10-2-0 in the team's ninth regular season in the Carrier Dome. MacPherson picked Daryl Johnston & Markus Paul to be the team captains for 1988. Another fine year! Syracuse finish with a great record. They got another great bowl invitation to the 1989 Hall of Fame bowl where they defeated LSU.

On Sept 3, in the season and home opener at the Carrier Dome, on the campus of Syracuse University in Syracuse, NY before 35,234, SU defeated Temple in a great opening match W (31-21). The Orangemen were off again. Unfortunately, the joy would ring out only until the following week on September 10 at Ohio State's huge Ohio Stadium in Columbus, OH as the Buckeyes defeated the Orangemen L (9–26) before 89,768. With an extra week to sweat out the loss to OSU, on Sept 24 at home, the Orangemen got their game together well enough to shut out the Hokies of Virginia Tech at the Carrier Dome W (35–0) before 41,118. Then, on Oct 1, at home, SU defeated Maryland W (20-9).

Remaining Games of the 1988 Season

On Oct 8 at home, SU defeated Rutgers W (34-20) before 48, 798. Then on Oct 15 at Penn State's Beaver Stadium in University Park, PA, SU beat the Nittany Lions W (24–10) before 85,916. On Oct 22 #19 SU defeated East Carolina at Ficklen Memorial Stadium, Greenville, NC W (38–14) before 16,450. Then, at home on Nov 5, the Orangemen beat Navy W (49-21). On Nov 12, #15 SU defeated Boston College at Alumni Stadium in Chestnut Hill, MA W (45–20) before 32,000.

Then, on Nov 19 at # 4 West Virginia, the #14 Orangemen were defeated by the Mountaineers L (9-31) before 65,127. Then, in the season closer at home in the carrier Dome, on Dev 3, Syracuse defeated Pittsburgh W (24-0) before49,860

Hall of Fame Bowl

On January 2 #17 Syracuse tangled with #16 LSU inside Tampa Stadium in Tampa, FL in the Hall of Fame Bowl. The Orangemen beat the Tigers W (23–10) before 49,860. The Orangemen finished #12 for the season.

Syracuse 23, Louisiana State 10
January 2, 1989
Tampa, Florida

Dick MacPherson had the Syracuse program screaming. So, it was natural that for the second straight season the Orangemen reached double figures in wins, culminated by dumping Southeastern Conference co-champion Louisiana State 23-10 in the third Hall of Fame Bowl at Tampa.

The Orange took the opening kickoff and went 80 yards, capped off by Robert Drummond's two-yard touchdown. Drummond ended his SU career in style, winning MVP honors with 122 yards and two touchdowns on 23 carries. David Holmes was the defensive star for the Orange, intercepting two passes, breaking up two more and coming up with six solo tackles. Daryl Johnston added 74 yards and Todd Philcox completed 16 of 23 passes for 130 yards and a TD.

Rob Moore had six catches for 56 yards. It was a great day for Syracuse. The SU defense was led by Terry Wooden and Rob Burnett, allowed the Tigers just 76 yards rushing. Dan Bucey had a game-high 10 tackles.

1989 Dick MacPherson Coach # 24

The 1989 Syracuse Orangemen football team competed in their one hundredth season of intercollegiate football. They were led by Dick MacPherson in his ninth of ten seasons as head coach of the Syracuse Orangemen. SU had its second-best season under McPherson this year–8-4-2 in the team's tenth regular season in the Carrier Dome. MacPherson picked Blake Bednarz, Dan Bucey, Rob Burnett, Michael Owens & Terry Wooden to be the team captains for 1989.

It was another fine year of football for Syracuse. As noted, the team finished with an 8–4-0 record and played in the 1989 Peach Bowl, where they beat Georgia, 19–18. They also played a regular season game in Tokyo, Japan, in the Coca-Cola Classic against Louisville.

On Sept 9, in the season opener at Temple, #14 ranked Syracuse defeated the Owls at Veterans Stadium in Philadelphia, PA in a blowout W 43–3 before 20,150. On Sept 16, in the home opener at the Carrier Dome, on the campus of Syracuse University in Syracuse, NY before 48,331, Syracuse barely got by a tough Army squad, W (10-3)

On Sept 23 at #13, the #10 ranked Orangemen lost to Pittsburgh at Pitt Stadium in Pittsburgh, PA L (23–30) before 45,762. On Oct 7 at home in the Carrier Dome, #17 Syracuse was beaten by #22 Florida State in a close match L (10–41) before 49,832. On Oct 14, at home, unranked Syracuse lost to #23 Penn State at the Carrier Dome L (12–34) before a packed house of 49,876

On Oct 21, at Rutgers, in Rutgers Stadium, Piscataway, NJ, Syracuse defeated the Scarlet Knights W (49–28) before 29,276. On Oct 28, at home in the Carrier Dome, Syracuse defeated East Carolina in a very tight match W (18–16) before 48,731. Again, at the Carrier Dome for a home game on Nov, Syracuse defeated the Eagles of Boston College W (23–11). Then, on Nov 11 at Navy at the Navy–Marine Corps Memorial Stadium in Annapolis, MD, the Orangemen defeated the Midshipmen W (38–17).

On Nov 23, SU lost another home game at the Carrier Dome—this one against #17 West Virginia L (17–24). In a special tribute game overseas, the Coca Cola Classic, SU defeated Louisville in the Tokyo, Tokyo, Japan W (24–13) before 50,000. SU finished the regular season 7-4-0.

The Peach Bowl

On December 30, one day before New Year's Eve, unranked Syracuse defeated unranked Georgia in the Peach Bowl in Atlanta, GA in a one point match W (19–18) before 44,911 stadium fans giving the Orangemen full record of 8-7 for 1989.

Syracuse 19, Georgia 18
December 30, 1989
Atlanta, Georgia

The newly Macpherson-invigorated Syracuse Orangemen found themselves in their third consecutive bowl season and they produced a spectacular come-from-behind, 19-18 victory over Georgia. John Biskup finished off a wild SU rally with a 26-yard field goal with just 25 seconds remaining. The Orange defense held Georgia to four first downs and 84 total yards in the second half.

SU trailed 18-7 before quarterback Mark McDonald came off the bench to replace Bill Scharr. McDonald guided SU to a 32-yard Biskup field goal to close the third quarter. Clutch running by game MVP Michael Owens (116 yards) and crisp passing by McDonald brought the Orange within striking distance. A 19-yard pass to Rob Moore cut the Bulldogs' lead to 18-16 with just a bit more than 10 minutes remaining. A potential game-tying conversion attempt fell incomplete.

SU began its final drive from its own 27 with 3:37 left. After moving to its own 43-yard line, the Orange faced a fourth and five.

McDonald then hit Owens down the sideline for 29 yards and a crucial first down to set up Biskup's game-winning field goal. It was a great victory for the Orangemen.

1990 Dick MacPherson Coach # 24

The 1990 Syracuse Orangemen football team competed in their one hundred-first season of intercollegiate football. They were led by Dick MacPherson in his tenth and last of ten seasons as head coach of the Syracuse Orangemen. SU had its third best season under McPherson this year–7-4-2. MacPherson picked John Flannery, Duane Kinnon, Gary McCummings & Rob Thomson to be the team captains for 1990. It was another fine year of football for Syracuse. With their season record of 6-4-2, the team was invited and played in the 1990 Aloha Bowl and shut out Arizona W (28-0)

This season marked the end of two eras for Syracuse football. First, it was Dick MacPherson's final year as head coach. He would leave to coach the 1991 New England Patriots. Second, it was the final season for Syracuse football as an independent. Starting with the 1991 season, the Big East Conference, of which Syracuse was a founding member, began sponsoring football competition.

In the first ever August football game in Syracuse football history, on Aug 31, in the season opener against USC at Giants Stadium in East Rutherford, New Jersey for the Raycom Kickoff Classic # VIII, Syracuse could not find what it needed and the Orangemen were defeated by the Trojans L (16–34) before 57,293. On Sept 8, in the home opener at the Carrier Dome, on the campus of Syracuse University in Syracuse, NY before 38,925, Syracuse had a difficult time in beating a tough Temple squad W (19-9). On Sept 15 in a rare night game at home, SU tied #19 Michigan State in the Carrier Dome T (23–23) before 49,822.

More games from 1990

On Sept 22 at home, Syracuse tied #25 Pittsburgh at the Carrier dome before 47, 996 T (20–20). Then on Oct 6 at Vanderbilt in

Vanderbilt Stadium, Nashville, Tennessee, the Orangemen defeated the Commodores, W 49–14 before 30,037. On Oct 13 at Penn State's Beaver Stadium, University Park, Pennsylvania, the Orangemen lost to the Nittany Lions in a close match L (21–27) before 86,002. On Oct 20 12:00 at home, the Orangemen shut-out the Scarlet Knights of Rutgers at the Carrier Dome Syracuse, New York, W (42–0) before 49,521. Then on Oct 27 at Army's Michie Stadium in West Point, New York, Syracuse beat the Cadets W (26–14) before a packed house of 41,153.

On Nov 3 at Boston College's Alumni Stadium in Chestnut Hill, Massachusetts, the Orangemen whipped the Eagles, W (35–6) before 32,213. Then, on Nov10, at home, The Green Wave of Tulane defeated the Orangemen in a very close match at the Carrier Dome L (24-26). On Nov 17 at West Virginia's Mountaineer Field in Morgantown, West Virginia, Syracuse prevailed W (31–7) before 44,669 fans. On Saturday, Nov 24 during Thanksgiving weekend, SU lost a big game against #2 Miami (FL) at the Miami Orange Bowl in Miami L (7–33) before 66,196.

The Aloha Bowl

On Christmas Day, December 25, 1990 at 3:30 PM, Syracuse squared off against Arizona in Aloha Stadium, Honolulu, Hawaii in the Aloha Bowl.). The Orangemen shut out the Wildcats W (28-0) before 32,217 while basking in the glow and the physical warmth of our nation's 50th state.

Lots more than the game was going on in Hawaii on Dec. 25, 1990. Syracuse snapped the Arizona Wildcats' 214-game scoring streak, the second-longest in NCAA history, with a 28-0 victory. Arizona hadn't been shut out since a 31-0 loss to Arizona State in 1971.

SU Quarterback Marvin Graves was voted Syracuse's most valuable player after running for two scores and throwing for two more TDs. Cornerback Todd Burden, with two interceptions and a forced fumble, was chosen the player of the game for Arizona (7-5).

Dick MacPherson moves on

The 1990 season at Syracuse was the last for Dick Macpherson. He could have coached as long as he wanted but he was ready to try his hand at professional football.

Those who have been reading this book like a book rather than using it as a reference know that the Syracuse University football team enjoyed few winning seasons during the 1970s. Then came Dick MacPherson followed immediately by Paul Pasqualoni and after twenty-dive years of these two coaches, Syracuse was a national power again.

In that 1970's decade, mostly post Schwartzwalder, the Orange made it to one postseason game. Syracuse defeated McNeese State 31-7 in the Independence Bowl on Dec. 15, 1979.

That was the only bowl game in which a Syracuse team led by head coach Frank Maloney ever played. Mr. Maloney compiled a record of 32-46-3 with the Orange. Syracuse football had definitely fallen on hard times.

And then came Dick MacPherson. He helped the football program regain its prestige, earning a record of 66-46-4 as its head coach for 10 seasons.

Richard F. MacPherson had a wonderful life. died Tuesday at Crouse Hospital in Syracuse at the age of 86. It was less than a year ago from when I began to put this book together--August 8, 2017. Here are some parts of his obituary as they tell nice story about the life of this great man and great coach:

He is survived by his wife, Sandra; his daughters Maureen and Janet; four grandchildren; and many friends and admirers.

He held various coaching positions at several other schools (Illinois, UMass, Cincinnati and Maryland) before arriving at Syracuse. He also served as an assistant coach for the Denver Broncos from 1967 to 1970 and the Cleveland Browns from 1978 to 1980.

Despite the potential, Mr. MacPherson didn't look like he would fare much better when he took over as Syracuse's head coach in 1981 than did his predecessor. His team went 4-6-1 in his first season and a dismal 2-9 in his second season at the helm. Syracuse was a in serious doldrums, and it was not until year three that Macpherson was able to begin the big turnaround. SU went 7-5 in 1985 and lost to Maryland in the Cherry Bowl 35-18.

Many fans turned on Mr. MacPherson in 1986 when, after some big successes, the Orange had a losing season at 5-6. Some of them formed the Sack Mac Pack, creating signs and bumper stickers urging the school to dump the head coach.

But athletic director Jake Crouthamel stuck by his longtime friend. Mr. MacPherson repaid this loyalty by leading the Orange to an undefeated season in 1987 and a No. 4 ranking.

On Jan. 1, 1988, Syracuse tied Auburn 16-16 in the Sugar Bowl. While the score kept the Orange from being beaten that season, the result irked the coach and the school's many fans.

"Of all the games MacPherson coached, the Sugar Bowl tie with Auburn, spoiling an undefeated season, may have rankled him the most. The game ended when coach Pat Dye of Auburn decided to attempt a 30-yard field goal with four seconds left rather than try to win the game with a touchdown," according to an Associated Press story published Wednesday in the New York Times. "The kick was successful, tying the score at 16-16. MacPherson was bitter about the rival coach's call. 'What did they come here for in the first place?' he said. He added, 'I gotta believe his menu was to stop us from being 12-0.'"

Mr. MacPherson left Syracuse after the 1990 season to serve as head coach of the New England Patriots for two years. Paul Pasqualoni succeeded him as the Orange's skipper and continued building the football program's winning tradition. Over 14 seasons, Mr. Pasqualoni compiled a record of 101-59-1 and led the team to nine bowl appearances.

In 2009, Mr. MacPherson was inducted into the College Football Hall of Fame. After retiring from coaching, he became a color commentator for Syracuse football on radio and television. His grandsons Cameron and Mackey both played for the Orange; Mackey is a graduate assistant coach with the team.

Those who knew Mr. MacPherson have lauded his passion for football and his rapport with players. He was an exceptional mentor to many people.

A native of Maine, he returned to Syracuse in retirement to continue his association with the school. He often spent his time in the Thousand Islands area. Dick MacPherson leaves a remarkable legacy, one that still enriches our region.

A full obit below:

Richard "Dick" F. MacPherson, age 86, passed away on August 8, 2017. He died peacefully in Syracuse, New York surrounded by family.

Coach Mac was born in Old Town, Maine on November 4, 1930, to Hugh and Ludovic (Moreau) MacPherson. He was the eleventh of twelve children. He attended Old Town High School, graduating in 1948. After serving in the United States Air Force, Mac graduated from Springfield College, where he played on the football team as a center and linebacker. At Springfield, he met the love of his life, Sandra. They were married in 1958, beginning Mac's 58 years as a loving, devoted husband.

Mac was the head coach of the UMass Minutemen from 1971 to 1977, during which time the team went from a struggling program to winners of the Boardwalk Bowl. He won four Yankee Conference championships and twice earned New England Coach of the Year honors. He then went to the Cleveland Browns, leaving there in 1981 when he accepted the favorite job of his life, head coach of the Syracuse Orangemen.

At Syracuse, Coach Mac's tenure included the 1987 undefeated season, five bowl appearances (four of which he won), and every single Coach of the Year honor given in 1987. Mac was then named head coach of the New England Patriots in 1991. He retired with 111 wins as a college head coach and was inducted into the College Football Hall of Fame in 2009.

To Coach Mac, the most important pillars of life were faith and family. A lifelong Catholic, Mac was known for his rosary beads, daily missals, and warm greetings. He loved golf, bridge, Time magazine, and watching his grandchildren play football, row crew, and cheerlead. More than anything, he loved caring for people and sharing his joyful love with those around him, family and stranger alike.

A proud Mainer with an accent to prove it, Coach Mac came to happily call Syracuse his home. He enthusiastically supported the Salvation Army, the Joslin Diabetes Center, and numerous other community charities. He was thrilled to lead Syracuse's St. Patrick's Day Parade as Grand Marshall in 2010.

Chapter 11 Paul Pasqualoni 1991 to 2004

Coach Paul Pasqualoni #25

Year	Coach	Record	Conf
1991	Paul Pasqualoni	10-2-0	Big East (5-0 #1)
1992	Paul Pasqualoni	10-2-0	Big East (6-1)
1993	Paul Pasqualoni	6-4-1	Big East (3-4)
1994	Paul Pasqualoni	7-4-0	Big East (4-3)
1995	Paul Pasqualoni	9-3-0	Big East (5-2)
1996	Paul Pasqualoni	9-3-0	Big East (6-1)
1997	Paul Pasqualoni	9-4-0	Big East (6-1 #1)
1998	Paul Pasqualoni	8-4-0	Big East (6-1 #1)
1999	Paul Pasqualoni	7-5-0	Big East (3-4)
2000	Paul Pasqualoni	6-5-0	Big East (4-3)
2001	Paul Pasqualoni	10-3-0	Big East (6-1)
2002	Paul Pasqualoni	4-8-0	Big East (2-5)
2003	Paul Pasqualoni	6-6-0	Big East (2-5)
2004	Paul Pasqualoni	6-6-0	Big East (4-2)

Coach Pasqualoni -- A little required fun after a win

Famous Coaches (From the Past) by SWC75.

Ben Schwartzwalder had been offered the job of being the first ever coach of the New England Patriots after the national championship season. When Coach Mac, a New Englander, got the same offer after the 1990 season, he took it. Since we were now a successful program, Jake Crouthamel decided to promote from within and we got our third straight linebacker coach elevated to the status of a head coach, Paul Pasqualoni.

Before coming to Syracuse he'd been a Penn State linebacker, (a Nittany Lion coaching the Orange!), and head coach at Western Connecticut State, a Division III team. He'd inherited a 1-8 squad from 1982 and took them to 9-1 by 1984. In 1985 they went 10-1 and made the DIII playoffs. Mac hired him in 1987. His youth and comparatively brief tenure with the program made him a surprise choice but that put him in a category with Coach Mac and Ben Schwartzwalder. Paul went on to become the 2nd winningest coach in Syracuse history, going 107-59-1.

He got off to a great start, going 10-2 in his first two years, crushing Steve Spurrier's Florida team in 1991 and coming up just short of upsetting #1 Miami in 1992. The 1993 team strangely fell apart, losing consecutive games to Miami and West Virginia by a combined 0-92. That team and the next broke the string of bowl teams at 6 in a row, (none of which we lost) but extended the string of winning seasons.

Then came the Donovan McNabb Era where we were very good but could never quite break through to greatness. We had a 41-0 Gator Bowl blow-out of Clemson, a 34-0 kick-off Classic rout of Wisconsin, ran Michigan out of the Big House, 38-28, (it was 38-7 at one point), and beat Miami back to back by 96-26. Who could imagine that we'd ever do such things?

But it created an intolerance for upset losses and uncompetitive performances, such as the two losses each to East Carolina, North Carolina State and later Rutgers and Temple when they were the dregs of the conference, as well as 0-62 and 7-51 losses at Virginia Tech, 13-45, 0-59 and 7-49 losses to Miami, and in his final season 0-51 to Purdue to open the season and 14-51 to Georgia Tech to close it. Eventually the talent and patience level declined and a new Athletic Director, Dr. Daryl Gross, fired him and brought in his own man, leaving us to argue about what really went wrong ever since.

1991 Paul Pasqualoni Coach # 25

The 1991 Syracuse Orangemen football team competed in their one hundred-second season of intercollegiate football. They were led by Paul Pasqualoni in his first of fourteen seasons as head coach of the Syracuse Orangemen. Coach Mac had left a fine nucleus for Coach Pasqualoni to work with. SU had its best season under its new coach this year and would have a similar 10-2-0 season next year and they were 5-0 in their first year in the Big East. This season matched Coach Mac's second-best season when Syracuse was independent.

Pasqualoni picked Andrew Dees, Mark McDonald, Tim Sandquist & Greg Walker to be the team captains for 1991. It was another fine year of football for Syracuse. With their season record of 10-2-0, the team was invited and played in the Hall of Fame Bowl v Ohio State on January 1.

Two new eras began for Syracuse football in 1991. It was the first season as head coach for Paul Pasqualoni, who was promoted from assistant after Dick MacPherson, who had led the Orangemen for the previous 10 seasons, left to take the head coaching job at the New England Patriots. More important in the long term, this was the first season in which the Big East Conference sponsored football—although the conference would not establish a full round-robin schedule in the sport until the 1993 season.

Syracuse as noted was 5-0 v Big East Teams this year. Miami, the #1 team in the nation was 2-0 in the Big East in 1991. SU and Miami did not play in 1991. Syracuse U was very fortunate after such a great coach as Dick Mac, to find another great one, Paul Pasqualoni. Picking an existing coach does not always work…but it sure worked with P.P.

On Sept 7, in the home opener at the Carrier Dome, on the campus of Syracuse University in Syracuse, NY before 35,541, Syracuse soundly beat a tough Vanderbilt squad W (37-10). On Sept 14 at Maryland, the #22 ranked Orangemen beat the Terrapins at Byrd Stadium in College Park, MD W (31–17) before 41,310.

On Sept 21, at home, #5 Florida engaged # 17 Syracuse in the Carrier Dome and they were defeated in a nice match W (38–21) before a packed house of 49,823.

It was Sept 21, 1991, that SU's Kirby Dar Dar took a handoff on the opening kickoff and reversed the field for a 95-yard touchdown, setting the stage for Syracuse's 38-21 beatdown of Florida. This was the third game in a four-game unbeaten streak to open the year for the Orange. Syracuse was ranked # 18 and climbed into the Top 10 after the win, while Florida came in at #5, Syracuse went on to finish 10-2 and win the Hall of Fame Bowl over Ohio State.

On Sept 28 in a night game at Tulane's Louisiana Superdome in New Orleans, LA, the Orangemen shut out the Green Wave W (24–0) before 19,729.

On Oct 5, #10 SU got to play the #1 ranked team in the nation, Florida State at Doak Campbell Stadium in Tallahassee, FL. The Seminoles were ready for the Orangemen and put them down handily L (14–46) before a nice crowd of 61,231. On Oct 12 at home, #15 ranked SU had not yet shaken in off the big loss and they lost again, this time to unranked East Carolina in a close Carrier Dome match L (20–23) before 37,767. Then, on Oct at #20 Pittsburgh in Pitt Stadium, Pittsburgh, PA, #24 Syracuse got the big win by a small shoe-nail, W (31–27) before 42,707. Then, on Oct 26 at Rutgers in Rutgers Stadium, Piscataway, NJ, #21 Syracuse won another W (21–7) before 30,162.

On Nov 2 at home, Temple came to beat #18th ranked SU at the Carrier Dome but fell to the Orangemen W (27–6) before 46,819. Then, on Nov 16 at home, at noon, Boston College faced off against #17 Syracuse at the Carrier Dome. The Orangemen got the best of the Eagles W (38–16) before 45,453. Then, on Nov 23 at home in the Carrier Dome. Unranked West Virginia got the loss against #16 Syracuse W (16-10). This brought the regular season record to 9-2-0 and SU earned a match in the Hall of Fame Bowl v Ohio State.

1991 Hall of Fame Bowl

On January 1, 1992 at 1:00 PM #16 Syracuse squared off vs. unranked Ohio State at Tampa Stadium in Tampa, FL for the Hall of Fame Bowl game. SU defeated the Buckeyes W (24–17) before 57,789 fans.

Syracuse 24, Ohio State 17
January 1, 1992
Tampa, Florida

Celebrated QB Marvin Graves of Syracuse won bowl MVP honors for the second straight year, leading the Orangemen in its win against Ohio State at the sixth Hall of Fame Bowl in Tampa. Graves, the 1990 Aloha Bowl MVP, completed 18 of 31 passes for a career-high 309 yards. His touchdown passes of 50 yards to Shelby Hill and the 60-yard game-winner to Antonio Johnson, were the two longest pass plays in Hall of Fame Bowl history.

The Orangemen led 14-3 at the half, with Graves accounting for the scoring on a pass to Hill and a three-yard run. SU opened the second half with a 32-yard John Biskup field goal, but the Buckeyes came right back with a touchdown by Carlos Snow to cut the lead to 17-10. Nothing was guaranteed without hard play.

Punter Pat O'Neill had a big day for SU (46.8-yard average), but had a punt blocked with eight minutes to play. This resulted in the ball being recovered by the opposition in the end zone, thus tying the game. It took just two minutes for the Syracuse offense to come up with the big play it needed. Johnson broke free on a play-action pass and Graves hit him for the deciding touchdown. It was a great game indeed. The D put in a great game also.

John Lusardi tallied 11 tackles and George Rooks had seven to lead the SU defense. The Orange sacked Ohio State quarterback Kirk Herbstreit four times.

1992 Paul Pasqualoni Coach # 25

The 1992 Syracuse Orangemen football team competed in their one hundred-third season of intercollegiate football. They were led by Paul Pasqualoni in his second of fourteen seasons as head coach of the Syracuse Orangemen. SU equaled its best season under new coach Pasqualoni this year after a similar 10-2-0 season in 1991. They were 6-1 in their second year in the Big East after a close loss to undefeated Miami.

Pasqualoni picked David Qalker and Geln Young to be the team captains for 1992. It was another fine year of football for Syracuse. With their season record of 10-2-0, the team was invited and played in the Fiesta Bowl v Colorado on January 1.

Games of the 1992 season

On Sept 5 at East Carolina's Ficklen Memorial Stadium in Greenville, North Carolina, the Orangemen defeated the Pirates W (42–21) On Sept 12, in the home opener at the Carrier Dome, on the campus of Syracuse University in Syracuse, NY before 49,238, #9 Syracuse beat a tough Texas team W (31-21). On Sept 19, Ohio State defeated #8 Syracuse at the Carrier Dome L (12–35) before 49,629. On Oct 3, at Louisville's Cardinal Stadium in Louisville, Kentucky, the #17 ranked Orangemen defeated the Cardinals W (15–9) before 37,323.

Then, on Oct 10 at home, #15 Syracuse defeated Rutgers in a high scoring match W (50-28). On October 17 at #24 West Virginia, at Mountaineer Field in Morgantown, West Virginia, for the (Ben Schwartzwalder Trophy), Syracuse beat the Mountaineers W (20-17) On Oct 24 at Temple in a game played at Veterans Stadium in Philadelphia, SU won the day W (38–7) before 11,221. On Oct 31 at home SU beat Pittsburgh at the Carrier Dome W (41–10) before 48,837 On Nov 7, #10 Syracuse beat the Hokies of Virginia Tech at the Carrier Dome W (28–9) in a packed house.

On Nov 14, before 33,298, at #17 Boston College, at Alumni Stadium, Chestnut Hill, Massachusetts #10 SU beat BC in the rivalry match W (27-10). On Nov 21, in its final game the #8 Syracuse Orangemen took their second loss of the season against the

#1 ranked Miami Hurricanes at the Carrier Dome in a very tight game L (10–16) before 49,857

1993 Fiesta Bowl

On January 1, 1993, #6 Syracuse teed off against #10 Colorado in SU n Devil Stadium, Tempe, Arizona in the Fiesta Bowl. Syracuse was becoming a regular bowl game winner and got the win in this game W (26–22) before 70,224.

Syracuse 26, Colorado 22
January 1, 1993
Tempe, Arizona

Marvin Graves was named the Offensive Player of the Game and Kevin Mitchell earned defensive honors as No. 6 Syracuse defeated No. 10 Colorado. Graves, who earned his third straight bowl MVP award, scored on a 28-yard run and led an SU attack that rushed for 201 yards. David Walker led the way with 80 yards on 16 carries and Terry Richardson added 63 yards on seven carries.

1993 Paul Pasqualoni Coach # 25

The 1993 Syracuse Orangemen football team competed in their one hundred-fourth season of intercollegiate football. They were led by Paul Pasqualoni in his third of fourteen seasons as head coach of the Syracuse Orangemen. SU had a winning season 6-4-1 but not at the level of the last several. They were 3-4- in their third year in the Big East. Pasqualoni picked Marvin Graves, Dwayne Joseph, and John Reagan to be the team captains for 1993. Syracuse did not play in a bowl game this year.

On Sept 4, in the home opener at the Carrier Dome, on the campus of Syracuse University in Syracuse, NY before 45,090, #6 ranked Syracuse beat a tough Ball State Team W (35-12). On Sept 9, at East Carolina's Dowdy–Ficklen Stadium in Greenville, NC, the #6 Orangemen defeated the Pirates W (41–22) before 33,055. Then, on Sept 18 at Texas's Texas Memorial Stadium in Austin, TX, SU tied the Longhorns T (21–21) before 65,897. On Sept 25 in a night game at the Carrier Dome, the #12 Orangemen squeaked out a win against Cincinnati W (24–21) before 48,312. Then, in another home match, on Oct 2, #13 Syracuse lost to Boston College L (29-33)

SU no longer had a rivalry with Penn State as Joe Paterno's Nittany Lions gave up independent status and began to play ball this year in the Big 10.

On Oct 16 at Pittsburgh's Pitt Stadium, Pittsburgh, PA #24 SU defeated Pitt W (24–21) before 34,268. On Oct 23 in a blowout, #23 Syracuse was pushed around by #6 Miami at the Miami Orange Bowl in Miami, FL L (0–49) before 63,194. On Oct 30, at home, SU was beaten again in a big shutout—this time by #13 West Virginia in the Ben Schwartzwalder Trophy game L (0–43) before 49,268. On Nov 6. At home SU defeated Temple in a blowout W (52-3).

On Nov 13 Syracuse lost to Virginia Tech at Lane Stadium in Blacksburg, VA L (24–45) before 44,722 fans. On Nov 26 at Rutgers in Giants Stadium, East Rutherford, NJ, the Orangemen beat the Scarlet Knights W (31–8) before 26,101.

1994 Paul Pasqualoni Coach # 25

The 1994 Syracuse Orangemen football team competed in their one hundred-fifth season of intercollegiate football. They were led by Paul Pasqualoni in his fourth of fourteen seasons as head coach of the Syracuse Orangemen. SU had picked up the pace winning one more game than last year -- 7-4-0. They were 4-3- in their fourth year in the Big East. Pasqualoni picked Wilky Bazile, Eric Chenoweth, Dan Conley, and Tony Jones to be the team captains for 1994. Syracuse was not selected for a bowl game this year.

On Sept 3, in the home opener at the Carrier Dome, on the campus of Syracuse University in Syracuse, NY before 45,090, unranked Syracuse was beaten in a one-point nail-biter against #16 ranked Oklahoma L 29-30). On Sept 10 at Cincinnati's Nippert Stadium in Cincinnati SU won W (34–19) before 21,735. On Sept 17 at home in the Carrier Dome, SU won a one-point battle against Rutgers W

(37–36) before 44,925. On Sept 24 at East Carolina's Ficklen Memorial Stadium, Greenville, North Carolina, SU beat the Pirates W (21–18). On October 1 SU beat #14 Virginia Tech W (28-20).

On Oct 8 at home in the Dome, #21 SU beat the Pittsburgh Panthers W (31–7). On Oct 22 at Temple in a game played at Veterans Stadium, SU defeated the Owls W (49–42) before a small crowd of 12,241. On Nov 5 at home, #10 ranked SU lost to #5 ranked Miami at the Carrier Dome L (6–27) before 49,565.

On Nov 12 at #25 Boston College at Alumni Stadium in Chestnut Hill, Massachusetts in the annual rivalry, the Eagles dominated and shutout the Orangemen L (0–31) before 44,500. On Nov 19, at home #24 SU defeated Maryland W (21-16). Then, in the season closer on Nov 24, Thanksgiving day at West Virginia's Mountaineer Field Morgantown, West Virginia, the Mountaineers captured the Ben Schwartzwalder Trophy L (0–13) before 40,369

1995 Paul Pasqualoni Coach # 25

The 1995 Syracuse Orangemen football team competed in their one hundred-sixth season of intercollegiate football. They were led by Paul Pasqualoni in his fifth of fourteen seasons as head coach of the Syracuse Orangemen. SU had picked up the pace again, winning nine games this year 9-3-0. They were 5-2- in their fifth year in the Big East. Pasqualoni picked Cy Ellsworth, Marvin Harrison, and Darrell Parker to be the team captains for 1995. Syracuse was selected for the Gator Bowl this year and they beat Clemson in a blowout shutout.

Games of the 1995 season

On Sept 2 at #20 North Carolina's Kenan Memorial Stadium in Chapel Hill, North Carolina, Syracuse won W (20–9) before 52,400. On Sept 9, in the home opener at the Carrier Dome, on the campus of Syracuse University in Syracuse, NY before 39,547, #22 ranked Syracuse was beaten by a flied goal against unranked East Carolina L 24-27). On Sept 23 at home, Syracuse defeated Minnesota at the Carrier Dome W (27–17) before 42,780. On Sept 30 at Rutgers

Stadium in Piscataway, NJ, SU won W (27–17). On Oct 7, at home, Syracuse defeated Temple W (31–14) before 40,646.

On Oct 14 at home, Syracuse put away Eastern Michigan at the Dome in a high scoring match W (52–24) before 38,902. Then, on Oct 21 at home against West Virginia Syracuse won the Ben Schwartzwalder Trophy W (30–7) before 48,880. On Nov 4 at Virginia Tech in Lane Stadium, Blacksburg, VA, SU lost to the Hokies L (7–31) before 51,239.

On Nov 11 at Pittsburgh's Pitt Stadium in Pittsburgh PA, SU got the win W (42–10) before 20,279. On Nov 18 at home v Boston College, #23 SU beat BC W (58–29) before 49,384. On Nov 25 in a tight match, #22 SU lost to #25 Miami at the Miami Orange Bowl venue in Miami FL L (24–35) before 47,544.

The 1996 Gator Bowl

On January 1, 1996, New Year's Day the Gator Bowl pitted then unranked Syracuse v #23 Clemson in the Gator Bowl game hosted in Jacksonville Municipal Stadium, Jacksonville, Florida. The Orangemen blew out the Tigers in a one-way game W (41-0) before 45,202

Game highlights

Syracuse 41, Clemson 0
January 1, 1996
Jacksonville, Florida

Syracuse fans loved this season finish as it was done in grand style. The Orangemen got credit for the most-lopsided victory of all of the 51 Gator Bowls. SU defeated Clemson, 41-0, in rain-soaked Jacksonville. SU scored early and more often than expected against a typically tough Clemson Tigers team. SU had a 20-0 lead after the first quarter. For Clemson, there was not much to write home about.

1996 Paul Pasqualoni Coach # 25

The 1996 Syracuse Orangemen football team competed in their one hundred-seventh season of intercollegiate football. They were led by Paul Pasqualoni in his sixth of fourteen seasons as head coach of the Syracuse Orangemen. SU had picked up the pace again, winning nine games again this year 9-3-0. They were 6-1 in their sixth year in the Big East. Pasqualoni picked Kevin Abrams, Harvey Pennypacker, and Malcolm Thomas to be the team captains for 1996. Syracuse was selected for the Liberty Bowl this year and they defeated Houston in a nice game. This was four bowl game wins of four played for Pasqualoni.

On Sept 7 in the season and home opener at the Carrier Dome, on the campus of Syracuse University in Syracuse, NY before 48,097, unranked Syracuse was out-muscled by #24 North Carolina's Tar heels L (10-27). On September 21 at Minnesota's Hubert H. Humphrey Metrodome in Minneapolis, MN, the Orangemen lost their second game by two points L (33–35) before 45,756 On Sept 28, back at the Carrier Dome, before 49,069, unranked Syracuse got the win against the Virginia Tech Hokies W (52-21). On Oct 5 at home, SU shut-out Rutgers in the Carrier Dome W (42–0) before 48,112. Then, on Oct 12 at home, SU beat Pitt in a big blowout W (55-7). Syracuse was on a roll.

On Oct 26, continuing the rivalry with Boston College at Alumni Stadium in Chestnut Hill, MA(Rivalry), SU lined up all the chips its way and took the game W (45–17) before 44,500. On Nov 2, at #18 West Virginia's Mountaineer Field in Morgantown, WV for the Ben Schwartzwalder Trophy, Syracuse got the prize W (30–7) before 56,312.

On Nov 9 at Tulane in the Louisiana Superdome, New Orleans, LA the Orangemen defeated the Green Wave W (31–7) before a sparse crowd of 13,537. On Nov 16, at home, a #19 ranked SU team played a reinvigorated #22 Cadets team at the Carrier Dome and defeated Army W (42–17) before 49,257. On Nov 23 at Temple, #16 Syracuse defeated the Owls at Veterans Stadium in Philadelphia, PA W (36015). Always having a tough time with Miami, this year on Nov 30, was no different as the Big East-powered-Hurricanes put out all the stops and in what for them was an away game at the dome. They barely got out with their skins in a close SU loss L (31-38). It could have been different. 49, 426 others thought it should have ended differently.

1996 Liberty Bowl

On December 27 at 3:00 PM, #23 Syracuse engaged Houston in the Liberty Bowl Game in Memphis, TN. Syracuse's eight game streak was preserved in this great win W (30–17) before 49,163

Syracuse 30, Houston 17
December 27, 1996
Memphis, Tennessee

The pundits have written that Syracuse put aside its usual balanced offense and rode its powerful running game to a 30-17 victory in the 1996 St. Jude Liberty Bowl in Memphis. For SU fans, it was as always, the past few years, a thing of beauty.

1997 Paul Pasqualoni Coach # 25

The 1997 Syracuse Orangemen football team competed in their one hundred-eighth season of intercollegiate football. They were led by Paul Pasqualoni in his seventh of fourteen seasons as head coach of the Syracuse Orangemen. SU had a great pace going winning nine games again this year for the third time in a row 9-4-0. They were 6-1 in their seventh year in the Big East. Pasqualoni picked Keith Downing, Donovin Darius, Rod Gadson, and Brad Patkochis to be the team captains for 1997. Syracuse was selected for the Fiesta Bowl and they were defeated by Kansas State in a nice game. This was the first bowl game loss for Pasqualoni out of five tries.

On Aug 24 in the season opener against #24 ranked Wisconsin in Giants Stadium, East Rutherford, New Jersey in the Kickoff Classic, Syracuse shutout the Badgers W (34–0) before 51,185. On Aug 30, in the home opener at the Carrier Dome, on the campus of Syracuse University in Syracuse, NY before 42, 742, #13 Syracuse was slightly out-muscled by North Carolina's Tar Heels by one-point L

(31-32). On Sept 6 at Oklahoma's Oklahoma Memorial Stadium in Norman, Oklahoma, SU lost its second of its first three games L (34–36) before 68,342. On Sept 13 at #22 Virginia Tech in Lane Stadium, Blacksburg, Virginia ESPN the Orangemen record went to 1-3 with the loss L (3–31) to the Hokies before 50,137.

Then, on Sept 20 at home, SU defeated Tulane in the Carrier Dome W (30–19_. On Oct 4, my wedding anniversary, before 44054, the Orangemen pummeled East Carolina W 56–0. Then, on Oct 9 at Rutgers in Rutgers Stadium, Piscataway, New Jersey, the Orangemen racked up another big win W (50–3) before 19,044 subdued fans. Then, on Oct 18 at home against Temple in the Carrier Dome, Syracuse delivered a walloping W (60–7) to the too-complacent Owls.

On Nov 1, #17 West Virginia played SU at the Carrier Dome and were whooped by Syracuse W (40–10) before 49,273. On Nov 8, at home #22 Syracuse defeated a stubborn Boston College team W (20-13) before a packed house of 49,153. On Nov 15 at Pittsburgh un-ranked Pitt were beaten by #19 Syracuse at Pitt Stadium in Pittsburgh, Pennsylvania in the annual rivalry game W 32–27) before 46,102. Then, on Nov 29 playing unranked Miami, the #16 Orangemen got a long-awaited win in Miami, FL at the Orange Bowl from the Hurricanes W 33–13 before 25,147

1997 Fiesta Bowl

On New Year's Eve, December 31, 1997 at 6:00 PM, a ready and able # 14 Syracuse Orangemen Squad faced off against the #10 national squad of Kansas State at SU n Devil Stadium in Tempe, Arizona in the annual Fiesta Bowl game. After winning seven games in a row, Syracuse dropped this game L (18–35) before 69,367.

Summarizing the game, Bishop threw for four touchdown passes, completing a career-high 14 passes for a career-best 317 yards. He was the offensive hero, finishing the game with 390 yards in total offense including 317 yards passing and 73 yards rushing. McDonald caught seven of Bishop's passes for a school-record of 206 yards and three touchdowns. His 77-yard reception in the fourth quarter was the longest in Fiesta Bowl history. Swift caught a career-high five passes for a career-high 98 yards and one touchdown.

QB McNabb was not at his best though he performed well, passing for 271 yards and running for 81 yards. Hiss accuracy was off as he completed just 16 of 39 passes and the rushing attack was not there to bail the QB out of jams. Syracuse's seven-game bowl game win streak had ended.

1998 Paul Pasqualoni Coach # 25

The 1998 Syracuse Orangemen football team competed in their one hundred-ninth season of intercollegiate football. They were led by Paul Pasqualoni in his eighth of fourteen seasons as head coach of the Syracuse Orangemen. SU had a fine season winning eight games against four losses. 8-4-0. They were 6-1 again in their eight year in the Big East. Pasqualoni picked Scott Kiernan, Rob Konrad, Donovan McNabb, and Jason Poles to be the team captains for 1998. Syracuse was selected for the Orange Bowl Fiesta Bowl and they were defeated by Florida in a nice game

On Sept 5 in the season and home opener against #10 ranked Tennessee at the Carrier Dome, on the campus of Syracuse University in Syracuse, NY before 49,550, #17 Syracuse lost by one point in a nail-biter L (33-34). On Sept 12 at #13 Michigan at Michigan Stadium (The Big House) in Ann Arbor, MI, Syracuse beat the Wolverines W (38–28) before the largest crowd to ever attend an SU game--111,012.

On Sept 19 at home Syracuse shellacked Rutgers in a blowout at the Carrier Dome W (70-14). On Oct 1 at NC State's Carter–Finley Stadium in Raleigh, NC. #11 Syracuse could not keep up with the Tar Heels and lost L (17–38) before

On Oct 10 at home, Syracuse beat Cincinnati in a blowout W (63–21) before 47,251. On Oct 17 in a major rivalry game at Boston College's Alumni Stadium in Chestnut Hill, MA, SU defeated the Eagles W (42–25) before 43,413. On Oct 31 at home, #17 Syracuse defeated Pittsburgh's Panthers W (45–28) before 49,012. On Nov 7 at West Virginia's Mountaineer Field in Morgantown, WV, Syracuse lost by a TD L (28–35) before 54,655

On Nov 14 at home, SU defeated Virginia Tech's Hokies in the Carrier Dome in a close match W (28–26) before 49,336. Then, on Nov 21 at Temple in a game played at Veterans Stadium, Philadelphia, PA, the Orangemen beat the Owls W (38–7) before 12,483. On Nov 28, at home, #21 SU pummeled #19 Miami (FL) W (66-13).

1999 Orange Bowl

On January 2, 1999, in the Orange Bowl game, Paul Pasqualoni's #18 ranked Syracuse Orangemen squared off against Steve Spurrier's # 7 Florida Gators at the Miami Orange Bowl field in Miami, FL. The Gators defeated the Orangemen L (10–31) 67,919

Florida 31, Syracuse 10
January 2, 1999
Miami, Florida

This was one of those games where as you replay it, should have gone the Orangemen's way. Donavan McNabb was either hot or not. This day, McNabb was not bad; but he was not hot.

1999 Paul Pasqualoni Coach # 25

The 1999 Syracuse Orangemen football team competed in their one hundred-tenth season of intercollegiate football. They were led by Paul Pasqualoni in his ninth of fourteen seasons as head coach of the Syracuse Orangemen. SU had a winning season again 7-5-0. They were 3-4 in their ninth year in the Big East. Pasqualoni picked Mark Baniewicz, Keith Bulluck, Donald Dinkins, Quinton Spotwood, and Nate Trout to be the team captains for 1999. Syracuse was selected for the Music City Bowl and they defeated Kentucky in a nice game.

On Sept 2 at Toledo in the season opener in the Glass Bowl—a stadium in Toledo, Ohio that was renamed after WWII, (The stadium has many glass components and may very well be a reflection of the Owens Illinois company that was headquartered in Toledo for many, many years.) Syracuse brought home the victory W (35–12) before 27,900. On Sept 11 in the home opener against Central Michigan at the Carrier Dome, on the campus of Syracuse University in Syracuse, NY before 45,563, Syracuse won in a blowout W (47-7).

On Sept 18 at home, SU was beaten by the Michigan Wolverines in a lose match L (13-18). On Sept 25 at home, for the Ben Schwartzwalder Trophy, Syracuse defeated West Virginia, W (30–7) before 44,890. On Oct 2 at home SU defeated the Tulane Green Wave by the score of W (47–17) before 48,286. On Oct 7 in the traditional rivalry game at Pittsburgh's Pitt Stadium in Pittsburgh, SU grabbed a tough victory W (24–17) before 45,455. Then, on Oct 16 at #4 Virginia Tech's Lane Stadium in Blacksburg, Virginia, SU was simply shellacked by the Hokies L (0–62) before 53,130.

Still not recovered from the trouncing from the prior week, at home on Oct 30 Syracuse gave up another loss to Boston College L (23-24) in hard fought close match before 48, 487. On Nov 6 at home SU beat Temple W (27-10). Then on Nov 13 at Rutgers in Rutgers Stadium, Piscataway, New Jersey, the Orangemen lost to the Scarlet Knights L (21–24) before 17,919. On the road on Nov 27 at Miami (FL)'s Miami Orange Bowl, the Hurricanes got the best of the Orangemen L (13–45) before 35,208

1999 Music City Bowl

On December 29, 1999 at 4:00 PM, Syracuse took on Kentucky at the Adelphia Coliseum in Nashville, Tennessee in the Music City Bowl and the Orangemen defeated the Wildcats W 20–13 before 59,221 stadium fans.

December 29, 1999 - Adelphia Coliseum
Syracuse 20, Kentucky 13
Attendance: 59,221

Syracuse had failed in its last three bowl games after winning seven in a row. This day, the Orangemen were ready to begin a new winning streak, but they scared a lot of fans in pulling it off.

2000 Paul Pasqualoni Coach # 25

The 2000 Syracuse Orangemen football team competed in their one hundred-eleventh season of intercollegiate football. They were led by Paul Pasqualoni in his tenth of fourteen seasons as head coach of the Syracuse Orangemen. SU had a winning season again 6-5-0. They were 4-3 in their tenth year in the Big East. Pasqualoni picked, Morlon Greenwood, Kyle Johnson, and Pat Woodcock, to be the team captains for 1999. Syracuse was not selected for a bowl game this year.

On Sept 2 in the home opener against Buffalo in the Carrier Dome, on the campus of Syracuse University in Syracuse, NY before 40,634, Syracuse won in a blowout W (63-7) On Sept 9 at Cincinnati's Nippert Stadium in Cincinnati, OH SU lost to the Bearcats L (10–12) before 17,717. SU lost two in a row on Sept 23 at East Carolina's Dowdy–Ficklen Stadium in Greenville, NC L (17-34) 33,026, On Sept 30 at home, SU defeated BYU at the Dome W (42–14) before 43,090. Then, in the rivalry against Pittsburgh at the Carrier Dome, SU triumphed W (24-17) before 40,699.

On Oct 14 at Boston College's Alumni Stadium in Chestnut Hill, MA SU lost to BC L (13–20) before 44,500. Then, on Oct 21, at home, #2 Virginia Tech beat Syracuse L (14–22) before 49,033. On Nov 4 at West Virginia's Mountaineer Field in Morgantown, WV, for the Ben Schwartzwalder Trophy), Syracuse played well and defeated the Mountaineers W (31–27) in a tough match before 51,422

On Nov 11, at Temple, in Veterans Stadium, Philadelphia, PA, the Orangemen defeated the Owls W (31–12) before 16,132. Then on Nov 18 at home, #2 Miami of Florida beat the Orangemen in a shutout L (0-26). In the season closer, at home, SU had its moxie all back and the Orangemen whipped Rutgers W (49-21) before 35, 589. There was no bowl game in 2000.

2001 Paul Pasqualoni Coach # 25

The 2001 Syracuse Orangemen football team competed in their one hundred-twelfth season of intercollegiate football. They were led by Paul Pasqualoni in his eleventh of fourteen seasons as head coach of the Syracuse Orangemen. SU had a fine winning season 10-3-0, which would be their last winning season under Coach Pasqualoni. They were 6-1 in their eleventh year in the Big East. Pasqualoni picked, P. J. Alexander, Dwight Freeney, Quentin Harris, Kyle Johnson, and Graham Manley to be the team captains for 2001. Syracuse played and won the Insight Bowl in 2001.

Games of the 2001 season

On Aug 26 v #10 Georgia Tech at Giants Stadium in East Rutherford, New Jersey in the 2001 College Kickoff Classic), Syracuse lost L (7–13) before 41,517. Then a week later on September 1, v #8 Tennessee at Neyland Stadium in Knoxville, Tennessee, SU went down L (9–33) before a huge crowd of 107,725. In week 3 of the 2001 season, on Sept 8 in the home opener against UCF in the Carrier Dome, on the campus of Syracuse University in Syracuse, NY before 35938, Syracuse won the game W (21-10) for the Orangemen's first win of the year. Then, on Sept 22 at home, SU defeated Auburn at the Carrier Dome W (31–14) before 43,403.

Then on Sept 29 at home against East Carolina, the Orangemen defeated the Pirates W (44–30) before 36,347. Then, on Oct 6 at Rutgers in Rutgers Stadium, Piscataway, New Jersey, SU beat the Scarlet Knights W (24–17) before 17,511, Moving on to Pittsburgh, PA on Oct 13 at the new Heinz Field, the Orangemen grabbed another win W (42–10) before 52,367. Then on Oct 20 at home, SU defeated Temple† at the Carrier Dome W (45–3).

On Oct 27 at #5 Virginia Tech at Lane Stadium in Blacksburg, Virginia, the Orangemen prevailed against the Hokies W (22–14) before 53,662. Two weeks later on Nov 10, at home in the Carrier Dome, # 18 SU defeated West Virginia W (24–13) before 43,753. Then, on Nov 17, SU played as #14 against #1 ranked Miami in the Miami Orange Bowl stadium, the Orangemen could not find a breath against the National Championship Hurricanes and went down in a shutout blowout L (0–59) before 52,896. The season was not over until all the games were played and so on Nov 24, at home SU defeated BC, #25 Boston College in the Carrier Dome, for another SU win in the rivalry W (39–28) before 45,063.

2001 Insight Bowl

On December 29, 2001. At 5:30 PM, #18 Syracuse took on Kansas State, playing at Bank One Ballpark, Phoenix, Arizona in the Insight.com Bowl. The Orangemen prevailed W (26–3) before 40,028 intrigued fans.

2002 Paul Pasqualoni Coach # 25

The 2002 Syracuse Orangemen football team competed in their one hundred-thirteenth season of intercollegiate football. They were led by Paul Pasqualoni in his twelfth of fourteen seasons as head coach of the Syracuse Orangemen. This was the worst year of Pasqualoni's coaching tenure and his first losing season 4-8-0. They were 2-5 in their twelfth year in the Big East. Pasqualoni picked Clifton Smith, Chris Davis, Will Hunter, Troy Nunes, and David Tyree, to be the team captains for 2001. Syracuse was not selected for a bowl game in 2002.

On Aug 29 at BYU's LaVell Edwards Stadium in Provo, the Cougars defeated the Orangemen L 21–42 before 65,612. In week 2 of the 2002season, on Sept 7 in the home opener against North Carolina in the Carrier Dome, on the campus of Syracuse University in Syracuse, NY before 39444 fans, Syracuse lost the game L (22-30 for the Orangemen's second loss of the year. Then, on Sept 14 at home, for their first win of the season, SU defeated Rhode Island at the Carrier Dome in a blow-out W (63-17) before 43,408. Then, on Sept 28 at 9:00 PM at #25 Auburn's Jordan–Hare Stadium in Auburn, AL, the Orangemen went down in a well-fought, very close match L (34–37) before 83,667

SU had beaten Pittsburgh 11 straight times until Oct 5 at home when SU lost big to Pittsburgh L (24-48) Then, on Oct 12 12:00 at Temple in Veterans Stadium, Philadelphia, PA, the Owls beat the Orangemen in a close game, L (16-17) before 17,220. Then for the fourth loss in a row, on Oct 18, the Orangemen traveled to the West Virginia Mountaineer Field, Morgantown, WV and were defeated L (7–34) before 45,088. Next up on Oct 25 at home was Rutgers. The Orangemen found their bearings and defeated the Scarlet Knights W (45–14) before 37,158.

On Nov 2 v UCF in a game played in the Citrus Bowl, Orlando, FL, the Orangemen grabbed the victory W 38–35 before 24,043. Then, on Nov 9, at home, the Orangemen won their first OT game against #8 Virginia Tech W (50–42) before 48,239.

On Nov 16, at rival Boston College's Alumni Stadium in Chestnut Hill, MA, the Orangemen took their seventh loss of the season L (20–41) before 36,221. Miami was in its prime, sitting in the #1 position when they came to the Carrier Dome on Nov 30 and beat the Orangemen at 1:00 PM by a big score L (7-49) before 45,679.

2003 Paul Pasqualoni Coach # 25

The 2003 Syracuse Orangemen football team competed in their one hundred-fourteenth season of intercollegiate football. They were led by Paul Pasqualoni in his thirteenth of fourteen seasons as head coach of the Syracuse Orangemen. This was a comeback year after the worst year of Pasqualoni's coaching tenure. The Orangemen had an even record of 6-6-0. It was two more wins than the prior season. They were 2-5 in their thirteenth year in the Big East. Pasqualoni picked R.J. Anderson, Keith Belton, and Rich Scanlon, to be the team captains for 2003. Syracuse was not selected for a bowl game in 2003.

This was the last season in which Syracuse used the "Orangemen" nickname. Beginning with the 2004–05 school year, the school adopted its current nickname of "Orange." Some pundits and alums persist in calling the new Orange, the Orangemen and that is OK—it's just not official.

On Sept 6 at North Carolina's Kenan Memorial Stadium in Chapel Hill, North Carolina, in triple overtime, SU got the victory W (49–47) before 47,000. In week 2 of the 2003 season, on Sept 13 in the home opener against Louisville in the Carrier Dome, on the campus of Syracuse University in Syracuse, NY before 38,550 fans, the Orangemen lost the game to the Cardinals L (20-30 for the team's first loss of the year. On Sept 20 at home, for their second win of the season, SU defeated UCF at the Carrier Dome W (38-14) before 35,103. On Sept 27 at home SU defeated Toledo at the Dome W (34–7) before 36,083

On Oct 11, at #4 Virginia Tech's Lane Stadium in Blacksburg, Virginia, the Hokeys beat the Orangemen in a blowout L (7–51) before 65,115. On Oct 18 at home, SU defeated Boston College in the annual rivalry W (39–14) before 45,313. In the Pittsburgh rivalry, Pitt won its second in a row against Syracuse on Oct 25 at Pittsburgh's Heinz Field in Pittsburgh, PA L (14–34) before 61,421. Then on Nov 8 at home, SU defeated Temple at the Carrier Dome W (41-17) before 43,149 fans.

On Nov 15, Syracuse traveled south to play #14 ranked Miami (FL) in the Miami Orange Facility in Miami but were beaten by the Hurricanes in a close match L (1017) before 48,130. On Nov22 at home, Syracuse lost another close match to #25 West Virginia and the Mountaineers went home with the Ben Schwartzwalder Trophy L (2334). On Nov 29, a tougher than usual Rutgers team would not give up an inch to the Orangemen as SU went down by three scores L (7-24). This game was played at Rutgers Stadium in Piscataway, New Jersey before 18,563.

2004 Paul Pasqualoni Coach # 25

The 2004 Syracuse Orangemen football team competed in their one hundred-fifteenth season of intercollegiate football. They were led by Paul Pasqualoni, a fine coach, and one of the best ever at SU, in his fourteenth and last season as head coach of the Syracuse Orange. This year was almost an exact duplicate of the prior year's record, 6-6-0. They were 4-2 in the Big East. Pasqualoni picked Julian Pollard,

Walter Reyes, Matt Tarullo, to be the team captains for 2004. Syracuse was not selected for a bowl game in 2004.

It was expected there would be controversy after this season if the plusses were not more than the minuses. There were many SU fans and alumni headhunters looking for Pasqualoni's scalp on a platter after three non-winning seasons in a row. The Orange had an even record of 6-6-0 again this year but it was not enough and there would be no fourth chance to make amends.

Dick Macpherson and Paul Pasqualoni were such great coaches they had given SU fans a taste of what it was to win consistently. It felt good. Just like when Ben Schwartzwalder had a few bad years at the end, there was little patience. When Pasqualoni had a few non-winning years, SU seemed to think that that could go "poof" and hire anybody off the street to take this great coach's place. Let's see how that works out as, after this season, for this book, we have just thirteen more seasons to go for this version of this coaches book.

I regret to tell you fine readers that this is not the worst news for the year. This was the first season in which Syracuse used the nickname of Orange. For some this is moot but for others, Orangemen was not something to be given up because Nike thought it was a good idea.

As most know, previously, Syracuse had respectively used "Orangemen" for men's sports, including football, and "Orangewomen" for women's sports. The equality movement in men and women's sports is intense, and it was determined by the "experts that a name without the sex of the participant in the name would be a better name than one with about a hundred-year tradition. To each his or her own. I express no opinion on that matter.

The games from Paul Pasqualoni's last season

On Sept 5 at # 25 Purdue's Ross–Ade Stadium in West Lafayette, IN, Syracuse took a KO to the chin in a huge shutout L (0–51) before 56,827. On Sept 11, at Buffalo in UB Stadium, Amherst, NY, SU beat the Bengals W (37–17) before 29,013. In week 3 of the 2004 season, on Sept 18 in the home opener against Cincinnati in the Carrier Dome, on the campus of Syracuse University in Syracuse,

NY before 32, 893 fans, the Orangemen beat the Bearcats W (19-7) for the team's second win loss of the year. On Sept 25 at No. 12 Virginia's Scott Stadium in Charlottesville, VA, Syracuse lost to the Wahoos L (0–31) before 59,699. Then to begin October, on Oct 2, at home, SU defeated Rutgers W (41–31)

On Oct 9 at home, in a close match against # 8 Florida State, the Seminoles defeated the Orange L (13–17) before 40,359. On Oct 21 at # 15 West Virginia Mountaineer Field in Morgantown, WV, SU lost to the Mountaineers L (6–27) before 52,909. On October 30 at home, Syracuse defeated Connecticut W (42–30) before 34,545. On Nov 6 at home for the Pittsburgh rivalry game, Syracuse beat the Panthers W (38–31) before 37,211.

On Nov 13 at Temple in a game played at the new Lincoln Financial Field in Philadelphia, Syracuse did not have enough to beat the supercharged Owls L (24–34) before 15,564. On Nov 27, SU beat #17 Boston College at Alumni Stadium in Chestnut Hill, MA W (43–17) before 44,500.

2004 Champs Sports Bowl

On December 21, 2004, with a 6-6-0 record SU qualified minimally for a bowl bid and agreed to play a tough Georgia tech team in the Champs Sports Bowl. The venue was the Citrus Bowl Stadium in Orlando, FL. The Champs Sports Bowl found Georgia Tech dominating Syracuse L (14–51) before 28,237.

Georgia Tech 51, Syracuse 14
December 21, 2004
Orlando, Florida

All Syracuse fans wanted a win. They were very pleased that a 6-5 record got the team to display its real prowess in a national bowl game Pasqualoni got them to the game, but everybody wanted a win or a good showing to feel good about the great coach and some vindication for the season. It was not coming in this game.

The Syracuse football team lost, 51-14, to Georgia Tech on Tuesday, December 21, in the Champs Sports Bowl at Florida Citrus Bowl Stadium in Orlando, Fla. Jared Jones finishes his career with 102 receptions and 1,189 yards, becoming the seventh SU receiver to tally over 100 receptions and 1000 yards.

Jones' 102 receptions ties him with Art Monk for sixth all-time at SU. Sophomore quarterback Perry Patterson threw for 219 yards on 21-of-34 passing with one touchdown and one interception.

Patterson also rushed for a score. Standout Senior tailback Walter Reyes left the game in the first half after aggravating a shoulder injury.

Georgia Tech quarterback Reggie Ball finished the game 12-of-19 for 207 yards, two touchdowns and one interception. Ball also ran for 38 yards and a touchdown. Running back P.J. Daniels finished with 119 yards on 17 carries and two touchdowns. Wide receiver Calvin Johnson had two catches for 61 yards and a touchdown and rushed twice for 12 yards and one touchdown. The stats all favored the Yellow Jackets.

The Yellow Jackets scored four unanswered touchdowns in the first half, including three in a span of 3:09. The Orange went three and out on its ensuing possession. Georgia Tech tacked on two touchdowns in the second half on runs by Ball and Daniels, to give the Yellow Jackets an insurmountable 49-6 lead. In this game the Orange were outmatched.

Patterson hooked up with Gregory at the 11:22 mark of the fourth quarter for a 25-yard touchdown. SU converted the two-point attempt on a pass from Rhodes to tight end Brandon Darlington, his first career reception. Georgia Tech recorded a safety late in the fourth quarter to make the final score 51-14. It was a less than proud moment in Syracuse football but not one that Pasqualoni should have been fired for—just my opinion.

Seattle Times on Pasqualoni Firing

Notebook: Syracuse fires coach Pasqualoni
Originally published December 30, 2004 at 12:00 am Updated December 29, 2004 at 8:52 pm
By The Associated Press

> SYRACUSE, N.Y. — Syracuse fired football coach Paul Pasqualoni yesterday, eight days after a 37-point loss in a bowl game — and less than a month after giving him a vote of confidence.
>
> "Sometimes you just know you need to make a change," athletic director Daryl Gross said. "He's had a long tenure here. He served the student-athletes well. He is a tremendous man. The things he's done here, you can marvel at.
>
> "I just think it's time to go in a different direction. We're going into the heart of the recruiting season right now. We needed to act one way or another."
>
> Pasqualoni, who was unavailable for comment, departs after 14 years with a 107-59-1 record and a 6-3 mark in bowl games. He is the second-winningest coach in school history, behind Ben Schwartzwalder, who had 153 victories.
>
> But the Orange struggled to break even after going 10-3 and finishing ranked No. 14 in 2001. They were 4-8 in 2002, Pasqualoni's only losing season, and 6-6 the last two years.
>
> Gross, a former assistant at USC who was hired two weeks ago to replace the retiring Jake Crouthamel, said a search for Pasqualoni's replacement will begin immediately.
>
> Pasqualoni, who had one year left on his contract, becomes the 11th Division I coach to be fired this year. His firing came after chancellor Nancy Cantor announced Dec. 6 that he would return for his 15th season. But Gross was hired 11 days later, and the Orange's 51-14 loss to Georgia Tech in the Champs Sports Bowl helped seal Pasqualoni's fate.

Greg Robinson Replaces Pasqualoni at Syracuse
By the Daily Orange, Student Newspaper

Just weeks after coming to Syracuse University, new Director of Athletics Daryl Gross decided it was time for a 'different direction' for the SU football program – one without head coach Paul Pasqualoni. [IMHO—as a long-time SU fan, who saw SU recover over the years, this was a big mistake]

And 13 days after Pasqualoni's Dec. 29 dismissal, Gross introduced his replacement: Greg Robinson, the former co-defensive coordinator of the Texas Longhorns. Despite Coach P's many contributions throughout the years, [according to the AD and the students] it was a necessary move for the new AD.

Pasqualoni stands out as one of the best coaches in SU football history. In 14 years as head coach, he boasts 11 straight winning seasons, nine bowl games and four Big East conference titles. That being said, recent history proved Pasqualoni was not the best person to be leading the program.

SU had not had a winning football season since 2002 and only appeared in one bowl game, which the Orange lost to Georgia Tech, 51-14, on Dec. 21. In the last few years, Pasqualoni also lost control of some of the recruiting elements necessary to build a winning team. While the blame doesn't lie solely on Pasqualoni, one of the realities of college sports is that if you can't produce the goods, you may be replaced. The change to Robinson may be just what the football program needs to get out of its slump.

With a tight search schedule and the coaching options rapidly evaporating, Gross came up with a great candidate to take over the program. Robinson is an experienced coach who has proven himself at both the collegiate and professional level. He coached in the NFL for 14 years and earned two SU per Bowl rings as the Denver Broncos' defensive coordinator. He's starting off with a clean slate and has the potential to do some great things with the football program.

While it may be difficult for Robinson to come in and immediately produce a winning team, it is important for him to strive to meet former AD Jake Crouthamel's criteria for success.

'The university's expectations of its football program are at a minimum: 1) finishing in the top three of the Big East; 2) finishing among the Top 25 annually; 3) frequent bowl participation; and 4) a high graduation rate,' Crouthamel said October 2002.

It is unfortunate that Pasqualoni is leaving the university at a low point in his career instead of a high one. He had to be replaced, though, and Greg Robinson should prove to be an excellent fit.

After we review the Robinson years, I will make some additional comments in Chapter 20.

General George S. Patton once said that "when everybody is thinking the same thing, somebody is not thinking. Paul Pasqualoni still has not been replaced at Syracuse, regardless of the consensus thinking that suggested he be fired. I sure hope Dino Babers turns out to be the replacement. Check Greg Robinson's record on the next page to get a perspective on whether Pasqualoni should have been fired.

Chapter 12 Greg Robinson 2005 to 2008

Coach Greg Robinson #26

Year	Coach	Record	Conf
2005	Greg Robinson	1-10-0	Big East (0-7)
2006	Greg Robinson	4-8-0	Big East (1-5)
2007	Greg Robinson	2-10-0	Big East (1-6)
2008	Greg Robinson	3-9-0	Big East (1-6)

Coach Robinson with Team

Famous Coaches (From the Past) by SWC75.

AD Gross had come from USC and his new man, on advice of Pete Carroll, was Greg Robinson, a handsome, silver-haired man with a ready smile and a confident gaze. He'd had a thirty-year career with several top college programs and NFL teams, including two Super Bowl rings earned as defensive coordinator of the Denver Broncos. His most recent job was with the Texas Longhorns who had re-emerged as a national power and would win the national championship with players Robinson coached during Greg's first year in Syracuse. The A-Team had arrived?

Except it turned out to be the " " team as we found out why Robinson had been an assistant for 30 years. His teams were out of shape. The game plans didn't seem to make much sense. New to the East, he didn't seem to know where to recruit. His first team went from 6-6 the previous year to 1-10, our worst record since 1892. His four-year record of 10-37 was the worst such stretch in SU history. That was it for "G-Rob". At least he lowered the bar for his successors. If Coach P had come after G-Rob, he'd be everyone's hero now. Maybe he still should be?

2005 Greg Robinson Coach # 26
*NCAA sanctions vacated SU's one season win

The 2005 Syracuse Orange football team competed in their one hundred-sixteenth season of intercollegiate football. They were led by Greg Robinson in his first of four seasons as head coach of the Syracuse Orange. After giving up on Coach Pasqualoni, the new consensus pick coach produced the worst football record in Syracuse history--1-10; 0-7 in the Big East. Syracuse was not selected for a bowl game in 2005.

In week 1 of the 2005 season, on Sept 4 in the home opener against West Virginia in the Carrier Dome, on the campus of Syracuse University in Syracuse, NY before 45,418 fans, the Orangemen lost in a close match to the eventual Big East Champion, Mountaineers L (7-15). On September 10 at home SU won its only game of the season against Buffalo W (31–0) before. The rest of the season, shown below in tabular form, were all losses

Date	Vs. /venue	Score	Attendance
Sept 17	home, #25 Virginia,	L (24-27,	40,027
Oct 1	away #6 Florida State	L (14–38)	83,717
Oct 7	away Connecticut	L (7–26)	40,000
Oct 15	home Rutgers	L (9-31)	39,022
Oct 22	away Pittsburgh	L (17–34)	33,059
Oct 29	home Cincinnati	L (16–22)	42,457
Nov 12	home South Florida	L (0–27)	40,144
Nov 19	away #6 Notre Dame	L (10–34)	80,795
Nov 26	away #17 Louisville	L (7–4)	37,896

2006 Greg Robinson Coach # 26
*NCAA sanctions vacated SU's four season wins

The 2006 Syracuse Orange football team competed in their one hundred-seventeenth season of intercollegiate football. They were led by Greg Robinson in his second of four seasons as head coach of the Syracuse Orange. This would be Coach Robinson's best record year at Syracuse (4-8), 1-5 in the Big East. Syracuse was not selected for a bowl game in 2006.

In week 1 of the 2005 season, on Sept 2 at Wake Forest's Groves Stadium, Winston-Salem, North Carolina the Orange lost to the Demon Deacons L (10–20) before 34,121. On Sept 9 in the home opener against Iowa in the Carrier Dome, on the campus of Syracuse University in Syracuse, NY before 37,199 fans, the Orange lost in a close match to the Hawkeyes L (13-20).

On Sept 16 at Illinois Memorial Stadium in Champaign, Illinois, the Orange beat the Fighting Illini W (31–21) before 40,657. Then, on Sept 23 at home against Miami (OH), SU won W (34–14) before 35,274. On Sept 30 at home, in the Carrier Dome, the Orange defeated the Cowboys W 40–34 in double OT.

On Oct 7, at home v Pittsburgh, SU lost to the Panthers L (11-21) before 41,870. Then, on Oct at #5 West Virginia's Mountaineer Field in Morgantown, West Virginia, the Mountaineers beat the Orange, L (17–41) before 60,051. On Oct 21 at home, #6 Louisville beat the Orange L (13–28) before 35,708. At Cincinnati's Nippert Stadium in Cincinnati. OH. On Oct 28, the Bearcats outscored the Orange L (3–17) before 20,146. Then, on November 11 at South Florida's Raymond James Stadium in Tampa, Florida, SU lost another L (10–27) before 43,413.

On Nov 18 at home, Syracuse defeated Connecticut in the Carrier Dome W (20-14) before 35,079. In the season closer, SU lost to #15 Rutgers, on Nov 25, at Rutgers Stadium in Piscataway, New Jersey L (7–38) before 43,791.

2007 Greg Robinson Coach # 26
*No NCAA sanctions or vacated wins this year

The 2007 Syracuse Orange football team competed in their one hundred-eighteenth season of intercollegiate football. They were led by Greg Robinson in his third of four seasons as head coach of the Syracuse Orange. This Orange record this year was 2-10. 1-6 in the Big East. Syracuse was not selected for a bowl game in 2007.

On Aug 31 in the home and season opener against Washington, at home in the Carrier Dome, on the campus of Syracuse University in Syracuse, NY before 40,329 fans, the Orange were overpowered the Huskies, L (42-12) On Sept 8 t Iowa's Kinnick Stadium in Iowa City, Iowa , the Orange were beaten by the Hawkeyes in a shutout L (0-35) before 70,585. On Sept 15 at home against Illinois in the Carrier Dome Syracuse lost their third in a row, L (20-41) before 34,188. At Louisville's Papa John's Cardinal Stadium in Louisville, Kentucky, on Sept 22, the Orange defeated the Cardinals by three points for their first win of the year before 40,922.

Paring against Miami (OH)* on Sept 29, at Yager Stadium in Oxford, Ohio, the Orange were defeated by the RedHawks L (17–14) before 16,800 in a very close game. On Oct 6, at home, #13 West Virginia came to the Carrier Dome meaning business and they won the game in a blowout L (55–14) against the Orange before 35,345. On Oct 13, and increasingly powerful Rutgers squad defeated the Orange at home at the Dome L (38-14) before 36,226. In another Carrier Dome matchup, Syracuse beat Buffalo on Oct 20 W (20–12) before 30,897. It was the last SU win of 2007.

On Nov 3 at Pittsburgh Heinz Field in Pittsburgh, Pennsylvania, the Panthers gained a close win from the Orange L (17-20) before 31,374. On Nov 10 at home the Orange lost to the Bulls of South Florida L (41–10) before 38,039. At #25 Connecticut, a week later on Nov 17, in a game played at Connecticut Rentschler Field in East Hartford, the Huskies defeated the Orange L (30–7) before 40,000. In the season finale on Nov 24, #24 Cincinnati overpowered the Orange L (52-31) before 30,040

You had to go way back past Paul Pasqualoni and Dick MacPherson to find opponents kicking around the Orangemen as they did in the Robinson years. Pasqualoni got three years with less than normal but not dismal records after proving himself while Robinson got a fourth season without showing any promise. What happened to the AD who forced Pasqualoni out? I bet I know!

In 2015, his proper fate caught up to Daryl Gross whose first move was to fire Paul Pasqualoni. Gross was fired but should have been ousted long before 2015. As you recall my comments about the firing of 14-year head coach Paul Pasqualoni, when Gross, the know-it-all exchanged a great grizzled veteran for flashy Greg Robinson, who arrived with a West Coast offense and a Southern California pedigree. Widely applauded at the time, the switch turned out to be a flop, with the football program bottoming out under Robinson and continuing to push toward average.

2008 Greg Robinson Coach # 26
*No NCAA sanctions or vacated wins this year

The 2008 Syracuse Orange football team competed in their one hundred-nineteenth season of intercollegiate football. They were led by Greg Robinson in his third of four seasons as head coach of the Syracuse Orange. This Orange record this year was 3-9. 1-6 in the Big East. Syracuse was not selected for a bowl game in 2008.

It was August 30 at Northwestern's Ryan Field in Evanston, IL that the Orange played its season opener and defeated the Wildcats L (10-30) before 20,015. Then the next week on Sept 6 in the home opener against Akron in the Carrier Dome, on the campus of Syracuse University in Syracuse, NY before 31,808, the Orange were beaten by the Zips L (28-42). On Sept 13, after a long hiatus, #17 Penn State, still led by Joe Paterno came into the Carrier Dome and were relentless in defeating the Orange L (13-55) before 45,745. On Sept 20 at home, SU got a close win against Northeastern W (30-21) before 34,694

On Sept 27, SU lost to long-time rival Pittsburgh at home L (24-34) before 27,549. On Oct 11, at West Virginia Mountaineer Field in Morgantown, WV in the Battle for the Schwartzwalder Trophy, SU left the trophy behind L (6-17) before 58,133. On Oct 18 at #19

South Florida at Raymond James Stadium in Tampa, FL, the Orange went town easy L (13-45) before 51,384

Back at home on Nov 1 in the Carrier Dome, the Orange managed to win a nice game against Louisville W (28-21) before 32,917. Rutgers still was not taking "no" for an answer as they again defeated the Orange, this time it was on Nov 8 at Rutgers Stadium in Piscataway, NJ L (17-35) before 42,172.

On Nov 15 at home against Connecticut, the Orange lost the game against the RedHawks, L (14-39) before 28,081. Somehow SU had ND's number and the scored a big win against the Charlie Weis version of The Fighting Irish on Nov 22 at Notre Dame Stadium, South Bend, IN W (24-23) before 80,795. Stranger things have happened but the same team that beat Notre Dame in an away game could not do the same against the team coached by Brian Kelly at Cincinnati on Nov 29 at # 16 Cincinnati's Nippert Stadium in Cincinnati, OH. The Orange lost to the next ND Coach's team, the Bearcats, L (10-30) before 34,603

Coach Greg Out at Syracuse

Football coaches are a dime a dozen but if you pay a dime, chances are you get no takers and if you get a taker for the dime a dozen price, you get no real results. Syracuse University's embattled AD, who I have not liked from the moment he fired Paul Pasqualoni bowed to pressure and fired a coach whose full win production in four years as head coach of just ten games would not be enough in some years to finish in the top ten rankings of national teams. Considering that Robinson had years of 1, 4, 2, and 3 wins, his record warranted the axe after year one.

> Syracuse University head football coach Greg Robinson was fired on a Sunday in November 2008, by director of athletics Daryl Gross, with two weeks left in the season. This seemed to end a turbulent era that began with great optimism only to deteriorate into misery, hopelessness and the worst four-year run in the program's 119 years of competition. Just like it is not good to fool Mother Nature, it is not good to mess with a team already mentored by a great coach, aka- Paul Pasqualoni.

Some say Robinson's record at Syracuse is 9-36 overall and 3-24 in the Big East, but I have found he achieved ten wins as described above. The Orange at this point in time in 2008 when this article was put together were 2-8 and 1-5 after losing to Connecticut 39-14 on Saturday night at the Carrier Dome.

At the time, the Orange had remaining games against Notre Dame on Saturday, which they won, and Cincinnati on November 29, which they lost. I think I could have coached better than Robinson simply by bringing Coach Paul back. Robinson, who had a year remaining on his contract earned $1.1 million per season. At a $100K per game, he was expected to coach the Orange for the last two games, and he did.

Chapter 13 Doug Marrone 2009 to 2012

Coach Doug Marrone # 27

Year	Coach	Record	Conf
2009	Doug Marrone	4-8	Big East (1-6)
2010	Doug Marrone	8-5	Big East (4-3)
2011	Doug Marrone	5-7	Big East (1-6)
2012	Doug Marrone	8-5	Big East (5-2)

Coach Doug Marrone Happy about the prospects of playing in the ACC

Famous Coaches (From the Past) by SWC75.

Doug Marrone came after G-Rob, another career assistant but one who had played here and had notebooks full of his plans for bringing the program back from the abyss. He immediately made it more competitive, even if he won only one more game than G-Rob's last year. The next year he won four league road games, thanks to Scott Shafer's excellent defense. Then came a mysterious collapse after a 5-2 start in 2011, followed by a second bowl win in three years, followed by a mysterious, (to us, anyway), exit to be replaced by Shafer.

Our thank you's to ESPN for permission to reprint their take on Doug Marrone's coming to Syracuse when Greg Robinson was fired.

Syracuse hires Doug Marrone as football coach
Updated: December 12, 2008, 6:01 PM ET
Associated Press

SYRACUSE, N.Y. -- Greg Robinson learned to bleed Orange. New Syracuse coach Doug Marrone already has that part down "When I went into coaching, I always prepared myself for this," the Bronx-born Marrone said Friday after being hired to replace Robinson as football coach. "This has been the job I have always wanted."

The offensive coordinator for the New Orleans Saints since 2006, Marrone is returning to the school where he played to try to resurrect a program that hasn't had a winning season since 2001. Robinson was fired in November after going 10-37 in four seasons.

"Not a lot of times in your life can you actually accomplish your dream," said Marrone, a three-year letterman at Syracuse under former coach Dick MacPherson in the mid-1980s. "Today is the greatest day of my life. This is my school and these are my people. You're going to be proud, and we're going to win football games."

Terms of Marrone's contract were not revealed. Robinson had one year left on a deal that paid $1.1 million per season.

Money wasn't on Marrone's mind as he contemplated working two jobs for a while.

"We need everyone to believe," he said. "We need the alumni, we need the fans. I love the people here."

The 44-year-old Marrone was selected by a football search committee that included former Syracuse players Tim Green, Art Monk, Don McPherson and Floyd Little, as well as MacPherson.

Athletic director Daryl Gross interviewed East Carolina coach Skip Holtz earlier in the week, but Holtz issued a statement through his athletic department on Thursday that he had withdrawn his name from consideration.

"We feel at the end of the day we got the best guy," Gross said. "He brings hope to our football program, brings hope to our student-athletes. He's got a group of kids that are just so hungry to win. It's time to rally around. He's going to be here a long time."

Like Robinson, this will be Marrone's first stint as a head coach. It doesn't figure to be a cakewalk. Robinson's tenure featured the only two 10-loss seasons in school history, too many of them by lopsided scores.

The team's poor performance under Robinson, who had three offensive coordinators in his four seasons, hurt the school financially. In 21 homes games over his first three seasons, more than 260,000 seats were not sold, average attendance fell to a 21-year low in 2007, and attendance numbers again were abysmal in 2008.

"For me to sit here and say that Doug Marrone is the right guy is what I would love to say, but I can't say that because I don't know at this point if Doug is the right guy for Syracuse football," said Green, a close friend of Marrone's in college. "

This is a daunting task that he's going to face. It's one of the most difficult things in the world of sports, to take a college football program that's down and resurrect it."

Marrone joins basketball coach Jim Boeheim and lacrosse coach John Desko as Syracuse alumni who returned to work at their alma mater. Of course, Boeheim and Desko have won national championships.

"We are not in a rebuilding process. We are in the process of rejuvenating this program," Marrone said as several players listened intently. "I don't have any options. I cannot fail. I cannot fail. My option is only to win, and that's what I'm going to do."

Marrone began his coaching career as an assistant at Cortland State, just south of Syracuse, and coached at Coast Guard, Northeastern, Georgia Tech, Georgia and Tennessee. He was a New York Jets assistant for three years before joining the Saints.

Marrone played for the Miami Dolphins in 1987 and the Saints in 1989, and was with the London Monarchs of the World league in 1991.

Under Marrone's guidance, the Saints have become one of the NFL's most explosive and consistent offenses. New Orleans set an NFL record with 440 completions in 2007 and also set team highs for passing first downs (222), attempts (652), touchdown passes (28) and completion percentage (67.5), also allowing the fewest sacks in the league with 16.

That Marrone has been out of the college ranks for several years doesn't figure to inhibit him at Syracuse.

"I knew someone would say, 'He doesn't have the recruiting ties.' Well, I kept those recruiting ties," said Marrone, whose interview presentation included three binders that he assembled and tailored specifically for the Syracuse job. "I know what we need to win. I've been setting this plan for a long time."

Marrone said he would evaluate the current coaching staff before naming his assistants. Dan Conley, a star at Syracuse for Paul Pasqualoni in the 1990s, just completed his first season as linebacker's coach and would appear to be a perfect fit for the new regime.

Copyright 2008 by The Associated Press. This story is from ESPN.com's automated news wire. Wire index

This piece was written so succinctly, and it said all I wanted to say that I decided to use this piece and thank ESPN for their kindness, rather than taking the raw facts from other pieces on the Internet and cobbling my own story about Marrone. So, far, from what I have read, I like Marrone. How about you?

2009 Doug Marrone Coach # 27

The 2009 Syracuse Orange football team competed in their one hundred-twentieth season of intercollegiate football. They were led by Doug Marrone in his first of four seasons as head coach of the Syracuse Orange. The Orange record this year was 4-8, And 1-6 in the Big East. Syracuse was not selected for a bowl game in 2009.

On Sept 5 SU played its home and season opener against Minnesota in the Carrier Dome, on the campus of Syracuse University in Syracuse, NY before 48,617. The Orange were beaten by the Golden Gophers in OT L (20-23) on Sept 12 at #5 Penn State's Beaver Stadium in State College, PA, the Orange lost in a tough battle L (7–28) before a huge crowd of 106,387.

On Sept 19 at home, SU defeated a tough Northwestern squad at the Carrier Dome W (37-34) before 40,251. Then, on Sept 26, at home the Orange defeated Maine at the Carrier Dome by the score of W (41–24) before 35,632

On Oct 3 at home, South Florida was the visiting team and they played well enough to beat the home team SU Orange L (20-34) before 40,147. On Oct 10 at home SU lost again to West Virginia at the Carrier Dome L (13–34) before 40,144. Akron came into the Dome on Oct 24 and they were ready for a win but SU held them back and got one for the Orange W (28–14) before 36,991. On Oct 31, at home a tough #7 Cincinnati team, coached by ND's Brian Kelly beat the Orange in a fair fight L (7-28).

On Nov 7, SU played rival #14 Pittsburgh M at Heinz Field in Pittsburgh, PA and the Orange was beaten by the Panthers L (10–37). At Louisville's Papa John's Cardinal Stadium in Louisville, KY on Nov 14, the Cardinals won again against the Orange L (9–10) before 33,223. Then on Nov 21 at home against Rutgers in the Carrier Dome, Syracuse defeated the Scarlet Knights W (31–13) before 36,759. In the last game of the year, on Nov 28 against Connecticut at its Rentschler Field in East Hartford, CONN, the Orange lost its eighth game of the season. L (31–56) before 40,000.

2010 Doug Marrone Coach # 27

The 2010 Syracuse Orange football team competed in their one hundred-twenty-first season of intercollegiate football. They were led by Doug Marrone in his second of four seasons as head coach of the Syracuse Orange. The Orange record this year was 8-5, their best in ten years. The team was 4-3 in the Big East. Syracuse was also selected for a bowl game in 2010. For the first time since Paul Pasqualoni was fired following the 2004 season, the Orange won enough games to become bowl eligible. Syracuse played Kansas State in the Inaugural Pinstripe Bowl at Yankee Stadium where they won 36–34 to finish the season 8–5, 4–3 in Big East. There was reason for hope at the Big Orange.

On Sept 4 at Akron in the InfoCision Stadium, Akron, Ohio, Syracuse came home with the win W (29–3) before 15,969. On Sept 11 at Washington Husky Stadium Seattle, WA, SU lost to the Huskies L (20–41) before 62,418. On Sept 18 SU played its home opener against Maine in the Carrier Dome, on the campus of Syracuse University in Syracuse, NY before 37,758. The Orange beaten by the Black Bears W (38-14). On Sept 25 at home, SU defeated Colgate W (42-7) Then, on Oct 9 at South Florida's Raymond James Stadium in Tampa, the Orange defeated the Bulls W (13–9) before 41,917.

In the yearly rivalry, on Oct 16 at home, the Orange lost to the Panthers of Pittsburgh† in the Carrier Dome before 40,168. On Oct 23, at #19 West Virginia at Mountaineer Field in Morgantown, WV, for the Ben Schwartzwalder Trophy, the Orange prevailed W (19–14) before 58,122. On Oct 30 at Cincinnati's Nippert Stadium, Cincinnati, OH, the Orange triumphed W (31–7) before 32,072. Then, in a tough game against Louisville at the carrier Dome, the Orange were barely defeated by the Cardinals L (20–28) before 40,735.

On Nov 13 at Rutgers in Rutgers Stadium, Piscataway, New Jersey the Orange tot by the Scarlet Knights in a close match W (13–10) before 49,911. On Nov 20, at home, Syracuse lost to Connecticut, L (6–23) before 41,635. In the final matchup of the season at home, it was rival Boston College defeating the Orange in the Carrier Dome L (7–16) before 42,191.

The Inaugural Pinstripe Bowl

On Dec 30, one day before New Year's Eve, Syracuse was matched with Kansas State for the Pinstripe Bowl at Yankee Stadium in The Bronx, New York. Syracuse won this close game W (36–34) before a cold crowd of 38,274 in 32-degree weather.

2011 Doug Marrone Coach # 27

The 2011 Syracuse Orange football team competed in their one hundred-twenty-second season of intercollegiate football. They were led by Doug Marrone in his third of four seasons as head coach of the Syracuse Orange. The Orange had a losing record this year at 5-7, their best in ten years. The team was 1-6 in Big East play to finish in a tie for seventh place. Syracuse was not selected for a bowl game in 2011.

On Sept 1 at home, Syracuse defeated Wake Forest W (36-29) in OT in its home and season opener in the Carrier Dome, on the campus of Syracuse University in Syracuse, NY before 40,833. On Sept 10 at home, Syracuse defeated Rhode Island W (21-14). On Sept 17 at USC in a game played at the Los Angeles Memorial Coliseum in Los Angeles, the Trojans defeated the Orange L (17-38) before 65,873. Then, on Sept 24 at home, Syracuse beat Toledo in OT W (33-30) before 39,116. On Oct 1, at home, in double overtime, Syracuse was defeated by Rutgers L (16-19) before 42,152

In a game against Tulane on Oct 8 in the Louisiana Superdome in New Orleans, Syracuse beat the Green Wave in a close match W (W 37-34) before 39,116. Two weeks later on Oct 21, at home Syracuse defeated #11 West Virginia in the Carrier Dome for the Ben Schwartzwalder Trophy W (49–23) before 45,265. Then, on Oct 29 at Louisville's Papa John's Cardinal Stadium in Louisville, the Orange lost to the Cardinals L (10–27) before 44,817

On Nov 5 at Connecticut's Rentschler Field in East Hartford, CT, the Huskies defeated the Orange by a TD L (21–28) before 38,769. At home against South Florida on Nov 11, Syracuse was beaten L (17-37 before 41,582. Then, on Nov 26 at home against Cincinnati, the Bearcats defeated the Orange L (13-30) before 38,159. In the final game of the season against rival Pittsburgh on Dec 3 at 12:00 PM at Heinz Field in Pittsburgh, the Panthers defeated the Orange L (20–33) before 40,058

2012 Doug Marrone Coach # 27

The 2012 Syracuse Orange football team competed in their one hundred-twenty-third season of intercollegiate football. They were led by Doug Marrone in his fourth and last season as head coach of the Syracuse Orange. The Orange had a winning record this year at 8-5, tied for their best in twelve years. The team was 5-2 in Big East play and finished with a share of the Big East Conference championship that was split four ways. They were invited to the Pinstripe Bowl where they defeated long-time rival West Virginia, whom they did not play in the regular season due to the Mountaineers' move to the Big 12 Conference.

The 2012 season also proved to be the final one for Marrone as the Orange head coach. After the conclusion of the season, head coach Doug Marrone was mentioned by several sportswriters as a possible candidate for a head coaching job in the National Football League. On January 6, 2013, Marrone was introduced as the head coach of the Buffalo Bills. Offensive coordinator Nathaniel Hackett departed for Buffalo as well, leaving a number of coaching positions open. On January 9, Syracuse announced the promotion of defensive coordinator Scott Shafer to head coach. Shortly thereafter, George McDonald was announced as the new offensive coordinator, and Chuck Bullough was announced as the new defensive coordinator.

I had a great feeling about Doug Marrone. I don't know why I just did. He moved on to Buffalo though he loved Syracuse. At Buffalo, after two years and bringing the team to 9-7, the owner died and Marrone had a chance to exercise a major contract opt-out if he did not want to stay with the new owners. He took a job as offensive coordinator with Jacksonville, had a great relationship with his head coach and then one day, the Jags fired that coach and promoted Marrone to be the head coach.

In his first year at the helm, Marrone's Jags posted a 10-6 record and were on top of the AFC South. In the Playoffs, they beat Buffalo W (10-3), and Pittsburgh W (45-42), and then lost in the AFC Championship to the Patriots L (20-24). Doug Marrone is destined to be a Parcells, or a Belichick and there will be other great coaches wanting to be a Marrone. That's about it. Too bad Syracuse could not hold onto him.

On offense for 2012, the Orange are returning senior quarterback Ryan Nassib, starting for his third consecutive season. Key offensive players such as Alec Lemon, Marcus Sales, Jerome Smith, and Prince-Tyson Gulley are also returning. On defense, key players returning include Shamarko Thomas, Marquis Spruill, and Deon Goggins.

In 2011, the program lost a number of significant contributors in the 2011 campaign, including tight end Nick Provo and defensive end Chandler Jones, and such losses left a number of questions regarding how a relatively young defense would be able to mature without many experienced players.

In its preseason rankings, College Football News ranked the Orange 57th in the country, and projected that they would go 6-6 in 2012. Their 2012 schedule is the 42nd-toughest in the nation, according to rankings compiled by statistician Jeff Sagarin. Marrone's last SU record of 8-5 fooled them all. Good for Marrone. Good for SU

2012 Season's games

On Sept 1 at home, Syracuse just barely lost to Northwestern in a shootout L (41-42) in its home and season opener in the Carrier Dome, on the campus of Syracuse University in Syracuse, NY before 37,830 A week later, on Sept 8, expecting a big crowd, SU lost another home game against #2 USC at MetLife Stadium (former Giants Stadium) in East Rutherford, NJ L (28–42) before a Carrier Dome size crowd of 39,507. On Sept 15 at home, SU beat

#17 FCS team Stony Brook W (28-17) before 34,512. Then, on Sept 22 at Minnesota's TCF Bank Stadium in Minneapolis, MN, the Orange lost their third game of the year, L (10–17) before 50,805.

On October 5 at home in a game against rival Pittsburgh, SU grabbed the victory in a one-point match W (14-13) before 40,394 Rutgers got its Rutgers Stadium a nice remodeling and a nice sponsor and a new name --High Point Solutions Stadium. The old Rutgers place had significant reconstruction from 2008 to 2009 to increase its capacity to 52,454.

And so, Syracuse got to test drive these new digs on October 12, when they were beaten by #19 Rutgers at High Point Solutions Stadium in Piscataway, NJ L (15–23) before a nice crowd of 48,011. On Oct 19 at home, SU defeated Connecticut W (40-10) before 36,715. Then on Oct 27 at South Florida's Raymond James Stadium in Tampa, SU won another W (37–36) before 38,562.

On Nov 3 at Cincinnati's Nippert Stadium in Cincinnati, OH, the Bearcats beat the Orange L (24–35). At home the next week on Nov 10, SU beat the Louisville Cardinals W (45–26) before 40,312. Then on Nov 17 at Missouri's Faurot Field in Columbia, MO. The Orange won again W (31–27) before 63,045. On Nov 23, SU defeated Temple at Lincoln Financial Field in Philadelphia, PA W (38–20) before 22,317

The 2012 Pinstripe Bowl

On December 29 at 3:15 PM, the Syracuse Orange defeated the West Virginia Mountaineers at Yankee Stadium in the Bronx, NY in the third Pinstripe Bowl W (38–14) before 39,098

The legacy of Doug Marrone
By Tyler Greenawalt
January 8, 2013

> Although he coached at Syracuse for only four seasons, former head football coach Doug Marrone helped revitalize a fading program.

It was only a matter of time before another team decided it needed Doug Marrone's help. Eight days after leading the Syracuse football team to its second bowl victory in three years, Marrone accepted the head coaching position at the Buffalo Bills.

"I had said that the Syracuse job was my dream job, and I meant what I said, and having had the opportunity to restore the great tradition of Syracuse football a reality," Marrone said at a Bills press conference Monday. "Today, I'm experiencing another dream come true."

"Doug has restored Syracuse football to its rightful place and we are appreciative of the foundation he has laid on and off the field for the future success of the program." -Syracuse Director of Athletics Dr. Daryl Gross

Regardless of what people think of Marrone's decision to leave the Orange, his four years of service have left a lasting impression on a program seemingly fading out of the spotlight. After a dismal three years of Greg Robinson that ended with a 10-37 record, Marrone was hired to rejuvenate the program.

Before coming to Syracuse on Dec. 8, 2008, Marrone coached on offensive side of the ball for the New York Jets from 2002-2005 and then for the New Orleans Saints from 2006-2008. As the Saints offensive coordinator, Marrone helped create the NFL's number one offense.

But it wasn't just his offensive-style that brought Marrone and Syracuse together; it was Marrone's collegiate connection. A three-year starter on the offensive line for the Orange from 1983-1985, Marrone was already knowledgeable about the SU football program.

"We've hired a guy that is a Syracuse graduate, who bleeds orange, who brings in tremendous, tremendous knowledge of football from his college and especially his pro experience," said SU athletic director Dr. Daryl Gross back in 2008. "He's someone that we can look forward to exciting offenses, seeing a lot of snaps per game. Better than that, he's somebody that brings leadership, who comes from the Bronx. When you talk about New York's College team, he fits the profile perfectly. He will be a tremendous recruiter in the Northeast, who knows the coaches. He's somebody that we believe will win at Syracuse."

Luckily for Syracuse, Marrone did just that in his four seasons. Picking up the pieces from Greg Robinson, Marrone and the Orange had a sub-par 2009 campaign. His 4-8 season was not the kind of start SU fans were hoping for, but Marrone did give them something to cheer about. Many statistical rankings increased significantly- all on the defensive side- most likely due to the hiring of defensive coordinator Scott Shafer in 2009. Shafer, who will reportedly replace Marrone in 2013, instilled a defense that consistently tried to put pressure on the quarterback.

It was not until Marrone's second season that Syracuse saw the switch from a BCS bottom-feeder to a bowl-contender, as the Orange finished with a 7-5 record. Syracuse also played in its first bowl game since 2004 against Kansas State in the New Era Pinstripe Bowl. SU won the game by a score of 36-24, its first bowl victory since 2001.

Two seasons in, and Marrone had already constructed a winning program. 2011 looked just as promising, with Syracuse winning five of its first seven games, including a 49-23 upset of No. 15 West Virginia. However, complacency seemed to set in, as the Orange finished Marrone's third season with a six-game losing streak, finishing with a 5-8 record.

2012 was the complete opposite of 2011 for Marrone and the Orange. Syracuse began the season with a 2-4 record but ended with a 7-5 record and another New Era Pinstripe Bowl berth, this time against former Big East rival West Virginia. Syracuse defeated the Mountaineers 38-14 for Marrone's second bowl victory in three years.

Unfortunately, that's where the story ends for Marrone with the Orange. The Buffalo Bills interviewed Marrone on Jan. 4 and he was hired the next day and signed a contract on Jan. 7.

"Doug has restored Syracuse football to its rightful place and we are appreciative of the foundation he has laid on and off the field for the future success of the program," Gross said in a statement released by university on Monday. "We wish him the absolute best in his opportunity in the NFL."

Syracuse University Chairman of the Board of Trustees Richard Thompson and Chancellor and President Nancy Cantor also released a statement, congratulating Marrone and praising his work over the past four years.

"We congratulate Coach Marrone on having this opportunity to become a head coach at the highest level. Under his leadership, we have restored the rich, winning football tradition at Syracuse, and we wish him continued success as he moves to the National Football League."

Marrone did exactly what he was brought in to do: build a program that could compete at a high level. He has multiple victories over top-25 teams, a couple of bowl wins, and changed the landscape of Syracuse football by instilling an idea of winning. He's coached players who moved on to the NFL level, including Mike Williams, Delone Carter and Chandler Jones, and it appears quarterback Ryan Nassib and offensive lineman Justin Pugh may also be heading to some NFL team as well.

Moving forward, it appears that Scott Shafer-hired by Marrone in 2009- will replace his former boss for the 2013 season, although no statements by the university have been made yet.

Chapter 14 Scott Shafer 2013 to 2015

Coach Scott Shafer # 28

Year	Coach	Record	Conf
2013	Scott Shafer	7-6	ACC (4-4)
2014	Scott Shafer	3-9	ACC (1-7)
2015	Scott Shafer	4-8	ACC (2-6)

Coach Shafer ready to take team onto the field

Famous Coaches (From the Past) by SWC75.

Scott's first year has been a roller-coaster ride, and nobody knows if he will be successful here, but we are hopeful because, launching ourselves into a new conference, we need him to be a success. If he isn't, we'll have to start all over again with someone else.

[At the time SWC75 wrote this piece on SU coaches, Shafer was in his first year of coaching. It would not work out and that is why Dino Babers is now the coach.] This is the third straight coach we've had who had never been a head coach before. We've never hired a coach in the post- World War II Era who had ever previously coached a major college football team. In our entire history we've hired two coaches who already had some measure of prominence as head coaches: Bill Hollenbeck, who filled in for Buck O'Neill when he was tending to his law practice in 1916 and Ossie Solem, who had had a losing record at Iowa.

2013 Scott Shafer Coach # 28

The 2013 Syracuse Orange football team competed in their one hundred-twenty-fourth season of intercollegiate football. They were led by Scott Shafer in his first of three season as head coach of the Syracuse Orange. The Orange had a winning record this year at 7-6. -5. The team was 4-4 in the ACC. They tied for third in the Atlantic Division of the ACC. They were invited to the Texas Bowl after the season where they defeated Minnesota.

On Aug 31, Syracuse played well but lost a close game to Penn State L (17-23) in its home and season opener played in MetLife Stadium, East Rutherford, NJ before 61,202 . Typically, SU home games are played at the Carrier Dome, on the campus of Syracuse University in Syracuse, NY. On Sept 7, #20 Northwestern beat Syracuse at Ryan Field in Evanston IL, L (27–48) before 38,033. On the home field for the first time in 2013, on Sept 14, at the Carrier Dome, SU shut out Wagner W (54-0) before 33,299.

Tulane came into the Carrier Dome hoping to extend their 2-1 record, but the Green Wave was beaten by the Orange in a shootout W (52-17) before 36,128. On Oct 5, Clemson defeated Syracuse in a blowout L (14-49).

The Orange traveled on Oct 12 to NC State's Carter–Finley Stadium in Raleigh, NC and played fine game beating the Tar Heels W (24-10) before 56,639. On Oct 19 against Georgia Tech in Bobby Dodd Stadium, Atlanta, GA, the Yellow Jackets whipped Syracuse in a blowout-shutout L (0–56) before 45,704. Then, on Nov 2 at home, Syracuse shut out Wake Forest at the Carrier Dome W (13-0).

On Nov 9, at Maryland's Byrd Stadium in College Park, MD, the Orange defeated the Terrapins W (20–3) before 37,213. In another blowout, Syracuse got walloped by #2 Florida State at Doak

Campbell Stadium in Tallahassee, FL L (3–59) before 74,491. The next game was the annual rivalry at home on Nov 23 against Pittsburgh at the Dome in a one-point loss L (16–17) before 35,317. In another rivalry in the last game of the season, SU got it together on Nv 30 at home to defeat Boston College's Eagles, in a close match W (34-31) before 37,406

The 2013 Texas Bowl

At 6-6, the Orange wee bowl eligible and they were invited to the Texas Bowl to play for a 5:00 PM December 27 6outing to play Minnesota at Reliant Stadium in Houston, TX, where they defeated the Cougars W (21–17) before a crowd of 32,327.

2014 Scott Shafer Coach # 28

The 2014 Syracuse Orange football team competed in their one hundred-twenty-fifth season of intercollegiate football. They were led by Scott Shafer in his second of three season as head coach of the Syracuse Orange. The Orange had a losing record this year at 3-9. The team was 1-7 in the ACC. They were not selected to play in a bowl game in 2014.

On Aug 29, SU played its season opener and home opener against #12 ranked (in FCS) Villanova, at the Carrier Dome, on the campus of Syracuse University in Syracuse, NY. SU won by one point (W (27-26) after a missed Villanova PAT in the 2nd OT. On Sept 13 at Central Michigan in Kelly/Shorts Stadium, Mount Pleasant, MI SU won the game W (40–3) before 25,531. On Sept 20 at home. The Maryland Terrapins defeated the Orange L (20–34) before 40,511. On Sept 27 8:00 PM SU was beaten by #8 Notre Dame at MetLife Stadium in East Rutherford, NJ L (15–31) before 76,802.

On Oct 3 at home, Louisville defeated Syracuse at the Carrier Dome L (6–28) before 37,569. On Oct 11 12:at home, #1 Florida State defeated Syracuse L (20–38) before 43,295. On Oct 18 at Wake Forest's BB&T Field in Winston-Salem, NC, the Orange prevailed W (30–7) before 25,107. Then on October 25 at #20 Clemson in a game played at Memorial Stadium in Clemson, SC. The Tigers defeated the Orange L (6–16) before 80,031

On Nov 1 at home, SU lost to NC State at the Carrier Dome L (17–24) before 40,787. Then, on Nov 8 at home SU lost to #22 Duke at the Carrier Dome L (10–27) before 39,331. In the rivalry with Pittsburgh, this year the game was played on Nov 22 at Heinz Field in Pittsburgh, PA, with the Panthers scoring the win L (7–30) before 32,549 In another major rivalry, on Nov 29, SU lost to Boston College at Alumni Stadium in Chestnut Hill, MA L (7-28) before 30,267 fans.

2015 Scott Shafer Coach # 28

The 2015 Syracuse Orange football team competed in their one hundred-twenty-sixth season of intercollegiate football. They were led by Scott Shafer in his third and last season as head coach of the Syracuse Orange. The Orange had a losing record this year at 4-8. The team was 2-6 in the ACC. They were not selected to play in a bowl game in 2015. On November 23, head coach Scott Shafer was fired. He stayed on to coach their final game on November 28. Shafer finished at Syracuse with a three-year record of 14–23.

On Sept 4, SU played its season opener and home opener against Rhode Island at the Carrier Dome, on the campus of Syracuse University in Syracuse, NY. SU won in a blowout (W 47-0). On Sept 12 at home, SU beat Wake Forest in the Carrier Dome W (30–17) before 26,670. In the Carrier Dome again on Sept 19 against Central Michigan, the Orange put the game in gear and prevailed W (30–27) in one OT, before 27,949. Then, on Sept 26, at home the Orange fell to # 8 LSU at the Carrier Dome L (24–34) before 43,101. Then, on 10 at 3:30 PM at South Florida in Raymond James Stadium, Tampa, FL, SU went down again L (24–45) before 27,235.

On Oct 17 at Virginia, in Scott Stadium, Charlottesville, VA, the Orange could not match the score L (38–44) with 3OT's to win but no cigar. Before 39,223. On Oct 24 at home in a major rivalry game v #25 Pittsburgh, the Orange could not pull it off and lost to the Panthers L (20–230 before 29,832. On Oct 31 SU travelled a thousand miles to fight #17 Florida State at Doak Campbell Stadium in Tallahassee, FL. The Seminoles had it all their way in a runaway game L (21–45) before 67,630.

On Nov 7 in an away game at Louisville's Papa John's Cardinal Stadium in Louisville, KY, the Orange took it on the chin again against the Cardinals L (17–41) before 46,158. Clemson was inching its way to the National Championship in one fine season after another. In this game on Nov 14 at home in the Carrier Dome against #1 Clemson, Syracuse lost a close one to the Tigers L (27–37) before 36,736. On Nov 21 at NC State's Carter–Finley Stadium in Raleigh, SU was stung by the Wolfpack L (29–42) before 55,260.

Then against an eternal rival in the last regular game of the year, on Nov 28, at home, the Orange got up the muster to defeat Boston College in the Carrier Dome in a close game W (20–17) before 30,317. No bowl games are offered for 4-8 teams.

Scott Shafer Out at Syracuse

By Stephen Bailey sbailey@syracuse.com on November 23, 2015 at 9:48 AM, updated November 23, 2015 at 11:35 PM

SCOTT SHAFER FIRED
Syracuse, N.Y. — Scott Shafer has been fired as Syracuse's head football coach, the school announced on Monday.

Shafer, who was promoted from defensive coordinator after Doug Marrone's departure in January 2013, is 13-23 in three seasons. The Orange is currently 3-8 this year heading into its season finale against Boston College. Shafer will coach in the final game.

Syracuse athletic director Mark Coyle expressed appreciation toward Shafer, who is in his third year at the helm, but said in a statement that a "change in leadership" was required.

"I want to thank Scott, his wife Missy, and their family for their seven years of dedication and service to SU Athletics and Syracuse University," Coyle said. "Scott has worked tirelessly to educate our students on and off the field and to build our program. However, I feel a change in leadership is needed at this time.

A national search will begin immediately." After coaching SU to a 7-6 record and Texas Bowl win in his first season, Shafer struggled through a 3-9 campaign mired in injury and lowlighted by the demotion of offensive coordinator George McDonald.

Facing one of the largest defensive rebuilds in college football history, Syracuse opened 2015 with its first 3-0 start since 1991 before losing its next eight contests — the longest in-season skid since 2005. An embattled fan base became more disgruntled as upset scares of No. 1 Clemson and then-No. 2 LSU weighed against a host of questionable in-game decisions.

Coyle, who started in July, has not spoken publicly since issuing a wait-and-see approach regarding Shafer's future in early September.

Shafer said he had one season left on his contract on Nov. 12 and likely would have had to been extended or bought out for the program to recruit in 2016.

Shafer arrived at Syracuse in 2009 and spent four years working as defensive coordinator under Marrone. In 2010, his unit was one of the best in the country, ranking seventh in total defense, 10th in pass defense and 13th in scoring defense. He was aa logical replacement for Marrone who left unexpectedly.

Shafer had previous defensive coordinator stops at Michigan (2008), Stanford (2007), Western Michigan (2005-06) and Northern Illinois (2000-03). Shafer also served as defensive backs coach at WMU (2004) and NIU (1996-99) after breaking into the coaching ranks as the secondary coach at Rhode Island from 1993-95.

After playing quarterback at Division III Baldwin-Wallace University in Ohio, Shafer was a graduate assistant at Indiana from 1991-92.

The news of Shafer's firing was first reported by Thayer Evans of Sports Illustrated. Contact Stephen Bailey anytime: Email | Twitter | 315-427-2168.

Syracuse over the years as we have portrayed in this book has had several great coaches and several who would have been even greater coaches if given time to mature with the program, or if they could have been convinced to stay.

Dino Babers was announced as the SU coach for 2016 onward. Babers has a great reputation and is a fine coach but so far, his record is poor. The most any of us have seen in the modern SU era is that SU accepts two years of poor records and then takes action or waits another year or at most two. Syracuse does want a winning team but after ten years, with some exceptions such as Ben Schwartzwalder, Dick MacPherson, Paul Pasqualoni and Doug Marrone.

The Institution's history shows that they do not appear to know how to attract great coaches or to keep a great coach when they get one. All Syracuse fans, including yours truly are hoping for an outstanding performance from Dino Babers team in 2018. We wish him the best.

Let's now take a look at where we stand from Coach Babers two years of experience with the Syracuse Orange.

Chapter 15 Dino Babers 2016 to ????

Coach Scott Shafer # 28

Year	Coach	Record	Conf
2016	Dino Babers	4-8	ACC (2-6)
2017	Dino Babers	4-8	ACC (2-6)
2018	Dino Babers	0-0	ACC (0-0

SU Football Coach Dino Babers with the team

2016 Dino Babers Coach # 29

The 2016 Syracuse Orange football team competed in their one hundred-twenty-seventh season of intercollegiate football. They were led by Dino Babers, in his first season as head coach of the Syracuse Orange. The Orange had a losing record this year at 4-8; the same record as in Scott Shafer's last year at the helm. The team was 2-6 in the ACC. They were not selected to play in a bowl game in 2016.

On Sept 2, SU played its season opener and home opener against Colgate, ranked #21 ranked in FCS). The game was played in the Carrier Dome, on the campus of Syracuse University in Syracuse, NY. SU won the match (W 33-7) before 31,336. On Sept 9, at home, Louisville defeated the Orange L (28–62) before 32,184. On Sept 17 at home, South Florida beat the Orange L (20–45) before 32,288.

In its first road game of the season, on Sept 24, Syracuse defeated Connecticut in Rentschler Field, East Hartford, CT W (31–24) before 31,899. On Oct 1, in a home game played at MetLife Stadium, East Rutherford, NJ, SU was defeated by Notre Dame L (33–50) before 62,794.

Back on the road, SU traveled on Oct 8 to Wake Forest's BB&T Field in Winston-Salem, NC and were defeated by the Demon Deacons L (9–28) before 25,162. On Oct 15 at home, SU beat the #17 ranked Hokies of Virginia Tech W (31-17) before 33,838. Then, on Oct 22 at Boston College's Alumni Stadium in Chestnut Hill, MA, Syracuse won its second game in a row, W (28–20) before 34,647. On Nov 5, playing against #3 ranked Clemson, soon to be National Champions, led by Heisman candidate Desean Watson, Syracuse lost in a blowout-shutout at Clemson Memorial Stadium L (0–54) before 80,609 fans.

On Nov 12 at home, Syracuse lost to the Wolfpack of NC State L (20–35) before 34,842. Again, at home, SU was defeated by Florida State L (14-45) before 32,340. Then in one of the highest scoring games of all time on Nov 26, at major rival Pittsburgh's Heinz Field in Pittsburgh, PA, neither defense showed up and Pittsburgh won the game with a huge score of L (61–76) before 34,049.

2017 Dino Babers Coach # 29

The 2017 Syracuse Orange football team competed in their one hundred-twenty-eighth season of intercollegiate football. They were led by Dino Babers in his second season as head coach of the Syracuse Orange. The Orange had a losing record this year of 4-8; the same exact record as in the last two seasons. The team was 2-6 in the ACC. They were not selected to play in a bowl game in 2016.

On Sept 1, SU played its season and home opener against Central Connecticut. The game was played in the Dome, on the campus of Syracuse University in Syracuse, NY. SU won the match W (50-7) before 31,336. On Sept 9, at home, the Orange lost to Middle Tennessee L (23-30 Before 29,731. SU got its second win of the season on Sept 16 at home against Central Michigan W (41-17) before 33,004.

On Sept 23 at #25 LSU in Tiger Stadium, Baton Rouge, Louisiana, the Orange put up a good fight but lost to the Tigers L (26–35) before a huge crowd of 96,044. Then in the final September game, Sept 30 at NC State's Carter–Finley Stadium in Raleigh, North Carolina, the Orange lost to the Wolfpack L (25–33) before 56,197

For its third win of the season, Syracuse beat rival Pittsburgh at home in the Carrier Dome on Oct 6, in a close match W (27–24) before 33,290.

Highlight SU Defeats Defending Champion Clemson

In the greatest game for the Syracuse Orange in decades, if not centuries, SU defeated the reigning National Champions, #2 ranked Clemson at home in the Carrier Dome in a hard-fought close match on Oct 13 W (27–24) before 42,475.

When you create a list of the best games SU has ever played so you can show them as highlights in a book about Great Coaches in Syracuse Football, October. 13, 2017 is a must-game for that list. My list would show the Friday win as the biggest for Syracuse since the Donovan McNabb era if not well before that.

Night game v Clemson at the Dome

The 27-24 win over No. 2 Clemson marked Syracuse's second win over a team ranked among the top two in football. Cole Murphy's 30-yard field goal with 9:41 remaining was the winning score. Quarterback Eric Dungey led the Orange with 278 yards passing and 61 yards rushing. BTW, I predict All-American in 2018 for Eric Dungey unless the NCAA sopped being able to spell Sceeerrrokuze.

A bit more detail:

Dungey on target. His 3 TD passes blows out #2 Clemson in a close match, 27-24

You bet the Syracuse Orange, who played like the vaunted Syracuse Orangemen from the Jim Brown days had a huge celebration in the SU locker room that could be heard through all of Syracuse. Finally, a great game from a team that is getting ready to be great.

Coach Dabo Swinney had a tough time believing what happened as this would not be a perfect season and Desean Watson would not bring back the Tigers. Syracuse under their collective breaths were singing Hold that Tiger the whole game.

Eric Dungey was well, and he threw for 278 yards and three touchdowns, Cole Murphy kicked a tiebreaking field goal in the fourth quarter, and Syracuse put a weird face on #2 Clemson 27-24 on this Friday night as the Tigers had to digest what it meant for their chances to repeat as national champions.

Clemson had won 12 consecutive games on the opponent's home field, the longest streak in Clemson history and they had tied for the second longest active streak in the nation. None of that mattered to the Orange-men who simply wanted to kick the opponents butts back to South Carolina. It's a football thing!

Dabo Swinney is a fine coach and he said: "It wasn't our night tonight. They were better than us," Swinney said. "There's nothing we're going to fix now. We're not going to be 12-0, that's for sure. That's not going to happen. This is going to hurt, but you move forward."

The Orangemen were (4-3, 2-1) are were 3-6 against the previous year's national champion, having also beaten Penn State in 1987 and Michigan in 1998. This was the program's first win in 13 tries against the No. 2 team in the nation. It was sweet.

SU Coach was elated. "This is truly one of the moments that you coach for. This is really special," said Syracuse coach Dino Babers, in his second year with the Orange. "This is big."

Reaming SU 2017 games

On Oct 21 at #8 Miami (FL) in Hard Rock Stadium, Miami Gardens, Florida SU put up a great fight against the Hurricanes losing by just 8 points L (19–27) before 56,158. On Nov4, at Florida State's Doak Campbell Stadium in Tallahassee, Florida, the Orange almost got an upset but lost L (24-27) before 71,805.

Then, on Nov 11 at home SU was beaten by Wake Forest at the Carrier Dome L (43–64) before 38,539. The Orange then traveled to Louisville on Nov 18 to Papa John's Cardinal Stadium in Louisville,

Kentucky and lost the game in a blowout L (10–56) before 34,265. In the rivalry game at home on Nov 25 at 12:20 p.m. SU lost to Boston College L (14-42) in the Carrier Dome before 30,202.

The two close losses after Clemson--Miami and then Florida State last year would have been blowouts. This year they were just losses. That is a definite improvement. Not good for the spirit but not bad like last year. The last three games seem to be because of the defense; but I think it was as much the fact that offensive star, QB Eric Dungey was injured and then in the BC game, running back Dontae Strickland could not play either.

The defense rarely got a break. SU also lost other starters earlier this fall. Many coaches will tell us all that you can't win without your best players or at least almost equal replacements. Syracuse in 2017 had neither.

2018 Dino Babers Coach # 29

The 2018 Syracuse Orange football team is preparing for their one hundred-twenty-ninth season of intercollegiate football. They are led by Dino Babers in his third season as head coach of the Syracuse Orange. The Orange have a losing record under Babers of 8-16 in two years but the margin of loss to some very powerful teams is much smaller than in prior years. Thus, there is great hope for the Syracuse Orange in the Fall 2018.

The recruiting class for 2018 also offers encouragement. Dino Babers brought in the best class in a decade and to top that, there are several big-name transfers that are on their way to play in Orange Country

Here's how SU stacks up nationally in the class of 2018

- National rank: 49
- 5 stars: 0
- 4 stars: 1
- 3 stars: 17

The 2018 Schedule is as follows:

Date	Opponent	Site
September 1, 2018	at Western Michigan*	Waldo Stadium Kalamazoo, MI
September 8, 2018	Wagner*	Carrier Dome Syracuse, NY
September 15, 2018	Florida State	Carrier Dome Syracuse, NY
September 22, 2018	Connecticut*	Carrier Dome Syracuse, NY
September 29, 2018	at Clemson	Memorial Stadium Clemson, SC
October 6, 2018	at Pittsburgh	Heinz Field Pittsburgh, PA (Rivalry)
October 20, 2018	North Carolina	Carrier Dome Syracuse, NY
October 27, 2018	NC State	Carrier Dome Syracuse, NY
November 3, 2018	at Wake Forest	BB&T Field Winston-Salem, NC
November 9, 2018	Louisville	Carrier Dome Syracuse, NY
November 17, 2018	vs. Notre Dame*	Yankee Stadium Bronx, NY
November 24, 2018	at Boston College	Alumni Stadium Chestnut Hill, MA

*Non-conference game. All times are in Eastern Time.

At syracusefan.com, this post from mlbball99 Scout Team offers great encouragement for 2018:

A couple of thoughts here:

Dino Babers is 56 years old. He is at a big school in a power six conference competing in arguably the best conference. He has embraced what the Carrier Dome can be. The football renovations have been done - practice facility, locker rooms, etc.

In his presser last night Dino raved about living in Syracuse and said how happy he was. Again, Dino is 56 years old. I do see schools trying to poach him after this year, but I think Dino has found a long-term home. I don't believe he wants to go try to rebuild something again at his age.

Wildhack and Dino have a fantastic relationship. Wildhack will play him ASAP.

We are so close to being a legit contender. We are a few plays away from being 7-0. Dungey is a legit Heisman candidate next year. The nation has noticed.

Also, do not forget, we have a 4-star QB grooming. Two 4-star OL on their way in.   Let's GO.

The Daily Orange Student Newspaper offers its thoughts on the probabilities of a Syracuse football turnaround

By Tomer Langer
SENIOR STAFF WRITER
UPDATED: Sept. 25, 2017 at 3:36 a.m.

When he was introduced as Syracuse's head coach on Dec. 5, 2015, Dino Babers asked for faith.

Belief without evidence, as he likes to specify. He said his goal is to make Syracuse a program that's "consistently good, not occasionally great." He didn't see any reason why SU couldn't reach the top of the Atlantic Coast Conference.

Babers has leaned on those mantras repeatedly since he arrived, asking for patience. He overhauled the offensive and defensive schemes and alluded to successful "cakes" the Orange would "bake," saying that SU was still working on the batter.

He also provided a timeline, saying that his system would be fully installed in the second year between the fourth and sixth games. On Monday, after beating Central Michigan, Babers stuck with his forecast.

"I think based off of the last game, it's probably about right," Babers said. "Again, I don't know, when you talk about the newness and guys being hurt and not being here the entire first year. But I'm not going to back away from a statement. This is when we normally get going, it just happens to be some of the toughest games on the schedule and that's how they fall so we have to see how we do."

The Orange (2-2) came close to proving Babers a soothsayer last night but fell, 35-26, to No. 25 Louisiana State (3-1, 0-1 Southeastern) in Baton Rouge, Louisiana. Some chalked it up to a likely blowout loss in the preseason, but several missed opportunities were the only things in the way of a Syracuse victory.

The steady performance of SU's defense and second-half offense highlighted the many reasons there are to believe that Babers can turn around the program.

But after dropping what could have been a signature win for the program, it's increasingly apparent the turnaround will take longer than expected.

Babers projected the timeline for SU because of the tangible results he'd had at previous coaching stops. He began coaching as a graduate assistant in 1984 and had a pair of two-year head coaching stints before he arrived at SU. At both Eastern Illinois and Bowling Green, his teams improved in the second year.

There have been clear areas of growth since Babers' arrival. A once-anemic offense stuffed the record books a year ago. The defense gave up more than 500 yards per game last year, but it has already shown vast improvements in Year 2.
In training camp, senior captain Zaire Franklin said the defense wasn't fully adjusted to the new Tampa-2 scheme being run in 2016. Though he said he felt the entire unit was much more prepared after a full year in the system.

"It would mean a lot to us," Franklin said last Tuesday about potentially getting a win at LSU, "to kind of start the Coach Babers era off the right way, the way it was supposed to."

Jimmy Garoppolo, the high-profile backup quarterback for the New England Patriots, was a junior starter when Babers' started at EIU. He also felt the difference between the first and second year. One play in particular, a 63-yard touchdown in the third game of the second season against Illinois State, sticks out for Garoppolo as the time when the offense fully clicked in the new system. The Panthers finished 12-2, compared to 7-5 the previous year and two 2-9 stints before Babers arrival.

"It fits his personality very well." Garoppolo said of Babers turning programs around. "He believes in what he's saying, and he has a way in making other people around him believe the same thing. That's what you need in a head coach. He does a great job of having guys buy in to the program. The coaches all buy in, and it makes for, in the words that he would say, it makes for a good 'La Familia.'"

There have been flashes of SU success but no concrete semblance of consistency. Last year's win over then-No. 17 Virginia Tech stands out as a high point that SU hadn't had since a 2013 bowl victory. Giving up 76 points in last year's season finale loss to Pittsburgh and blowing a home game against Middle Tennessee State this year are among the times SU has not performed.

Consistent moments escaped Syracuse on Saturday. Eric Dungey's first pass was picked off by top corner Greedy Williams and returned to the SU one-yard line. LSU scored on the next play. In the second quarter, wide receiver Sean Riley dropped a pass in the end zone while he was wide open, costing SU the go-ahead touchdown.

"We didn't get it done and that's the bottom line," senior wide receiver Ervin Philips said. "People can look at the game and say that we played well. But at the end of the day it's about getting it done, it's about winning."

If anything, the LSU loss showed that it would be foolish to count Syracuse out of any game moving forward. SU has three more games against opponents currently ranked inside the Top 25. Another high-caliber opponent, Florida State, lost to North Carolina State and fell out of the rankings. Syracuse faces the Wolfpack next week. The Orange could win its next two games and take the next step toward bowl eligibility.

Neither of those wins would make as much of a statement as the one SU let slip away Saturday night. Not against a Top 25 team in the SEC at what Babers called "one of the top five venues in America when it comes to college football."

Babers stressed postgame that he was disappointed, not upset. He wanted his players to have that one memorable win that they could tell their kids and grandkids about.

"They don't realize how close they were," Babers said, "and I'm disappointed they didn't get it right now at this time."
Based on his previous stops, Babers expected his team to get that win. Despite how close the Orange got, Babers' timeline will face a minor delay.

Another 2018 perspective

5 things to know about Syracuse football 2018 schedule
Updated Jan 17; Posted Jan 17

By Nate Mink
nmink@syracuse.com,
syracuse.com

> Syracuse football is entering its third year under head coach Dino Babers and the team and fans and alums are looking to improve upon back-to-back 4-8 seasons.(*Dennis Nett | dnett@syracuse.com*)

Dino Babers doing his job

Syracuse, N.Y. -- Syracuse football's complete 2018 schedule was released Wednesday with announcement of the ACC slate.

[The schedule is shown above.]

The Orange is entering its third year under head coach Dino Babers and is looking to improve upon back-to-back 4-8 seasons. This year's schedule carries the familiar national powers of previous years: Clemson, Florida State and Notre Dame are on it.

And, while the ACC has improved its overall health in recent years, making no game any small task, there is reason to believe this season's slate of games won't be as challenging as last year's.

There are seven teams on this year's schedule that played in a bowl game last season (Western Michigan was bowl eligible with six wins but was not invited to a bowl).

To put that in perspective, 10 of the 12 teams Syracuse faced last season went to a bowl.

Here are four more thoughts on the schedule:

1. The opener will tell us something
Syracuse for the past four seasons has opened against an FCS opponent that was mostly overmatched from the opening kick. The Orange felt good about itself, but it really didn't know how it would respond against any semblance of resistance.

Syracuse goes on the road in Week 1 at a healthy Mid-American conference opponent that has staff familiar with some of SU's veteran personnel.

2. Syracuse will get ACC heavyweights in September
Getting Florida State and Clemson in September should give SU a chance at the conference heavyweights with its roster intact. FSU will be playing its first road game under new coach Willie Taggart, who defeated Babers when he coached at South Florida two seasons ago.

Clemson will be carrying a loaded roster and will be seeking revenge for last season's loss at the Carrier Dome.

Depth is always a concern for Syracuse, so the health of its roster will be vitally important heading into October, which looks like the month where progress will or will not reveal itself.

3. Louisville a Friday night upset?
Nobody forgot what happened the last time an ACC opponent came to the Carrier Dome on a Friday night, when Syracuse handed Clemson a stunning, 27-24 loss.

For the second time in three years, Louisville is coming to the Dome on a Friday night (this time, without star quarterback Lamar Jackson).

Dino Babers and his team have pulled off stunning victories in each of his first two seasons.

Scalping Florida State at home or Notre Dame at Yankee Stadium would also make for another memorable moment.

4. October will reveal program progress
Syracuse will play three opponents in October that will go a long way toward deciding whether the program is able to take a step forward.

Games at Pittsburgh and at home against North Carolina and North Carolina State are three perfect examples of the kinds of wins the program needs to snare if it wants to continue to build momentum on the recruiting trail.

One is against a Northeast rival, and the other two are home games against good but not overwhelming rosters.

Take it another step forward, and the Nov. 3 contest at Wake Forest provides another opportunity for SU to show it can consistently defeat peer programs or programs with slightly better talent than SU.

Contact Nate Mink anytime: 315-430-8253.

278 Great Coaches in Syracuse Football

Other books by Brian Kelly: (amazon.com, & Kindle)

Other books by Brian Kelly: (amazon.com, & Kindle)

Great Moments in Pittsburgh Steelers Football All the best from the Pittsburgh Steelers
Great Moments in New England Patriots Football Great football moments from Boston to New England
Great Moments in Philadelphia Eagles Football. The best from the Eagles from the beginning of football.
Great Moments in Syracuse Football The great moments, coaches & players in Syracuse Football
Boost Social Security Now! Hey Buddy Can You Spare a Dime?
The Birth of American Football. From the first college game in 1869 to the last Super Bowl
Obamacare: A One-Line Repeal Congress must get this done.
A Wilkes-Barre Christmas Story A wonderful town makes Christmas all the better
A Boy, A Bike, A Train, and a Christmas Miracle A Christmas story that will melt your heart
Pay-to-Go   America-First Immigration Fix
Legalizing Illegal Aliens Via Resident Visas Americans-first plan saves $Trillions. Learn how!
60 Million Illegal Aliens in America!!! A simple, America-first solution.
The Bill of Rights By Founder James Madison Refresh *your knowledge of the specific rights for all*
Great Players in Army Football Great Army Football played by great players..
Great Coaches in Army Football Army's coaches are all great.
Great Moments in Army Football Army Football at its best.
Great Moments in Florida Gators Football Gators Football from the start. This is the book.
Great Moments in Clemson Football CU Football at its best. This is the book.
Great Moments in Florida Gators Football Gators Football from the start. This is the book.
The Constitution Companion. A Guide to Reading and Comprehending the Constitution
The Constitution by Hamilton, Jefferson, & Madison – Big type and in English
PATERNO: The Dark Days After Win # 409. Sky began to fall within days of win # 409.
JoePa 409 Victories: Say No More! Winningest Division I-A football coach ever
American College Football: The Beginning From before day one football was played.
Great Coaches in Alabama Football Challenging the coaches of every other program!
Great Coaches in Penn State Football the Best Coaches in PSU's football program
Great Players in Penn State Football The best players in PSU's football program
Great Players in Notre Dame Football The best players in ND's football program
Great Coaches in Notre Dame Football The best coaches in any football program
Great Players in Alabama Football from Quarterbacks to offensive Linemen Greats!
Great Moments in Alabama Football AU Football from the start. This is the book.
Great Moments in Penn State Football PSU Football, start--games, coaches, players,
Great Moments in Notre Dame Football ND Football, start, games, coaches, players
Cross Country with the Parents A great trip from East Coast to West with the kids
Seniors, Social Security & the Minimum Wage. Things seniors need to know.
How to Write Your First Book and Publish It with CreateSpace
The US Immigration Fix--It's all in here. Finally, an answer.
I had a Dream IBM Could be #1 Again The title is self-explanatory
WineDiets.Com Presents The Wine Diet Learn how to lose weight while having fun.
Wilkes-Barre, PA; Return to Glory Wilkes-Barre City's return to glory
Geoffrey Parsons' Epoch... The Land of Fair Play Better than the original.
The Bill of Rights 4 Dummmies! This is the best book to learn about your rights.
Sol Bloom's Epoch ...Story of the Constitution The best book to learn the Constitution
America 4 Dummmies! All Americans should read to learn about this great country.
The Electoral College 4 Dummmies! How does it really work?
The All-Everything Machine Story about IBM's finest computer server.
ThankYou IBM! This book explains how IBM was beaten in the computer marketplace by neophytes

Brian has written 161 books in total. Other books can be found at amazon.com/author/brianwkelly

www.ingramcontent.com/pod-product-compliance
Lightning Source LLC
Chambersburg PA
CBHW071653090426
42738CB00009B/1515